The First Crusade

The Call from the East

PETER FRANKOPAN

THE BODLEY HEAD
LONDON

Published by The Bodley Head 2012

2 4 6 8 10 9 7 5 3 1

First published in Great Britain in 2011 by
The Bodley Head
Random House, 20 Vauxhall Bridge Road,
London SW1V 2SA

www.bodleyhead.co.uk
www.vintage-books.co.uk

Addresses for companies within The Random House Group Limited can be found at:
www.randomhouse.co.uk/offices.htm

The Random House Group Limited Reg. No. 954009

A CIP catalogue record for this book
is available from the British Library

ISBN 9781847921550

The Random House Group Limited supports The Forest
Stewardship Council (FSC®), the leading international forest
certification organisation. Our books carrying the FSC label are printed on
FSC® certified paper. FSC is the only forest certification scheme endorsed
by the leading environmental organisations, including Greenpeace.
Our paper procurement policy can be found at
www.randomhouse.co.uk/environment

Typeset in Dante MT by Palimpsest Book Production Limited,
Falkirk, Stirlingshire
Printed and bound in Great Britain by
Clays Ltd, St Ives plc

To my wife, Jessica

Disturbing news has emerged from Jerusalem and the city of Constantinople and is now constantly at the forefront of our mind: namely that the race of the Persians, a foreign people and a people rejected by God . . . has invaded the lands of the Christians [and has] depopulated them by slaughter and plunder and arson.

Robert of Rheims

An embassy of the emperor of Constantinople came to the synod and implored his lordship the Pope and all the faithful of Christ to bring assistance against the heathen for the defence of this holy church, which had now been nearly annihilated in that region by the infidels who had conquered her as far as the walls of Constantinople. Our Lord Pope called upon many to perform this service, to promise by oaths to journey there by God's will and to bring the emperor the most faithful assistance against the heathen as very best as they were able.

Bernold of Constance

Kelts assembled from all parts, one after another, with arms and horses and all the other equipment for war. Full of enthusiasm and ardour they thronged every highway, and with these warriors came a host of civilians, outnumbering the sand of the seashore or the stars of heaven, carrying palms and bearing crosses on their shoulders . . . like tributaries joining a river from all directions, they streamed towards us in full force.

Anna Komnene

In his essence, the emperor was like a scorpion; for while you have nothing to fear from its face, you do well to avoid injury from its tail.

William of Tyre

Contents

Illustrations

Alp Arslan and Romanos IV after the battle of Manzikert (*Bibliothèque nationale de France*).

Christ and the Virgin Mary, mosaic in the south vestibule of Hagia Sophia, late tenth century (*akg-images/Erich Lessing*).

Reliquary for the wood from the True Cross, *c.*950 (*akg-images/Erich Lessing*).

The walls of Constantinople (*akg-images/Gerard Degeorge*).

Emperor Alexios I Komnenos (*Vatican Library/Giraudon/Bridgeman Art Library*).

Hyperpyron of Alexios I Komnenos, mint of Constantinople (*The Barber Institute Coin Collection, University of Birmingham, B5543*).

Pope Urban II arrives at the council of Clermont, from *Le Roman de Godefroi de Bouillon*, fourteenth century (*Bibliothèque nationale de France/Giraudon/Bridgeman Art Library, Ms Fr 22495 f. 15*).

Emperor Alexios receives Peter the Hermit (*RMN, Château de Versailles/Gérard Blot*).

The Crusaders at Nicaea, 1097, from *Estoire d'Outremer* by William of Tyre, twelfth century (*Bibliothèque nationale de France/Bridgeman Art Library, Fr 2630 f. 22v*).

The siege of Antioch, 1097–8, from *Estoire d'Outremer* by William of Tyre, twelfth century (*Bibliothèque municipale de Lyon/Bridgeman Art Library, Ms 828 f. 33r*).

The massacre at Antioch, 1098 (*Bibliothèque nationale de France*).

The Crusader assault on Jerusalem, 1099 from *Le Roman de Godefroi de Bouillon*, fourteenth century (*Bibliothèque nationale de France/Bridgeman Art Library, Fr 22495 f. 69v*).

The looting of Jerusalem, 1099, illuminated miniature from a universal chronicle, fifteenth century ((*Bibliothèque nationale de France/Bridgeman Art Library, Fr 20124 f. 331*).

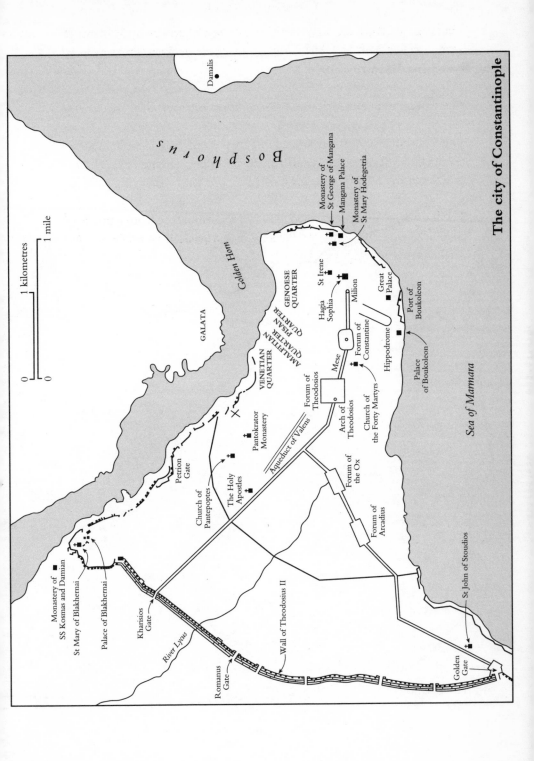

The city of Constantinople

Bosphorus

Damalis

1 kilometres
1 mile

Golden Horn

GALATA

Monastery of
St George of Mangana
Mangana Palace
Monastery of
St Mary Hodegetria

St Irene

GENOESE
QUARTER

PISAN
QUARTER

AMALFITAN
QUARTER

VENETIAN
QUARTER

Hagia
Sophia

Milion

Forum of
Constantine

Great
Palace

Port of
Boukoleon

Mese

Hippodrome

Palace of
Boukoleon

Forum of
Theodosios

Arch of
Theodosios

Church of
the Forty Martyrs

Sea of Marmara

Aqueduct of Valens

Pantokrator
Monastery

The Holy
Apostles

Forum of
the Ox

Church of
Pantepoptes

Petrion
Gate

Forum of
Arcadius

Monastery of
SS Kosmas and Damian

St Mary of Blakhernai

Palace of Blakhernai

Kharisios
Gate

River Lycus

Wall of Theodosius II

St John of Stoudios

Romanus
Gate

Golden
Gate

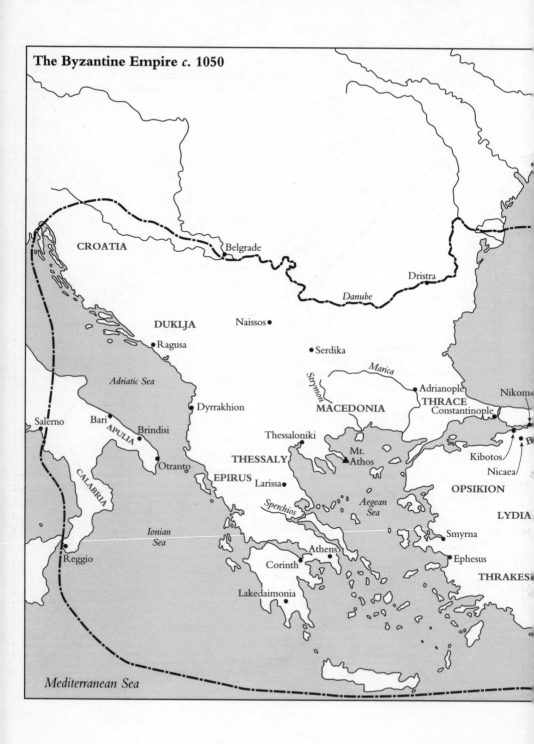

The Byzantine Empire *c.* 1050

CROATIA

Belgrade

Dristra

Danube

DUKLJA

Naissos

Ragusa

Adriatic Sea

Serdika

Marica

Strymon

Adrianople

MACEDONIA

THRACE

Nikom

Dyrrakhion

Constantinople

Salerno

Bari

APULIA

Brindisi

Thessaloniki

Mt.
Athos

Kibotos

B

THESSALY

Nicaea

Otranto

EPIRUS

Larissa

OPSIKION

CALABRIA

Sperchios

*Aegean
Sea*

LYDIA

*Ionian
Sea*

Smyrna

Reggio

Athens

Ephesus

Corinth

THRAKES

Lakedaimonia

Mediterranean Sea

Kherson

Black Sea

Sinope

PAPHLAGONIA

Trebizond

Ani

KHALDIA

Theodosioupolis

Amaseia

Manzikert

NIA

GALATIA

Sebasteia

Lake Van

Ankyra

MESOPOTAMIA

Halys

PHRYGIA

CAPPADOCIA

Kaisereia

Melitene

norion

Koloneia

Tigris

NATOLIKON

Samosata

Marash

Ikonion

CILICIA

Edessa

Mopsuetia (Mamistra)

Mosul

Adana

Tarsos

Attaleia

PAMPHYLIA

Antioch

Seleukeia

Euphrates

Triploi

0   100   200   300   400 kilometres

0   50   100   150   200 miles

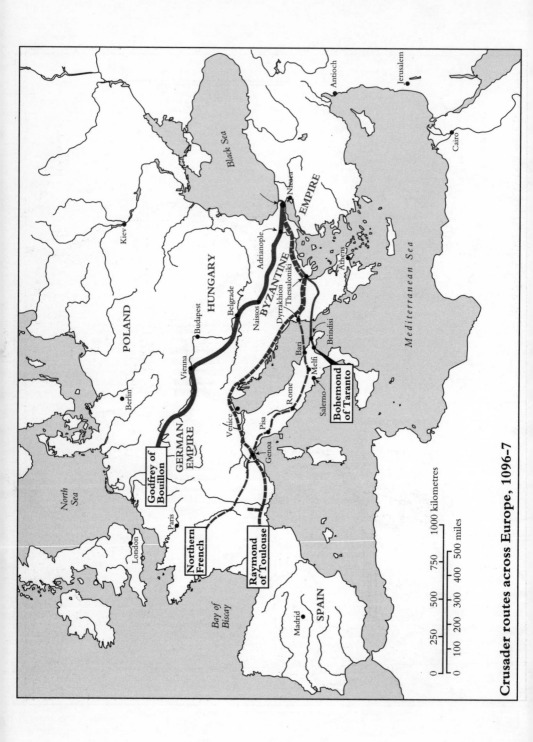

Crusader routes across Europe, 1096–7

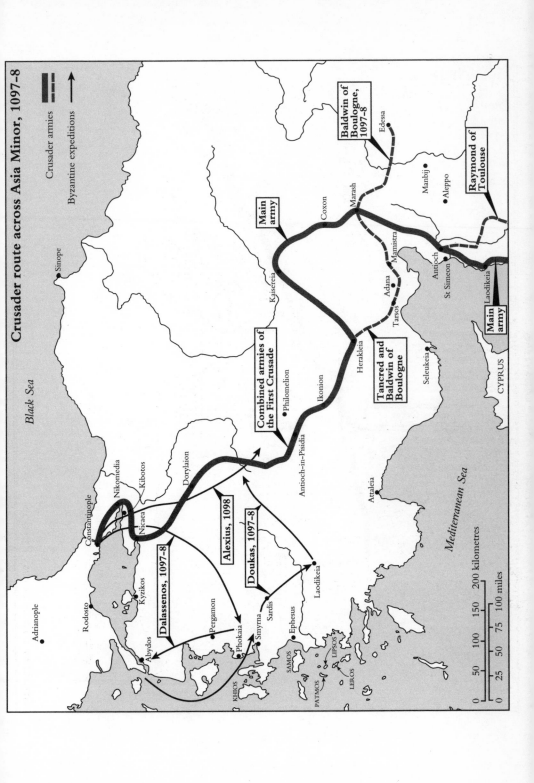

Crusader route across Asia Minor, 1097–8

Crusader armies

Byzantine expeditions

Black Sea

Mediterranean Sea

Adrianople

Constantinople
Rodosto
Nikomedia
Kibotos
Nicaea
Dorylaion
Sinope

Kyzikos
Pergamon
Abydos
Phokaia
Smyrna
Sardis
Ephesus
KHIOS
SAMOS
PATMOS
LEROS
LIPSOS
Laodikeia
Attaleia

Dalassenos, 1097–8
Alexius, 1098
Doukas, 1097–8

Combined armies of the First Crusade

Philomelion
Ikonion
Antioch-in-Pisidia
Kaisereia

Herakleia
Tarsos
Adana
Mamistra
St Simeon
Antioch
Seleukeia
Laodikeia
CYPRUS

Main army

Coxon
Marash
Manbij
Aleppo
Edessa

Baldwin of Boulogne, 1097–8

Raymond of Toulouse

Tancred and Baldwin of Boulogne

Main army

0   25   50   75   100   150   200 kilometres
0   25   50   75   100 miles

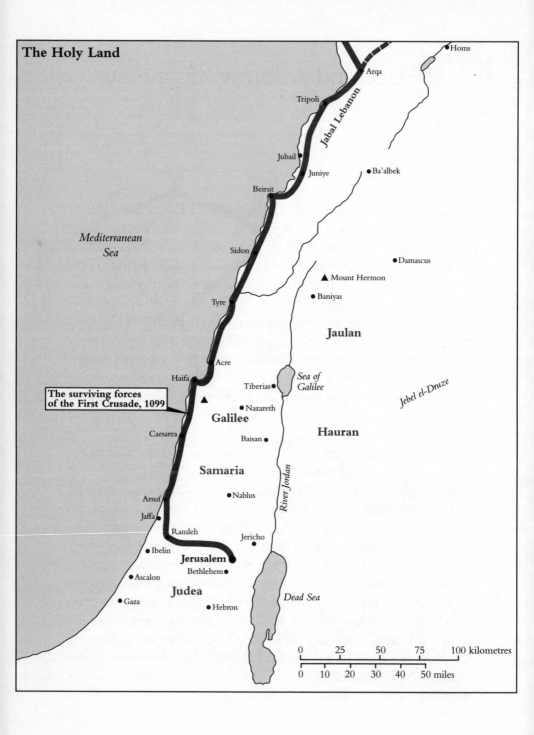

The Holy Land

Mediterranean
Sea

Homs

Arqa

Tripoli

Jabal Lebanon

Jubail

Juniye

Ba'albek

Beirut

Sidon

Damascus

Mount Hermon

Baniyas

Tyre

Jaulan

Acre

Sea of
Galilee

Haifa

Tiberias

Jebel el-Druze

The surviving forces
of the First Crusade, 1099

Nazareth

Galilee

Hauran

Caesarea

Baisan

Samaria

River Jordan

Arsuf

Nablus

Jaffa

Ramleh

Jericho

Ibelin

Jerusalem

Bethlehem

Ascalon

Judea

Dead Sea

Gaza

Hebron

| 0 | 25 | 50 | 75 | 100 kilometres |

| 0 | 10 | 20 | 30 | 40 | 50 miles |

Preface and Acknowledgements

As most undergraduates find, at one point in the course of their studies, the prospect of a lecture starting at 9 a.m. can feel unfair and almost cruel. I remember wearily climbing the stairs of the History Faculty in Cambridge in 1992, having to shake myself awake to take a seat to listen to the first lecture of the term on the paper I had chosen, called 'Byzantium and its neighbours, 800–1200'. Five minutes later, I was suddenly alert and transfixed, as though I had just been given a triple espresso. I was hearing about the ruthless Pecheneg steppe nomads and how they would do anything in return for pepper, scarlet silk and strips of Middle Eastern leather; I was wondering about why pagan Bulgar leaders would choose to become Christians in the ninth century; I was hearing about New Rome – the imperial city of Constantinople.

The excitement of that first lecture triggered a voracious appetite about the Byzantine Empire and its neighbours. It was a matter of course that I should want to carry on to do postgraduate research, and the only difficulty was choosing a topic. It was the reign of the emperor Alexios I Komnenos that caught my eye, with its wonderfully rich sources and many unanswered questions. It soon became clear, however, that in order to gain any real insight into the Byzantine Empire in the late eleventh and early twelfth centuries, I had to understand the literature of this period, and the *Alexiad* in particular; then the Greek and Latin sources of southern Italy; then the world of the steppe nomads; then the archaeology and material culture of Constantinople, the Balkans and Asia Minor; then the history of the Crusades, the medieval papacy, the establishment of Latin colonies in the Holy Land . . . What had started, innocently enough, with an early morning lecture became a passion; occasionally overwhelming, sometimes frustrating, always exciting.

There are many who deserve thanks for their support and help over the years. The provost and fellows of Worcester College have provided a wonderful and sympathetic home since 1997, outstanding in their generosity and modest in the demands they have made. I owe thanks to Princeton University for awarding me a Stanley J. Seeger Visiting Fellowship, which allowed me a chance to open new avenues of research. The fellows of Harvard are also owed a debt of gratitude for making me a summer fellow at Dumbarton Oaks, where some of the ideas here took shape many moons ago. The staff of the Bodleian Library, above all the Lower Reading Room, and of the History Faculty Library have been wonderfully patient and good-humoured. The same is true of my many colleagues in Oxford where I have had the great privilege to work alongside some of the finest scholars in the field of Late Antique and Byzantine Studies.

I owe thanks to many of my colleagues in Oxford, but particularly to Mark Whittow, Catherine Holmes, Cyril and Marlia Mango, Elizabeth and Michael Jeffreys, Marc Lauxtermann and James Howard-Johnston who have been generous in sharing their views of the eleventh and twelfth centuries. I am particularly grateful to Jonathan Shepard, who gave that first lecture in Cambridge, for steering me towards Byzantium and for proving an important influence since. Many others, from my undergraduate and graduate students to colleagues with whom I have discussed Constantinople, Alexios and the Crusades late into the night at conferences, are also owed my gratitude. If I have failed to take their good advice, and that of others, I can only apologise.

Catherine Clarke has been wonderful, encouraging me to tell the story of the First Crusade afresh. This book would not have been written without her guidance and the help of her fantastic team at Felicity Bryan. Will Sulkin at The Bodley Head and Joyce Seltzer at Harvard University Press have been generous and supportive throughout. I owe thanks to Jörg Hensgen for asking difficult questions and making this book better than it would otherwise have been. Chloe Campbell has been a guardian angel, her patience and advice consistent and invaluable. Many thanks to Anthony Hippisley, and also to Martin Lubikowski for his maps. I could not be more grateful to my parents, who have inspired me since I was a boy.

My greatest debt is to my wife Jessica, who heard about nomads, Byzantium and the eastern Mediterranean on the same day that I did, as I told her excitedly about the new world I had encountered that morning. She listened patiently as I told her I had found my dream subject, and encouraged me to pursue it over the first of many cappuccinos in Clowns; this book is dedicated to her.

Peter Frankopan
July 2011

Author's Note

I have not followed a consistent rule when transliterating from Greek, as it would seem churlish not to use well-established English forms of well-known names. Naturally, this leads to some personal judgements, which I hope are not off-putting. I have used Constantinople, Nicaea and Cappadocia, for example, but Dyrrakhion, Thessaloniki and Nikomedia. Likewise with individuals, I have used George, Isaac and Constantine, but Alexios, Nikephoros, Palaiologos and Komnenos. Western names are given in their modern form, hence William rather than Guillermus and Robert rather than Robertus. Turkish names follow the *Encyclopaedia of Islam*.

Where possible, I have used English translations of the major sources, rather than direct readers to the original texts. This is not always ideal, since in some cases, there are outstanding modern critical editions which will in due course lead to better and finer translations than some of those cited. Nevertheless, it seems preferable to aim for some consistency of approach than to cite some modern translations but provide my own versions of others. As with the names, I very much hope that this does not detract from the wider enjoyment of the subject matter.

Introduction

On 27 November 1095, in the town of Clermont in central France, Pope Urban II stood up to deliver one of the most electrifying speeches in history. He had spent the previous week presiding over a church council attended by twelve archbishops, eighty bishops and other senior clergy, before announcing that he wanted to give an address of special importance to the faithful. Rather than speak from the pulpit of the church in Clermont, Urban decided to deliver his words in a nearby field so all who had gathered in anticipation could hear him.

The setting was spectacular. Nestled at the heart of a chain of dormant volcanoes, with the mightiest of the lava domes, the Puy-de-Dôme, clearly visible just five miles away, the Pope had chosen a spectacular setting. The crowd strained to hear him as he began to speak on a cold winter's day: 'Dearest brethren,' he said, 'I, Urban, supreme pontiff and by the permission of God prelate of the whole world, have come in this time of urgent necessity to you, the servants of God in these regions, as a messenger for divine admonition.'[1]

The Pope was about to make a dramatic call to arms, on the point of urging men with military experience to march thousands of miles to the Holy City of Jerusalem. The speech was intended to inform and to provoke, to exhort and to anger; to generate a reaction of unprecedented scale. And it did precisely that. Less than four years later, western knights were camped by the walls of the city where Jesus Christ was crucified, about to take Jerusalem in God's name. Tens of thousands had left their homes and crossed Europe, spurred on by Urban's words at Clermont, determined to liberate the Holy City.

'We want you to know', the Pope explained in his speech at Clermont, 'what sad cause has brought us to your land and what emergency of yours and all the faithful it is that has brought us here'. Disturbing news had reached him, he said, both from Jerusalem and from the city of Constantinople: the Muslims, 'a foreign people and a people rejected by God, had invaded lands belonging to Christians, destroying them and plundering the local population'. Many had been brutally murdered; others had been taken prisoner and carried off into captivity.[2]

The Pope graphically described the atrocities being committed in the east by the 'Persians' – by which he meant the Turks. 'They throw down altars, after soiling them with their own filth, circumcise Christians, and pour the resulting blood either on the altars or into the baptismal vessels. When they feel like inflicting a truly painful death on some they pierce their navels, pull out the end of their intestines, tie them to a pole and whip them around it until, all their bowels pulled out, they fall lifeless to the ground. They shoot arrows at others tied to stakes; others again they attack having stretched out their necks, unsheathing their swords to see if they can manage to hack off their heads with one blow. And what can I say about the appalling treatment of women, which is better to pass over in silence than to spell out in detail?'[3]

Urban did not mean to inform the crowd which had gathered, but to galvanise it: 'Not I but God exhorts you as heralds of Christ to repeatedly urge men of all ranks whatsoever, knights as well as foot soldiers, rich and poor, to hasten to exterminate this vile race from our lands and to aid the Christian inhabitants in time.'[4]

The knighthood of Europe should rise up and advance boldly as warriors of Christ and rush as quickly as they could to the defence of the Eastern Church. A battle line of Christian knights should form and march to Jerusalem, driving out the Turks on the way. 'May you deem it a beautiful thing to die for Christ in the city where he died for us.'[5] God had blessed the knights of Europe with an outstanding ability in battle, great courage and strength. The time had come, he said, for them to make use of their powers and avenge the sufferings of the Christians in the east and to deliver the Holy Sepulchre to the hands of the faithful.[6]

The various accounts of what Urban said at Clermont leave little doubt that the Pope's speech was an oratorical masterpiece, his exhortations carefully weighted, his gruesome examples of Turkish oppression perfectly chosen.[7] He went on to describe the rewards awaiting those who took up arms: whoever made the journey east would be eternally blessed. All were encouraged to take up this offer. Crooks and thieves were urged to become 'soldiers of Christ', while those who had previously fought against their brothers and kinsmen were told to now join forces and fight lawfully against the barbarians. Whoever went on the journey, inspired by their devotion rather than for the love of money or glory, would receive remission of all their sins. It was, in the words of one observer, 'a new way to attain salvation'.[8]

The response to Urban's speech was rapturous. Up went the cry: '*Deus vult! Deus vult! Deus vult!*' – 'God wills it! God wills it! God wills it!' The crowd listened intently to hear what the Pope would say next. 'Let that be a war-cry for you in battle because it came from God. When you mass together to attack the enemy, this cry sent by God will be the cry of all – "God wills it! God wills it!"'[9]

Many who heard the Pope's speech were gripped by enthusiasm, hurrying home to begin preparations. Clerics dispersed to spread the word, while Urban undertook a gruelling schedule, criss-crossing France to promote the expedition, dispatching stirring letters to regions he did not have time to visit. Soon all of France was abuzz with crusading fever. Leading noblemen and knights hurried to join the expedition. Men like Raymond of Toulouse, one of the richest and most powerful figures in Europe, agreed to participate, as did Godfrey, Duke of Lorraine, who was so eager that before setting out, he minted coins bearing the legend 'GODEFRIDUS IEROSOLIMITANUS' – 'Godfrey the Jerusalem pilgrim'.[10] News of the expedition to Jerusalem spread quickly and feverishly.[11] The First Crusade was under way.

Four years later, in early July 1099, a battered, bedraggled yet supremely determined force of knights took up position by the walls of Jerusalem. The holiest location in Christendom was about to be attacked and seized from the Muslims. Siege engines had been built and were ready for action. Solemn prayers had been offered. The knights were about to achieve one of the most astonishing feats of endeavour in history.

The ambition of the First Crusade stemmed in part from the scale of the enterprise. In the past, armies had marched long distances and defied the odds to make sweeping conquests. The campaigns of the great generals of antiquity, such as Alexander the Great, Julius Caesar and Belisarius, showed how vast tracts of territory could be swallowed up by well-led, disciplined soldiers. What made the Crusade different was the fact that the western force was not an army of conquest but of liberation. At Clermont, Urban did not urge the knighthood of Europe to seize places as they journeyed east, benefiting from the resources of newly conquered towns and regions; rather, the aim was to free Jerusalem – and the churches of the east – from the oppression of the so-called pagans.[12]

Things had not proved quite so simple, however. The journey across thousands of miles had brought terrible suffering and hardship, countless casualties and enormous sacrifice. Of the 70,000–80,000 soldiers of Christ who had responded to the Pope's call, no more than a third reached Jerusalem. Urban's envoy, travelling with the main Crusade leaders and writing back to Rome in the autumn of 1099, put the ratio of survivors to those lost in battle and disease well below this, suggesting that fewer than ten per cent of those who set out ever saw the walls of the Holy City.[13]

Pontius Rainaud and his brother Peter, 'most noble princes', for example, were murdered by robbers after travelling from Provence through northern Italy and down the Dalmatian coast; they did not even make it halfway to Jerusalem. Walter of Verva got considerably further when he went out to forage for food one day with a band of fellow knights near Sidon (in modern Lebanon). He never came back. Perhaps he was ambushed and killed; maybe he was taken prisoner and sent as a captive deep into the bowels of the Muslim world, never to be heard of again; or perhaps his end was altogether more mundane: a missed step by a heavily laden horse on mountainous terrain could easily have fatal consequences.[14]

There was Godevere, a noblewoman who chose to accompany her husband, Count Baldwin of Bouillon, on his journey east. She fell ill near Marash (in modern Turkey) and faded quickly, her condition worsening daily before she slipped away and died. This English-born aristocrat was laid to rest in an obscure and exotic corner of Asia Minor, far away from home, in a place her ancestors and kinsmen would never have heard of.[15]

Then there were others, like Raimbold Cretons, a young knight from Chartres, who reached Jerusalem and took part in the assault on the city. He was the first knight to scale the ladders that had been placed against the walls, no doubt striving for the kudos heaped on the first man to break into the city. But Raimbold's ascent had been watched by a defender of the fortifications who was no less eager, and who dealt him a blow that took one arm clean off and severed the other almost completely; Raimbold at least survived to witness the fall of Jerusalem.[16]

And then there were the men whose mission ended in glory. The great leaders of the First Crusade – Bohemond, Raymond of Toulouse, Godfrey and Baldwin of Bouillon, Tancred and others – became household names all over Europe as a result of the capture of the Holy City. Their achievements were commemorated in countless histories, in verse and song, and in a new form of literature: medieval romance. Their success was to provide the benchmark for all later Crusades. It was a tough act to follow.

The First Crusade is one of the best-known and most written-about events in history. The story of knights taking up arms and crossing Europe to liberate Jerusalem enthralled writers at the time and has thrilled historians and readers ever since. Tales of astounding heroism, of the first encounters with the Muslim Turks, of the hardships suffered by the armed pilgrims on their journey east – ending with the bloody slaughter of the population of Jerusalem in 1099 – have echoed through western culture for nearly a thousand years. Imagery and themes from the Crusade proliferated in the music, literature and art of Europe. Even the word 'Crusade' itself – literally, the way of the Cross – came to take on a wider meaning: a dangerous but ultimately successful quest by the forces of good against evil.

The First Crusade captured the popular imagination because of its drama and violence. But it was not just theatre: the expedition has held its grip on the west because it shaped so much of what was to come: the rise of papal power, the confrontation between Christianity and Islam, the evolution of the concepts of holy war, knightly piety and religious devotion, the emergence of the Italian maritime states and the establishment of colonies in the Middle East. All had their roots in the First Crusade.[17]

Not surprisingly, literature on the subject continues to flourish. Although generations of historians have written about the expedition, a remarkable school of modern scholars has produced outstanding and original work over the last few decades. Subjects such as the marching speed of the Crusader army, its provisioning and the coinage it used have been examined in detail.[18] The interrelationship between the main narrative western sources has been looked at, recently provocatively so.[19] In the past few years, attention has turned to understanding the apocalyptic backdrop to the expedition to Jerusalem and to the early medieval world in general.[20]

Innovative approaches to the Crusade have been taken: psychoanalysts have suggested that the knights who went to Jerusalem were looking for an outlet to relieve pent-up sexual tension, while economists have examined supply/demand imbalances in the late eleventh century and explored the expedition in terms of the allocation of resources in early medieval Europe and the Mediterranean.[21] Geneticists have assessed mitochondrial evidence from southern Anatolia in an effort to understand population movements in the late eleventh century.[22] Others have pointed out that the period around the Crusade was the only time before the end of the twentieth century that GDP outstripped population growth, the implication being that there are parallels to be found between medieval and modern demographics and economic boom.[23]

And yet, in spite of our perennial fascination with the First Crusade, remarkably little attention has ever been paid to its real origins. For nearly ten centuries, the focus of writers and scholars has been on Pope Urban II, his rousing speech at Clermont and the galvanising of the knighthood of Europe. However, the catalyst for the expedition to Jerusalem was not the Pope, but another figure entirely: the call to arms issued by Urban was the result of a direct appeal for help from the emperor of Constantinople, Alexios I Komnenos, in the east.

Founded in the fourth century as a second capital from which the Roman Empire could govern its sprawling provinces in the eastern Mediterranean, the 'New Rome' soon became known as the city of its founder, the emperor Constantine. Constantinople, nestled on the western bank of the Bosphorus, grew to become the largest city in Europe, adorned with triumphal arches, palaces, statues of emperors and countless churches and monasteries built in the centuries after Constantine adopted Christianity.

The Eastern Roman Empire continued to flourish after the western provinces faded and 'Old Rome' fell in the fifth century. By 1025, it controlled most of the Balkans, southern Italy, Asia Minor as well as large parts of the Caucasus and northern Syria, and it had expanding ambitions in Sicily. Seventy years later, the picture was rather different. Turkish raiders had swarmed into Anatolia, sacking several important cities and severely disrupting provincial society. The Balkans had been subject to decades of near incessant attack, with much the same consequences. The empire's territories in Apulia and Calabria, meanwhile, had been lost altogether, taken by Norman adventurers who conquered southern Italy in less than two decades.

The man who stood between the collapse of the empire and its salvation was Alexios Komnenos. An outstanding young general, Alexios had not inherited the throne, but seized it in a military coup in 1081 at the age of around twenty-five. His first years in power were uncomfortable as he struggled to deal with the external threats facing Byzantium while at the same time imposing himself over the empire. As a usurper, lacking the legitimacy of power through succession, Alexios took a pragmatic approach to secure his position, centralising authority and promoting close allies and members of his family to the most important positions in Byzantium. But by the mid-1090s, he was losing his political authority and the Byzantine Empire was reeling from violent incursions on all sides.

In 1095, Alexios sent envoys to Urban II, with an urgent message. Finding the Pope at Piacenza, they 'implored his lordship and all the faithful of Christ to bring assistance against the heathen for the defence of this holy church, which had now been nearly annihilated in that region by the infidels who had conquered her as far as the walls of Constantinople'.[24] Urban reacted immediately, declaring that he would head north, to France, to gather together forces to aid the emperor. It was this appeal from Alexios that triggered the First Crusade.

Although the arrival of Byzantine ambassadors is regularly noted in modern histories of the First Crusade, what the emperor was asking for – and why – has been glossed over. As a result, the Crusade is commonly seen as the Pope's call to arms; as Christian soldiers fighting their way to Jerusalem in the name of the Lord. This, certainly, is what the story became, almost as soon as the knights stood on the walls of the city in 1099, and it has been almost uniformly adopted by writers, artists, film-makers and others ever since. But the true origins of the First Crusade lie in what was happening in and around Constantinople at the end of the eleventh century. This book will show that the roots of the expedition lay not in the west but in the east.

Why did Alexios request help in 1095? Why did he appeal to the Pope, a religious leader, without significant military resources of his own? Following a spectacular falling-out between the Catholic and Orthodox churches in 1054, why was Urban willing to provide assistance to the emperor in the first place? Why did Alexios wait till 1095 to make his plea for support when the Turks had made themselves masters of Asia Minor in 1071, after the disastrous defeat of the Byzantine army at the battle of Manzikert? In short, why was there a First Crusade?

There are two reasons why the history of the Crusade has been so distorted. First, after the capture of Jerusalem a powerful school of history writing in western Europe, dominated almost exclusively by monks and clerics, went to great lengths to stress the centrality of the role played by the Pope in conceiving the expedition. This was in turn reinforced by the creation of a string of Crusader states in the Levant based on Jerusalem, Edessa, Tripoli, and above all on Antioch. These new states needed stories that explained how they came to be under the control of western knights. In the case of both the origins of the Crusade and its aftermath, the role of Byzantium and of Alexios I Komnenos were extremely inconvenient – not least since many successes of the Crusaders came at the Eastern Roman empire's expense. It suited western historians to explain the expedition from the perspective of the papacy and the Christian knighthood, and to leave the eastern emperor to one side.

The second reason for the heavy focus on the west stems from the problems of the historical sources. The Latin sources for the First Crusade are well known – and are wonderfully juicy. Narrative accounts such as the anonymous *Gesta Francorum* provide one-sided reports of the personal bravery of individuals such as the heroic Bohemond on the one hand, and the skulduggery of the 'wretched' Emperor Alexios, scheming to outdo the Crusaders with his cunning and fraud on the other. Authors like Raymond of Aguilers, Albert of Aachen and Fulcher of Chartres provide no less lively and opinionated guides to an expedition which saw the competing egos of its leaders clash repeatedly, and where duplicity and treachery were regular features. They record conflicts where success frequently flirted with disaster; they report how morale plunged as the heads of captured knights were catapulted into the Crusaders' camp during the sieges of towns; they note their horror at priests being suspended upside down over city walls and beaten to antagonise the westerners; they tell of noblemen cavorting with lady-friends in orchards, ambushed and gruesomely executed by Turkish scouts.

The primary sources from the east, by contrast, are more complex. The problem is not the quantity of material, for there are a great many accounts, letters, speeches, reports and other documents written in Greek, Armenian, Syriac, Hebrew and Arabic that offer precious glimpses into the prelude of the Crusade. The issue, rather, is that these have been much more poorly exploited than their Latin counterparts.

The most important and difficult of these texts from the east is the *Alexiad*. Written in the middle of the twelfth century by Alexios' eldest daughter, Anna Komnene, this account of the emperor's reign has been both misused and misunderstood. The text, written in florid Greek, is full of nuances, allusions and hidden meanings that are easily overlooked. In particular, the chronological sequence of events provided by the author is often unreliable: events are frequently misplaced, split into two or duplicated.

Writing nearly five decades after the episodes she describes, Anna Komnene can be forgiven for making occasional mistakes about the order in which events happened – a point the author herself acknowledges in the text: 'As I write these words, it is nearly time to light the lamps; my pen moves slowly over the paper and I feel myself almost too drowsy to write as the words escape me. I have to use barbaric names and I am compelled to describe in detail a mass of events which occurred in rapid succession. The result is that the main body of the history and the continuous narrative are bound to become disjointed because of interruptions. Let those who are enjoying the text not bear me a grudge for this.'[25]

The image of the historian crouching over a script, working late into the night, is an emotive and charming one; but here it is a literary device, as is the author's crafted apology about her mistakes, a standard disclaimer used by the writers from classical antiquity whose works provide a template for the *Alexiad*. In fact, Anna Komnene's work is extremely well researched, drawing on an impressive archive of letters, official documents, campaign notes, family histories and other written material.[26]

While some problems of the *Alexiad*'s chronology have been identified by scholars, a great many have not. This in turn has led to major errors in the commonly accepted sequence of events that took place in the reign of Alexios I Komnenos. The most significant of these concerns the state of Asia Minor on the eve of the Crusade. The picture presented by Anna Komnene's account is misleading; in fact, careful re-evaluation of the *Alexiad* – taken together with other source material – reveals startling conclusions, sharply at odds with long-established views. In the past, it has been assumed that the Byzantine emperor sought military assistance from the west to undertake an ambitious and opportunistic reconquest of Asia Minor from a position of strength. The reality was very different. His call for help was a desperate last roll of the dice for a ruler whose regime and empire was teetering on the brink of collapse.

The fact that the situation in Asia Minor on the eve of the First Crusade has not been properly understood in the past is highly significant. The knights were heading east to take on the Turks, a formidable enemy, who had brought the Byzantine Empire to its knees. Originally part of the Oguzz tribal confederation which Arab historians located to the east of the Caspian Sea, the Turks were a steppe people whose military prowess gave them increasing influence over the caliphate in Baghdad as it fragmented in the later tenth century. From the 1030s, not long after their adoption of Islam, the Turks were the dominant force in the region, less than a generation later becoming masters of Baghdad itself after their leader, Tughril Beg, was appointed sultan with full executive powers by the caliph.

Their progress westwards was relentless. Raids soon began on the Caucasus and Asia Minor, causing disruption and provoking panic among the local population. The Turks could move quickly and seemingly without trace on squat central Asian horses whose strength and stamina made them well suited for the mountainous terrain and steep ravines of this region; they were 'swift as eagles, with hooves as solid as rock', according to one source. The Turks reportedly attacked those they came across like wolves devouring their food.[27]

By the time of Urban's speech at Clermont, the Turks had demolished the provincial and military administration of Anatolia that had stood intact for centuries and captured some of the most important towns of early Christianity: places like Ephesus, home of St John the Evangelist, Nicaea, the location of the famous early church council, and Antioch, the original see of St Peter himself, were all lost to the Turks in the years before the Crusade. Little wonder, then, that the Pope pleaded for the salvation of the church in the east in his speeches and letters in the mid-1090s.

The context of the First Crusade is to be found not in the foothills of Clermont or in the Vatican, but in Asia Minor and in Constantinople. For too long, the narrative of the Crusade has been dominated by western voices. But the knights who set out in high expectation in 1096 were reacting to a developing crisis on the other side of the Mediterranean. Military collapse, civil war and attempted coups had brought the Byzantine Empire to the edge. It was to the west that Alexios I Komnenos was forced to turn, and his appeal to Pope Urban II became the catalyst for all that followed.

I

Europe in Crisis

The First Crusade defined the Middle Ages. It established a common identity for the knighthood of Europe, pinned firmly on the Christian faith. It influenced behaviour, with piety and service emerging as highly prized personal qualities, extolled in verse, prose, song and art. It idealised the concept of the devout knight, fighting for God. It established the Pope as a leader not just of spiritual significance but of political importance. It gave common purpose to western principalities, creating a framework where the defence of the church was not just desirable but an obligation. Out of the First Crusade grew the ideas and structures which shaped Europe until the Reformation.

Ironically, the Crusade was itself the product of discord and disunity, for Europe was riven by turmoil and crisis in the second half of the eleventh century. This was a time of conquest and upheaval across the continent. England was under Norman occupation, having barely managed to resist persistent attacks from Scandinavia. Apulia, Calabria and Sicily were also in the process of being transformed by immigrants from Normandy, first mercenaries and then opportunists, who were drawn south by the rich financial rewards on offer. Spain was in transition, its Muslim occupiers being evicted town by town after more than three centuries of control over the peninsula. Germany too was in upheaval, with major uprisings breaking out against the crown on a regular basis. The Byzantine Empire, meanwhile, was under chronic pressure, with its northern, eastern and western frontiers threatened, assaulted and overrun by increasingly aggressive neighbours.

The eleventh century was also a time of violent dispute between the papacy and the leading magnates of Europe which saw rulers being dramatically excommunicated, then sometimes rehabilitated only to be thrown out of communion once again. Almost all the main figures of this period – Henry IV of Germany, Philip I of France, King Harold of England, the Byzantine emperor Alexios I Komnenos and the Norman duke Robert Guiscard – were excommunicated at least once by the papacy as part of its attempts to assert authority over the secular world.

So great were the divisions even within the church that in the late eleventh century there were rival popes, each claiming to be the legitimate heir to the throne of St Peter and backed up by rival clergies claiming to be the legitimate electing body. Then there was the Byzantine church, which was sharply at odds with the practices and teachings that were standard in the west, and in a state of schism with the papacy. Yet the most poisonous and sustained of the arguments engulfing Europe in this period threatened the viability of the church as a whole: a major fallout had devastated relations between Pope Gregory VII and the most powerful man in Europe, Henry IV of Germany. Henry's predecessors had established control over northern Italy and made themselves emperors of Rome in the 960s; as a result they paid close and careful attention to the papacy, retaining a right to be involved in papal elections. Relations between Gregory VII and Henry IV started promisingly enough after the appointment in April 1073 of Gregory, 'a religious man, well versed in both branches [sacred and secular] of knowledge, a most pre-eminent lover of equity and righteousness, strong in adversity . . . honourable, modest, sober, chaste, hospitable'.[1] The Pope took heart from messages sent by the emperor after his election. Henry, he wrote to one supporter, 'has sent us words full of pleasantness and obedience, and such as we remember that neither he nor his predecessors ever sent to Roman pontiffs'.[2]

It did not take long, though, for relations to degenerate. Even before becoming pope, Gregory had been a pragmatist with strong views about reforming the church and centralising Rome's power more effectively. Of particular concern was the issue of appointments to high offices in the church, many of which were being sold in what amounted to little better than organised corruption. Some senior positions brought lucrative stipends as well as influence and authority, making them a highly desirable sinecure – useful rewards to be handed out by powerful rulers.[3]

Gregory's attempts at reform by banning the sale of religious offices and asserting that he alone had the right to make appointments set him on a collision course with Henry, who deeply resented the Pope's interference in the affairs of the German church. By 1076, relations had broken down to such an extent that the Pope excommunicated Henry, declaring that 'on behalf of Almighty God, the Father, Son and the Holy Spirit, through your power and authority, I deny to King Henry, son of the emperor Henry, who has risen up with unheard of pride against your church, the government of the entire kingdom of the Germans and of Italy, and I absolve all Christians from the bond of any oath that they have taken, or shall take, to him; and I forbid anyone to serve him as king'.[4]

Not surprisingly, this inflamed tensions, with Henry's supporters declaring that the Pope was a criminal and bishops loyal to the German sovereign passing the sentence of excommunication on the pontiff himself.[5] Although the two men were briefly reconciled in the later 1070s, their relationship broke down once and for all after the Pope was persuaded to give his backing to powerful enemies of the emperor in Germany, who were seeking to depose him. After Gregory endorsed the claims of one of these rivals to the throne, praising his humility, obedience and love of truth in contrast to Henry's pride, disobedience and deceit, the emperor took drastic steps.[6]

The bishops of Germany and northern Italy were summoned to a church council at Brixen in June 1080. There it was proposed that Gregory should be expelled from Rome by force and replaced by an 'orthodox' pope. Wibert, archbishop of Ravenna, was nominated as pope elect, with his coronation to take place in Rome the following spring.[7] After being delayed by uprisings in Germany, Henry IV finally marched into Italy, advancing on Rome and taking the city in 1084. Wibert was immediately crowned as Pope Clement III in the basilica of St Peter. A week later, Henry himself was crowned as emperor of Rome. 'We have been ordained by Pope Clement', he wrote, 'and have been consecrated emperor by consent of all the Romans on the Holy Day of Easter with the exultation of the whole Roman people.'[8]

The establishment of Clement as a rival pope, claiming to be the true heir to the throne of St Peter and supported by a swathe of senior clergy, threatened to split the Roman church in two. Although Gregory himself took refuge in the Lateran and eventually escaped from Rome to Salerno, where he died in exile in 1085, uncertainty and confusion continued to cloud the papacy. It took nearly a year for a successor to be named to take Gregory VII's place, and even then the candidate chosen as pope, Victor III, had to be installed more or less by force. His death after barely eighteen months in office led to a new election and created further upheaval. In March 1088, Odo, cardinal bishop of Ostia, was named pope, taking the name Urban II; yet he was not recognised in lands subject to Henry IV in Germany or northern Italy. The church was in disarray.

The schism in the Western Church showed little sign of healing in the years that followed. In the decade before the Council of Clermont in 1095, it was Clement III – and not Urban II – who was in the stronger position. The latter, after all, was rarely even able to get inside the walls of Rome in the first years of his pontificate: even his election had taken place in Terracina, well away from the Eternal City, which was still firmly held by forces loyal to the emperor. Although he briefly managed to enter Rome in 1089, celebrating with a procession, a coronation Mass and proclaiming an encyclical, he quickly withdrew again, not daring to risk staying in the city for any length of time.[9] When he returned at Christmas in 1091 and 1092, he was forced to camp outside the city walls, unable to undertake the most basic duties of the Pope, including saying Mass in St Peter's.[10]

The idea that Urban might be ble to move and inspire the Christian knights of Europe to rise up, bear arms and march on Jerusalem would have been laughable at the time of his election. Although the Pope followed developments in Spain closely, where gains were being made at the expense of the Muslims, he could do little more than send enthusiastic letters of support and encouragement.[11] But given Urban's predicament at home, his concern for the fate of the faithful in the east, while perhaps heartfelt, would have carried little weight and no influence in a world where he struggled to rally supporters even in Rome, let alone elsewhere in Europe.

In contrast, Clement III was relentlessly reinforcing his position as the true head of the Catholic Church. In the late 1080s, he sent a spate of letters to Lanfranc, archbishop of Canterbury, inviting him to Rome, asking for Peter's pence to be sent to him, and offering to intervene in disputes in England. He also urged the king of England and the bishops to provide help to the mother church.[12] Clement communicated with the Serbs, confirming clerical appointments and sending a special ecclesiastical vestment, a pallium, to the archbishop of

Antivari.[13] He made contact with the head of the church in Kiev, the capital of the medieval Russian state, sending him messages of good-will.[14] He was behaving exactly as the Pope should: officiously contacting, advising and supporting leading figures in the Christian world. It was Clement III, and not Urban, who looked likely to deliver the sort of speech and produce the sort of reaction that might unite the church in the mid-1090s.

Where Urban II did have an advantage over his rival was in his relationship with the Eastern Church – though this itself was not without difficulty. Originally, Rome and Constantinople had been two of the five primary sees of Christendom, along with Antioch, Alexandria and Jerusalem. The fall of the last three to the Islamic conquests of the seventh century elevated the status of the remaining two cities to the point of endemic rivalry. Disputes about their relative importance, as well as about matters of doctrine and practice, flared up on a regular basis, and furious exchanges between Pope Nicholas I and the head of the church in Constantinople, the patriarch Photios, had brought relations to a particular low point in the ninth century.

Normally, though, time soothed tensions and these quarrels were broken up by long periods of co-operation. A tenth-century Byzantine manual reveals how letters sent by the emperor in Constantinople to the Pope should be addressed, following a set formula: 'In the name of the Father and of the Son and of the Holy Spirit, our one and only God. [name left blank] and [name left blank], emperors of the Romans, faithful to God, to [name left blank] most holy Pope of Rome and our spiritual father'. Likewise, respectful terms with which to address the emperor were set out for ambassadors from Rome.[15] These formulas suggest that co-operation between east and west was the norm rather than the exception.

In the middle of the eleventh century, however, relations between Rome and Constantinople emphatically broke down. A mission sent by Pope Leo IX in 1054 to explore common interests in Italy, where Byzantium controlled the regions of Apulia and Calabria, went spectacularly awry. Negotiations started off on the wrong foot, with discussion turning not to a possible alliance but to differences between the Latin and Greek rites in celebrating the Eucharist. As the excitable source material shows, it was of real significance to resolve whether leavened or unleavened bread should be used for the body of Christ. Most important of all, however, was the addition of the so-called *filioque* clause to the Creed, by which it was claimed that the Holy Spirit proceeded not just from the Father, but also from the Son. Initially proposed at a church council in Spain in the sixth century, which was, significantly, not attended by many leading clerics, its use had been initially condemned even by the papacy. However, the controversial *filioque* clause became increasingly prevalent in a world where it was not always easy to regulate practices. By the early eleventh century it was used so widely that it was formally accepted as a standard part of the Creed. The addition of the clause by Rome was furiously decried in the eastern Mediterranean, above all in Constantinople.

After the embassy reached the Byzantine capital, matters quickly came to a head. On 16 July 1054, the papal legate, Cardinal Humbert of Silva Candida, along with other envoys from Rome, strode into the great church of Hagia Sophia in Constantinople as the Eucharist was being celebrated. In a moment of high drama, they walked directly up to the front of the church, not pausing to pray. Before the clergy and the congregation, they produced a document and brazenly placed it on the high altar. The patriarch of Constantinople, it read, had abused his office and was guilty of many errors in his beliefs and teaching. He was forthwith excommunicated, to suffer with all the worst heretics in hell, who were listed carefully. The patriarch and his supporters were condemned to eternal damnation, to suffer with 'the Devil himself and his angels, unless they should repent. Amen, Amen, Amen.' With that, Humbert turned around and walked out of the church, pausing to pat the dust from his sandals as he reached the doors of Hagia Sophia. He then turned to the congregation and declared solemnly: 'Let God see and judge'.[16]

This was the nadir in relations between Rome and Constantinople, to this day known as the Great Schism. The animosity between east and west now became almost institutionalised. In 1078, for example, Gregory VII issued a notice excommunicating Nikephoros III Botaneiates, even though the new emperor had not had any contact with Rome; three years later, the Pope did the same to Alexios I Komnenos after the latter deposed Nikephoros.[17] Around the same time, the Pope not only sanctioned an attack on Byzantium, but issued its leader with a banner to carry into battle against the imperial army. He even went so far as to endorse Robert Guiscard, the architect of the assault, as the legitimate candidate for the throne of Constantinople itself, even though the Norman had neither a genuine claim nor a realistic chance of installing himself as emperor.[18]

This puts Urban's call to arms at Clermont into sharp relief. As the contemporary sources from late 1095 and early 1096 make clear, the Pope drew careful attention to the suffering of Christians in Asia Minor and to the persecution of the churches in the east – that is to say, the churches following the Greek rite.[19] What led to this remarkable turnaround in the relations between Rome and Constantinople? The reasons for this extraordinary shift lay in the struggle for control of the church as a whole in the later eleventh century and, in particular, with the weakness of Urban's position in the west.

When he became pope, Urban was keenly aware that he was being outmanoeuvred by Clement III and his protector Henry IV; he was forced to build bridges wherever he could. One of the first steps he took was to conciliate with Constantinople. Soon after his election in 1088, the Pope sent a small delegation to the imperial capital to discuss the sensitive topics that had provoked the falling-out three decades earlier. After being received by the emperor, they set out the issues in 'a gentle and fatherly way', as one contemporary commentator put it, covering topics such as the Greek use of leavened bread, as well as the removal of the Pope's name from the holy diptychs of Constantinople, which contained the lists of the bishops, living and dead, considered to be in communion with the church.[20]

The emperor, Alexios I, was a former general with spartan tastes and a no-nonsense approach to his faith – a man who stayed awake late into the night with his wife immersed in study of the Holy Scriptures, according to their eldest daughter.[21] He listened to the Pope's ambassadors and ordered a synod to be convened to discuss their grievances, which included the complaint that churches following the Latin rite in the capital had been closed down, thereby preventing westerners living in the city from worshipping. The emperor also personally presided over a meeting attended by the patriarchs of Constantinople and Antioch, two archbishops and eighteen bishops, and asked to see the documents relating to the decision to remove the Pope's name from the diptychs. When informed that these did not exist, and furthermore that there appeared to be no canonical basis for the absence of the Pope's name, he ordered that it be reinserted, according to custom.[22]

Alexios went further. Through the envoys, the emperor urged the Pope to come to Constantinople to put an end to the disputes which had been so damaging to the church in the past. In a document stamped with the imperial gold seal, he suggested that a special council should be convened, made up of senior Greek and Latin clergy, to discuss the major areas of difference. For his part, the emperor promised to abide by the conclusions reached in order to achieve a united definition of the Church of God.[23]

The patriarch of Constantinople, Nicholas III Grammatikos, then wrote separately to the Pope in October 1089, expressing his delight that Urban was keen to affect an end to ecclesiastical dispute. The Pope was wrong, Nicholas wrote politely, to think that the patriarch personally harboured animosity to Latin Christians. He was mistaken too to think that churches using the western rite in the capital had been closed; in fact, the westerners living in Constantinople were allowed to worship using the Latin rite. 'We desire with all our heart, more than anything, the unity of the church', Nicholas wrote.[24]

These steps reopened dialogue with Rome and paved the way for a major realignment of the Byzantine Empire on the eve of the First Crusade. A senior Byzantine cleric, Theophylact Hephaistos, was commissioned to prepare a document deliberately playing down the significance of the differences between Greek and Latin customs to soothe misgivings in the Eastern Church. Many were petty, he wrote. Latin priests observed a fast on Saturdays, rather than on Sundays; they fasted incorrectly during Lent; unlike Orthodox priests, they thought nothing of wearing rings on their fingers, and also cut their hair and shaved their beards; they were not dressed in black while celebrating the liturgy but wore coloured silk vestments; they did not genuflect correctly; and unlike Greek monks who were strict vegetarians, Latin monks were only too happy to eat lard and various meats. All these issues could be easily resolved, the cleric argued, as could the question of leavening bread for use in the Eucharist.[25] The *filioque* addition to the Creed was an altogether more serious problem, he acknowledged, and those who accepted the clause would descend into the flames of hell.[26] Nevertheless, he was still hopeful that the clause would be removed.[27]

This careful repositioning was intended to close the gap between Constantinople and Rome, not just in religious affairs, but to pave the way for a political and even a military alliance. It was a crucial staging post in the genesis of the First Crusade, and a prerequisite for the Pope's appeal to the knighthood of Europe to march to Byzantium's defence just a few years later.

Urban reacted quickly to the positive signs from Constantinople. He travelled south to meet with one of his few supporters, Count Roger of Sicily, and seek his approval for improving links with Byzantium. Roger had long been concerned by Henry IV's aggressive intervention in Italy. In the mid-1080s some of the German emperor's supporters had called on Henry to advance to Constantinople and then to Jerusalem where glorious coronations would await him; along the way he should also establish himself over the Normans by taking control of Apulia and Calabria, the latter at Roger's expense.[28] Roger gave an unequivocal reply when he heard about Alexios' invitation to hold a council to mend relations: the Pope should attend, and rid the church of the Great Schism.[29]

This was exactly what Urban wanted to hear: it gave him the chance to take on the role of unifier of the Church. In the context of his struggle with Clement III, Urban's breakthrough was invaluable – and Clement knew it. The latter found out about his rival's exchanges with Constantinople from Basil of Calabria, a hard-line Byzantine cleric who had become disaffected by being prevented by Urban from taking up his see in southern Italy. Basil had been present at the Council of Melfi in the autumn of 1089 when it was made plain that he would be installed in Reggio if he recognised the Pope's authority. Appalled to see two of his colleagues do just that, Basil exploded with fury.[30] In his eyes, Urban was unworthy of the office of pope, just like his 'three times cursed' predecessor Gregory VII. He wrote to the patriarch of Constantinople describing the Pope as a cowardly wolf who ran away when faced with the most basic questions about Christian doctrine. He was a heretic who had also taken to selling ecclesiastical offices to the highest bidder.[31]

Basil's personal misgivings mask the fact that the Council of Melfi was a significant moment for rebuilding relations between Rome and

Constantinople. What Basil saw as the unforgivable submission of his colleagues to take up their sees at Rossano and Santa Severina were in fact more likely to be important cases of new co-operation between the Pope and Byzantium in southern Italy.[32]

Basil nevertheless took matters into his own hands. As soon as he learnt about the conciliatory moves in Constantinople, he made contact with Clement III. The antipope replied immediately. 'Please send us quickly the letter from our holy brother the Patriarch of Constantinople which you have mentioned', referring to the instructions Basil had been sent in order to reconcile with Rome. 'We also must reply to him about the subject which is of such concern; he should know that everything has been duly prepared by us – for we too wish, and welcome, peace and unity.'[33] Clement reassured Basil about his own grievances, promising him that these would soon be revolved in his favour.[34] Yet if Clement did try to initiate dialogue of his own with Constantinople, it did not get far. Although he had shown an interest in building bridges with the Greek church – writing to John, the Byzantine-born metropolitan, or archbishop, of Kiev to raise the prospect of closer ties with the Greek church – his overtures came to nothing. For Alexios, Urban was a more attractive ally than his German-backed counterpart.[35]

For one thing, Urban still retained influence in southern Italy, a region that had been under Byzantine control for centuries until a disastrous set of reversals in the 1050s and 1060s at the hands of Norman conquerors whose power spread, according to Anna Komnene, like gangrene – 'for gangrene, once established in a body, never rests until it has invaded and corrupted the whole of it'.[36] Although the fall of Bari to the Normans in 1071 brought imperial rule of Apulia and Calabria to an ignominious end, the provinces were still home to a primarily Greek-speaking population who looked naturally to Constantinople for their lead. This link was now reactivated in the wake of rapprochement between Rome and Constantinople. Since the Norman conquest, wills, sales charters and other formal documents had carried the name of the Norman duke to date them. But from the start of the 1090s, Alexios' name and regnal year began to appear with increasing frequency, a clear sign that the locals were looking once again to the emperor for leadership.[37] The rehabilitation of Byzantium went a step further when Urban lifted the excommunication that had been passed on Alexios in 1081.[38]

There were other signs of a realignment of interests between east and west. In the early 1090s, the Greek monastery of San Filippo di Fragalà benefited from a surge of favours. Several churches were placed under its authority and additional lands were granted to its community of monks by Count Roger of Sicily, who issued a decree that the monastery would be free from the interference of the Latin clergy, and from 'the barons, the *strategoi*, the viscounts as well as all others'.[39] And there were examples of significant co-operation else-where, specifically with regard to military matters. Faced with major invasions across the Balkans in the early 1090s, Alexios I sent appeals to all quarters to bolster his forces. Imperial envoys were also sent to Urban in Campania, who promptly dispatched men in the spring of 1091 to help Alexios fight Pecheneg steppe nomads who had launched a massive invasion from the Danube deep into Thrace. The subsequent battle of Lebounion, which saw the annihilation of this fearsome nomadic tribe, was one of the most important battles in the empire's history.[40]

By 1095, therefore, much had been done to heal the long-standing rift between Rome and Constantinople. Although the council proposed by Alexios a few years earlier had yet to take place, emperor and Pope had struck up a good working relationship. Indeed, if a later addition to a twelfth-century source is to be believed, together they had already developed a plan. Envoys reportedly arrived at the court of King Zvonimir of Croatia early in 1090, sent jointly by Urban and Alexios, appealing for knights to provide assistance to the beleaguered church in Byzantium and to relieve Muslim oppression in Jerusalem. If true, this was a dry run for the Pope's appeal at Clermont: a call for help from Old and New Rome; the lure of Jerusalem; and military service as an act of devotion. In Zvonimir's case, however, it did not have the desired effect: according to the interpolation, his knights were so appalled that Zvonimir was prepared to fight somebody else's war that they murdered him (although other sources claim that the king died peacefully of old age).[41]

By pursuing reconciliation with Constantinople, Urban deliberately positioned himself as the leader of the Christian world, which had been ravaged by years of intense competition, struggle and strife. As one contemporary chronicler put it, at the end of the eleventh century the church was in a state of chaos. 'In all parts of Europe', wrote

Fulcher of Chartres, 'peace, virtue and faith were brutally trampled upon by stronger men and lesser, inside the church and out. It was necessary to put an end to all these evils.'[42] Yet Urban needed a wider scheme to establish himself at the heart of Christendom. The headway he had made in his dealings with the Greek church was not enough on its own to have any wider meaning when it came to the rivalry with Clement III in Rome, let alone strengthen his position elsewhere in Europe.

In the mid-1090s, however, the situation began to change. First, sudden and unexpected developments in Germany offered an extraordinary opportunity to outflank the antipope and his chief supporter, the emperor Henry IV. Urban was boosted by high-profile defections from Henry's camp, frustrated by the emperor's heavy-handedness. One was Henry's beautiful young wife, who sought out the Pope to complain that she had been forced to commit so many 'unusual filthy acts of fornication with so many men that even her enemies would excuse her flight [from the emperor]. All Catholics should be moved to compassion because of her treatment.'[43] In a highly charged climate where the Pope's supporters were desperate to seize on anything that could be used to discredit the emperor, sordid gossip was circulated gleefully by polemicists.[44] More important still was Conrad, Henry IV's son and heir, a serious young man who decided to renounce his father and together with his vassals offered his support to Urban, exhausted by the never-ending quarrels within the church and unsettled by doubts about his prospects as a result of military setbacks suffered by his father in northern Italy.

These developments gave the Pope an immediate and emphatic boost. Urban announced that he would hold a council in March 1095 in Piacenza, in the heart of territory previously loyal to Henry IV and in the heart of Clement III's original archbishopric of Ravenna. With Henry's estranged wife appearing at the council to condemn her husband, the antipope was fiercely denounced, before an amnesty was offered to all the clergy who had previously sided with the emperor. Immediately after the council, Conrad met with Urban at Cremona where he greeted the Pope by acting the part of a groom, holding the bridle of the pontiff's horse in a ritual mark of deference and public humility.[45] At a second meeting a few days later, Conrad swore an oath to protect the Pope, his office and his property. In return,

Urban promised to recognise Conrad's claim to the imperial throne.[46] He also proposed a marriage between his new ally and the daughter of Count Roger of Sicily, Urban's principal supporter in Italy. It would be much to Roger's honour and to his future profit if a marriage was arranged, the Pope wrote to the count. The marriage was duly concluded in Pisa in splendid style, and Conrad was settled with lavish gifts from his wealthy father-in-law.[47] This helped bring about a dramatic improvement in Urban's position, taking him from an isolated figure forced to camp outside the walls of Rome to a figure of central importance in the politics of Europe.

Something else happened at Piacenza, however, that would change the position of the papacy forever. As the council met to discuss ecclesiastical affairs – definitions of heresy, the excommunication of the king of France on the charge of adultery, matters relating to the priesthood – envoys arrived from Constantinople.[48] They brought terrible news: the Byzantine Empire was on the point of collapse, and help was urgently needed. Urban grasped the implications immediately. Here was the chance to unite the church once and for all. He announced he was heading north – to Clermont.

Crusade historians – medieval and modern – have followed him there. But what were the disasters that had taken place in the east? Why was help so desperately needed? What had gone wrong in Byzantium? To understand the origins of the Crusade, it is not to the foothills of central France we must turn, but to the imperial city of Constantinople.

2

The Recovery of Constantinople

Constantinople was designed to inspire awe. Like Old Rome, it was a vast and immensely imposing capital. A visitor approaching over land would have first seen the massive walls and the huge aqueducts carrying water into the city. Fortified to a height of twelve metres, the Land Walls ran from the Golden Horn to the Sea of Marmara. Rebuilt by the emperor Theodosios in the fifth century, they were designed to deter even the most ambitious enemy. Five metres thick, the walls were protected by ninety-six towers, offering views over the approaches from the west and the north. Entry was controlled by nine well-guarded gates, but those only provided access past the outer walls. The traveller then had to cross a deep moat and pass through another ring of walls before passage opened up along one of the main roads leading into the heart of the city.

If anything, arrival by sea was even more spectacular. Constantinople lay on the north bank of the Sea of Marmara at the narrowest point separating Europe and Asia Minor. The monuments, churches and palaces of the city, glimpsed from the deck of a boat, gave an awesome first impression. The capital stretched as far as the eye could see, covering 30,000 hectares. Its population, numbering in the hundreds of thousands, was about ten times greater than that of the largest cities in Europe.

Constantinople's principal buildings too were astonishing. Most astounding of all was the magnificent church of Hagia Sophia, constructed by the emperor Justinian in the sixth century. Its enormous suspended dome, over thirty metres wide and fifty-five metres high, seemed to float like 'a tent of the heavens'. It was a marvel of engineering and the church was magnificent in its beauty. Golden mosaics twinkled, caught by the light streaming through the windows.[1] Yet

Constantinople was strewn with outstanding landmarks: hundreds of churches and monasteries, a vast hippodrome for chariot and horse racing, bathhouses, the Great Palace and even a zoo. One poem extolling Constantinople suggested that where there were once Seven Wonders of the world, there were now Seven Wonders of Constantinople.[2]

Such a bustling city needed to be provisioned. Markets were monitored and regulated by the office of the eparch, the governor of Constantinople, whose agents made sure that weights were standardised and maintained control of the consistency of produce being sold. Quality was also ensured by a system of guilds: grocers and fishmongers, butchers and chandlers, rope makers and saddlers, all had clear rules and codes of conduct as to what they were allowed to sell, and where they could sell it. There were even clear guidelines as to pricing, at least on staple goods, to control inflation. The result was a steady supply of fruit and vegetables, dairy products, meat and fish, alongside more exotic goods such as spices, wax, silverware and silk – the commodity for which Byzantium was most famous.[3]

One eleventh-century tourist marvelled at the cosmopolitan population of the city and at the magnificence of its buildings, also recording with wonder the religious processions which took place around the capital. He was fortunate enough to witness the miracle of the icon of the Virgin in the church of the Theotokos of Blakhernai, where the Virgin's veil slowly rose to reveal her face, before falling back into place.[4] Another visitor from the late eleventh century could also barely contain his awe: 'Oh, what a noble and beautiful city is Constantinople! How many monasteries and palaces it contains, constructed with wonderful skill! How many remarkable things may be seen in the principal avenues and even in the lesser streets! It would be very tedious to enumerate the wealth that is there of every kind, of gold, of silver, of robes of many kinds, and of holy relics. Merchants constantly bring to the city by frequent voyages all necessities of man. About 20,000 eunuchs, I judge, are always living there.'[5]

The city had long been a magnet for traders and adventurers, seeking to find fame and fortune. There were many like Bolli Bollason, who journeyed to Constantinople from Iceland in the 1020s, to see and experience the capital for themselves. 'I have always wanted to travel to southern lands one day,' he told his peers, 'for a man is thought to grow ignorant if he doesn't ever travel beyond the country of his birth.'[6] It was to Constantinople, many thousands of miles away, that he journeyed. When he reached Byzantium, Bolli joined the Varangian guard, a corps of mercenaries from Scandinavia, Russia and, by the eleventh century, the British Isles who formed the emperor's bodyguard. 'They fight like madmen, as if set on fire with anger', wrote one eleventh-century writer, 'they do not spare themselves and do not care about their wounds.'[7] When Bolli eventually returned to Iceland, he made a striking appearance: 'He had on the clothes of fur which the Garth-king [the Byzantine emperor] had given him, and on top of them a scarlet cape; and he had [an outstanding sword] with him, the hilt of which was brilliant with gold, and the grip woven with gold; he had a gilded helmet on his head, and a red shield on his flank, with a knight painted on it in gold. He had a dagger in his hand, as is the custom in foreign lands. Wherever he went, women paid heed to nothing but gazing at Bolli and his grandeur.'[8]

Bolli was just one of many drawn to Constantinople. Harald Hardrada, later king of Norway, whose exploits appear in the *Heimskringla*, the cycle of sagas about the rulers of Norway, journeyed to Byzantium where he served on galleys, scouted for pirates in the Aegean, and took part in an attack on Sicily in the early 1040s. While in imperial service, he came up with an ingenious flying bomb, coating young birds with pine resin mixed with wax and sulphur before setting fire to them and dispatching them back to their nests inside the walls of the city he was besieging. Serving the great emperor of Constantinople, or Miklegarth – the old Norse name for the city – was exotic, exciting and awesome. It was both an honour and a rite of passage for many Scandinavians.[9]

Then there were men like Odo of Stigand, a young Norman who trained as a doctor and vet in Constantinople in the 1050s, picking up a smattering of several foreign languages in the process. His brother, Robert, also spent time in the capital, bringing gold, precious stones and relics of St Barbara with him when he eventually came home to Normandy.[10] Knights with military experience were welcomed in Byzantium, with several rising to high positions in the imperial army. Some of the Anglo-Saxon leaders who fled England after the battle of Hastings in 1066 also found their way to Byzantium, looking for a new start in the wake of William's conquest.[11]

By the end of the eleventh century, therefore, a great swathe of different nationalities could be found in Constantinople and elsewhere in the empire. Armenians, Syrians, Lombards, Englishmen, Hungarians, Franks, Jews, Arabs and Turks were all living, visiting and trading in the capital.[12] Amalfitan traders even carved out their own quarter in Constantinople;[13] one became so favoured by the emperor that he was given the unusual privilege of having bronze doors cast in the imperial foundries to send back to Amalfi, where they hang to this day at the entrance to the cathedral of St Andrew.[14] Byzantium was diverse, cosmopolitan, and well connected: trade networks and diplomatic links, as well as the connections of the immigrant population, meant that the empire was famous in the most distant corners of Europe.

The sharp increase in the number of foreigners visiting and settling in the city was due in part to a rapid acceleration in the economic prosperity of the empire following a series of major military successes by the great emperor-generals of the tenth century. Arab pirates who had interrupted maritime traffic in the Aegean and the eastern Mediterranean for centuries were finally dealt with, their attack bases systematically knocked out. The frontiers both in the Balkans and in the east were first stabilised and then rolled back by a succession of competent and ambitious military commanders, who heralded a golden age for the empire.

Major new projects were commissioned in Constantinople, including the magnificent complex of St George on Mangana, which included a hospital, homes for the aged and the poor, a sumptuous palace, and a monastic church where Constantine IX, the emperor who commissioned the works, was eventually buried. Schools of law and philosophy opened to cater to an increasingly socially mobile population. Traders and merchants grew wealthy and as a result found the doors of the senate opened to them. Private individuals began to use their disposable income to invest in land and precious objects. Men like Eustathios Boilas, a landowner in Cappadocia, were encouraged by the empire's stability and prosperity to develop barren land that was 'foul and unmanageable . . . inhabited by snakes, scorpions and wild beasts' and lovingly transform it into vineyards and gardens, supplied by watermills and aqueducts.[15]

Around the middle of the eleventh century, however, Constantinople's progress began to falter. Norman mercenaries, who had originally been recruited by central Italy's city-states, began to realise that they could exploit the fractious competition between Amalfi, Salerno, Capua, Benevento and Naples. Within a matter of decades, they had used this rivalry effectively to build up their own power base, and by the mid-1050s the Normans were starting to challenge the Byzantine provinces of Apulia and Calabria. The empire found itself under pressure elsewhere too. Constantinople had long had to keep a careful watch over the steppe lands to the north of the Black Sea. For centuries, these tracts of land had been populated by nomads who were volatile and dangerous if not carefully dealt with. One of the most aggressive tribes was the Pechenegs, who excelled in raiding poorly defended targets. Based on the northern banks of the Danube, the Pechenegs now turned on Byzantium, intensifying their assaults from the 1040s onwards and causing havoc in the Balkans.

In the east the empire was threatened by the Turks' spectacular rise to power. While they had been on the periphery of the caliphate of Baghdad at the start of the eleventh century, their military prowess became highly valued by rival factions in the Muslim world, and they soon involved themselves in the tangled politics of Baghdad itself. In 1055, one of the tribal leaders, Tughril Beg, became sultan – effectively the secular leader of Sunni Islam in the Middle East. And this was not the end of Turkish ambition. Even before becoming masters of Baghdad, bands of Turks had made their way westwards to the edges of Asia Minor and begun launching small-scale attacks into the subcontinent's Byzantine interior.

The empire did not just struggle to respond to these threats: it spectacularly failed to deal with them altogether. Southern Italy was left to its own devices and fell swiftly to the Normans, who turned their attention to attacking Muslim Sicily after capturing the southern Italian city of Bari in 1071. The Byzantines also did little to counter the Pechenegs, with the empire feebly resorting time and again to bribery, paying tribute in return for peace. There was at least some co-ordinated defence in the east, but only after major towns like Trebizond, Koloneia and Melitene had been raided. In 1067, after a band of Turks reached and sacked Kaisereia, desecrating the tomb of St Basil and carrying off the doors to the church, which were covered with gold, pearls and precious stones, the clamour for decisive action became overwhelming. All eyes turned to Romanos IV Diogenes, a general elevated to the throne after marrying the widow of the previous emperor.

Romanos set off on several expensive campaigns that achieved little. But then, in the summer of 1071, the emperor allowed himself to get drawn into battle near the important fort of Manzikert by Turkish forces which he believed to be modest in number and easy to defeat. They were in fact part of the main Turkish army, under the personal command of the sultan, Alp Arslan. Faulty intelligence, poor decision-making and bad leadership contributed to a defeat that was less significant from a military point of view, but humiliating in terms of prestige. Romanos IV himself was captured and, dishevelled and caked in the dust of battle, brought before the sultan, who initially refused to believe that the man being presented to him was really the emperor. The encounter, during which Alp Arslan behaved with conspicuous kindness and dignity before releasing Diogenes, was celebrated soon after by writers and poets, quickly becoming a defining event in Turkish history and identity.[16]

The campaign that ended at Manzikert in 1071 had been intended to reinforce Byzantium's eastern frontier and protect the interior of Asia Minor from the debilitating and demoralising raids that scarred it. Its failure – and the lack of corrective action in its aftermath – led to a growing sense of panic. Many Byzantines abandoned the region, fleeing to Constantinople for fear of further Turkish raids. One was the future patriarch, Nicholas Grammatikos, who left Antioch-in-Pisidia to set up a new monastery in the capital; an archdeacon from Kaisereia made the same decision, gathering up the treasures from his church in Cappadocia to head for the safety of the capital.[17]

The influx of refugees put a strain on the resources of Constantinople. As it was, the pressure on the provinces had thrown the empire's finances into disarray, sharply reducing the tax revenues. In addition, military operations like the Manzikert campaign, or more limited efforts against the Pechenegs, were costly. Increasing military commitments also meant that agricultural production fell as manpower was diverted from the fields by conscription, adding to the depopulation of the countryside as the rural population fled to the safety of the cities.

Attempts to deal with the mounting financial crisis were not successful. The government attempted to correct the fiscal imbalance by debasing the coinage – lowering the gold content while maintaining the same notional value. This might have helped had it been managed carefully, but by the 1070s, debasement was spiralling out of control, the precious-metal content being further degraded with almost every issue.[18] Tax collection became rapacious and chronic inflation set in, with the price of wheat driven up by a factor of eighteen in the mid-1070s.[19]

Economic meltdown was accompanied by political chaos, as aristocrats rose in revolt against the government in protest at the rising demands being made of them and at the deteriorating situation within the empire. In the late 1070s, one leading magnate after another rebelled, plunging Byzantium into civil war. Although many of the most serious uprisings were eventually put down, the disruption they caused was profound. And the empire's neighbours were quick to take advantage. Having made themselves masters of southern Italy, the Normans set about preparing an attack on Epirus, the gateway to the empire's western provinces. In Croatia and Duklja, the ruling dynasties sought to realign themselves with Old Rome rather than Constantinople, contacting the Pope to ask that their leaders be recognised as sovereign rulers – an unequivocal challenge to Byzantine claims over this region.[20]

In Asia Minor, the empire's crisis offered opportunities that were too good to miss. Bands of Turkish marauders continued to make forays deep into the region, meeting with little opposition. In 1080, for example, some reached as far west as Kyzikos, duly sacking the city, and plunging the emperor into deep despair.[21] The lure of plunder was only one attraction that drew Turks into Byzantine territory. Another was the insatiable appetite of rebellious aristocrats for military support. Almost every rebel in this period employed Turkish auxiliaries, often after competitive auctions between rival factions for the same band of mercenaries.[22] Byzantines seemed more than willing to make common cause with Turks in their squabbles with each other.[23]

By 1081, things could scarcely have been worse. The Balkans were in flames with Pecheneg raids and uprisings by local leaders who rejected imperial control over some of the most important towns of the region. A major Norman attack from southern Italy was also under way, led by Robert Guiscard, one of the most ruthless and successful military commanders of the early Middle Ages. Meanwhile, the Turks had reached the shore of the Bosphorus, the neighbouring regions completely exposed to their raids. 'The Byzantines saw them living absolutely unafraid and unmolested in the little villages on the coast and in sacred buildings', reported Anna Komnene. 'The sight filled them with horror. They had no idea what to do.'[24] The Roman Empire had once ruled from the straits of Gibraltar in the west to India in the east, from Britain in the north deep into Africa. Now little remained beyond the imperial capital itself.[25] The Turks had ravaged Asia Minor, wrote Anna, destroying towns and staining the land with Christian blood. Those who were not gruesomely murdered or taken prisoner 'hurried to seek refuge from impending disaster by hiding in caves, forests, mountains and hills'.[26]

With the eastern provinces seemingly lost to the Turks and the empire on its knees, Byzantium was in crisis long before imperial envoys reached Pope Urban at Piacenza to appeal for help against the Turkish threat. Why then, was a sudden, dramatic request for support sent from Constantinople in 1095 if Asia Minor had fallen nearly fifteen years earlier? The timing of this passionate plea for help and the Pope's spectacular response were both politically driven. The Byzantine appeal was strategic; Urban's response was motivated by self-interest and the desire to establish himself over his rivals in the Western Church. At the heart of the First Crusade, therefore, lies a knotty story of crisis and realpolitik emanating from Asia Minor. And behind the spark that ignited the expedition was the young man who emerged as the ruler of the Byzantine Empire exactly ten years after the disaster at Manzikert: Alexios Komnenos.

In the early 1080s, Constantinople desperately needed a man of action, who would reverse the decline of the empire. There were several self-appointed candidates to save New Rome: Nikephoros Bryennios, Nikephoros Basilakios, Nikephoros Botaneiates and Nikephoros Melissenos – all owing their first names, 'the one who brings victory', to a different age, when the empire could look forward to continued success and prosperity. None of these men, though, could provide the answer to Byzantium's problems. Alexios Komnenos, however, inspired hope.

Alexios Komnenos came from a respected and well-connected family in Byzantium. There was also a dash of imperial purple in the blood,

for Isaac Komnenos, Alexios' uncle, had held the throne for two years
in 1057–9 before being deposed by a group of disgruntled senior officers
whose personal ambitions had not been sufficiently tended to.
Although this background provided the Komnenos family with an
imperial pedigree, few can have thought that the young man who, as
one account reveals, begged to go on campaign against the Turks
while barely old enough to shave, would end up ruling the empire
for thirty-seven years and laying the cornerstone of a dynasty that
would rule for more than a century.[27]

One person who did have this vision, however, was Alexios' mother.
A tough, determined woman, Anna Dalassene came from one of the
empire's leading families, many of whose members had served
Byzantium in important positions in the civilian and military administrations. Anna had serious ambitions for her five sons. The eldest,
Manuel, rose quickly through the ranks of the army to become a
senior commander during the ill-fated reign of Romanos IV Diogenes,
but was killed in battle. The rise of two of Anna's other sons, Isaac
and Alexios, was meteoric and nigh on unstoppable.

As Byzantium began to disintegrate, a vacuum opened up for ambitious young men who were able and loyal. The Komnenos brothers
were the prime beneficiaries, with Isaac, the older of the two,
appointed first to command the army of the eastern provinces and
then governor of the city of Antioch, while Alexios was repeatedly
promoted for his outstanding success defeating rebels in central Asia
Minor and the western Balkans in the 1070s.

By the end of the decade, speculation mounted in Constantinople
about the brothers' ambitions, spurred by their successful cultivation
of both the emperor Nikephoros III and of his wife, the empress
Maria. Gossip swirled through the capital about Alexios' relationship
with the latter, described as a striking woman, 'very tall, like a cypress
tree; her skin was snow white, her face oval, her complexion wholly
reminiscent of a spring flower or a rose'.[28] The emperor, meanwhile,
a doddery old man with a keen eye for fashion, was enthralled by the
clothes made from fine materials which Isaac Komnenos brought him
from Syria.[29]

Speculation about the brothers' ambitions proved correct. Around
the end of 1080, they decided that the time had come to try to
take the throne for themselves, prompted by rival figures at court

who began openly briefing against them. They were spurred on too by the moves of other leading aristocrats like Nikephoros Melissenos, who had already minted coins depicting himself as ruler and produced a seal that bore the uncompromising legend: 'Nikephoros Melissenos, emperor of the Romans'.[30] Such was Melissenos' progress that the emperor considered formally naming him as his heir in a bid to appease him.[31]

Isaac and Alexios realised that they had to move quickly. Although he was the younger of the two, it was agreed that Alexios should take the throne if the coup was successful, his marriage to a member of the powerful Doukas family proving vital in winning the support of one of the most powerful families in Byzantium. The decisive moment came when news reached Constantinople that a major Norman attack had begun on the empire's western flank at Epirus. For once, the emperor reacted decisively, entrusting a major force to his leading commander – Alexios Komnenos. Yet having reached Thrace with his army, the young general did what all Roman rulers feared most: he turned round to march back on the capital.[32]

The city's defences were formidable; there was no real prospect that the Komnenoi would be able to take it by storm. Contact was therefore made with the German mercenary contingent that was protecting the Kharisios gate, one of the main entry points on the western side of the city. After terms had been agreed with its commander, the huge wooden doors were swung open and the Komnenoi and their supporters surged into the city.[33] Alexios and his men advanced swiftly through the city as support for the emperor melted away. Met with only limited opposition, they looted wildly. Even Anna Komnene could not hide her horror at the scenes which accompanied the entry of her father's supporters: 'No writer, however earnest could possibly do justice to the terrors by which the city was enveloped in those days. Churches, sanctuaries, property both public and private were all victims of universal pillage, while the ears of its citizens were deafened by cries and shouts raised on every side. An onlooker might well have thought an earthquake was taking place.'[34]

Violence was directed particularly at the capital's elites. Senators were pulled from their horses; some were stripped naked and left humiliated in the street.[35] The emperor himself yielded meekly as he slunk away from the palace, his imperial vestments stolen by courtiers who put them on and mocked him.[36] Captured and handed over to the Komnenoi, Nikephoros was placed in a monastery where he is reported to have taken to the life of prayer and contemplation – although he was not impressed by the strict vegetarian regime on offer.[37]

Soon after taking control of the city, Alexios I Komnenos was crowned emperor of the Romans in the Great Church of St Sophia in Constantinople. The elaborate coronation ceremony would have followed the rituals laid out in a tenth-century text, with Alexios arriving at Hagia Sophia, changing into the imperial robes and then entering the church with the patriarch. After being prayed for and acclaimed with the chant 'O great emperor and autocrat! May you reign for many years!', Alexios would have been crowned, before dignitaries came forward one by one to kiss the new sovereign's knees.[38]

To consolidate his position, the new emperor quickly appointed allies to key posts in the empire. A new commander-in-chief of the western armies was named, and a new governor was appointed for the town of Dyrrakhion, the focus of the ongoing Norman attack.[39] The support of Nikephoros Melissenos was diplomatically ensured by giving him a prominent role, as well as the gift of the tax revenues of Thessaloniki, one of the largest towns in the empire. Isaac Komnenos, meanwhile, was appointed to a newly created rank, placing him second to the emperor in the hierarchy of government. Many members of the new emperor's immediate family also received promotions, status and rewards to mark them out as part of the new establishment.[40] This creation of a new tier of loyalists provided Alexios with the secure power base he needed to contend with external threats, as well as with the empire's economic meltdown.

From the outset, Alexios took control of military affairs himself, rather than leaving them in the hands of subordinates, as most of his predecessors had done. A few months after taking the throne he personally led an army to Epirus to confront the Normans, who promptly inflicted a disastrous defeat on Alexios and his forces at Dyrrakhion in October 1081. Over the next two years, as the Normans penetrated deep into Macedonia and Thessaly, the emperor himself commanded the army in a series of exhaustive operations which finally resulted in the withdrawal of the invading army back to Italy. In 1084, when the Normans launched a second invasion on the empire's western flank, it was Alexios again who set out from Constantinople in person to repel the attack – and on this occasion with rather more success. After supplies and communications were cut, the Normans sustained heavy casualties from starvation and disease and were slowly strangled into submission. 'Greece, freed of its enemies, was liberated and rejoiced fully', acknowledged one Norman contemporary.[41]

Alexios' success was a powerful vindication for the young usurper. He had seized the throne promising a new future for the empire, and although his efforts against the Normans were not without regular setbacks, he had done something that the Muslims of Sicily and King Harold of England had failed to achieve: successfully resist a large-scale Norman invasion.

The new emperor now turned his attention to the Pechenegs, whose raids were continuing unabated in spite of major Byzantine successes achieved by one of Alexios' new appointees, in 1083. 'I am convinced', wrote the commander in question after one such victory, 'that even for many years after my death the miraculous act of Almighty God which happened will not be forgotten.'[42] He was wrong: the Pechenegs remained a huge problem in the 1080s, ravaging Byzantine territory on a regular basis. 'Their attack is like lightning', wrote one contemporary, 'their retreat both slow and swift – slow because of the weight of booty they are carrying, swift because of the speed of their flight . . . They leave no trace at all for those pursuing them. Even if a bridge was built across the Danube, they would still not be caught.'[43]

Alexios repeatedly led the army out to meet the waves of invasion, to little effect. By the winter of 1090, the threat had become critical, with a vast body of Pecheneg nomads invading the empire and reaching southern Thrace with the intention of settling permanently in the rich pastureland around the mouth of the river Ainos – and dangerously close to Constantinople. The emperor gathered troops from wherever he could, set camp at the foot of a hill named Lebounion, and prepared for battle.

The engagement that followed at the end of April 1091 provided one of the most startling military victories in Byzantine history: 'It was an extraordinary spectacle', wrote Anna Komnene. 'A whole people, numbered not in these tens of thousands but in countless multitudes, with their women and children was utterly wiped out on that day. It was the twenty-ninth of April, a Tuesday. Hence the ditty chanted by the Byzantines: "All because of one day the [Pechenegs] never saw the month of May." '[44] To all intents and purposes, the Pechenegs were annihilated. Many survivors of the battle were executed shortly afterwards; the remainder were dispersed across the Balkans. They would never again pose a threat to the empire.[45]

Alexios' first decade in power thus appears to have been remarkably successful. The threat of two aggressive and dangerous neighbours had been seen off, in the case of the Pechenegs permanently. The emperor had installed himself securely on the throne, surrounding himself with reliable family members whose interests were closely aligned with his own. There was little evidence, furthermore, of internal opposition to his rule – no challenges from those who had been removed from power in 1081, or other rivals to the throne. This was undoubtedly the result of the measures Alexios put in place to control the aristocracy. Leading rivals were brought on campaign by the emperor, keeping them close to him and away from Constantinople.[46] During Alexios' absence Isaac was left behind in the capital with an uncompromising brief to deal with any criticism of the new ruling family.[47] Yet despite this apparent nervousness about opposition, it seemed that Alexios was widely welcomed as emperor, his leadership a breath of fresh air to an empire that had become stale.

The emperor's style of rule was certainly not self-indulgent, unlike that of some of his predecessors who were more concerned with what they wore or what they ate: Constantine VIII (1025–8), for example, had spent little time dealing with matters of state, instead setting himself up in the imperial kitchens where he experimented endlessly with flavours and colours.[48] By contrast, Alexios was a diffident character with a soldier's habits, who had simple tastes and disavowed life's luxuries. Severe and serious, he also had no time for small talk and kept his own counsel.[49] He was a man who spurned mirrors, reported his son-in-law, Nikephoros Bryennios, because he believed that 'for a man and a warrior, arms and simplicity and purity of way of life are adornment'.[50] He had similarly puritan views when it came to history writing. Alexios was unimpressed that his eldest daughter wanted to write an account of his reign, encouraging her instead to compose elegies and dirges. His response to his wife, when he learned that she wanted to commission an account of his life for future generations, was even more blunt: 'It would be better, he said, to grieve for him and deplore his misfortunes.'[51]

Alexios was a devout man, whose main relaxation came from studying the Bible. He would often sit late into the night reading the Scriptures in silence alongside his wife, who had similar inclinations.[52] He shared such piety with other members of his family; his brother Isaac was much admired by the clergy for his religious zeal.[53] And his mother too was similarly devout. The founder of a beautifully appointed church and monastery overlooking the Golden Horn in the capital, she was a strong supporter of monks and clerics throughout the empire, often intervening on their behalf and arranging tax exemptions. Her seal testified to her as not just the mother of the emperor, but also as a nun. The emperor's daughter reported that it was Anna Dalassene who had 'deeply implanted the fear of the Lord' into her son's soul when he was a boy.[54]

With Alexios' rule, Byzantium entered a period of sombre asceticism. Soon after taking power in 1081, the emperor resolved to wear a hair shirt and to sleep on a stone floor to atone for the behaviour of his troops during the coup. He apologised to the clergy the following year for taking unused church treasures to help fund efforts against the Normans, vowing never to do so again. Within the imperial palace, the 'utter depravity' of previous generations was replaced by solemn singing of sacred hymns and strictly regimented mealtimes.[55]

In addition, Alexios was at pains to impose his orthodox religious views. From the start of his reign, stern action was taken against those with opinions and beliefs that were deemed heretic, with the sovereign himself regularly presiding over trials and administering punishment to those found guilty. Championing the interests of the church was of course an entirely sensible policy, especially for a usurper who had seized the throne by force. But in Alexios' case, it was sincere.

Yet the emperor had no trouble taking on senior members of the clergy: in his first three years on the throne, he engineered the replacement of not one but two patriarchs of Constantinople, until the appointment of Nicholas III Grammatikos provided him with a man willing to co-operate with him. Other leading clerics were also dealt with forcefully, such as the bishop of Chalcedon, who was tried and exiled after criticising the emperor and his policies. Furthermore, as we have seen, Alexios was the driving force behind the rapprochement with Rome at the end of the 1080s, overseeing a meeting of the synod in the capital, and all but insisting on reconciliation with the papacy.

The force of Alexios' character fashioned the empire. Under his leadership, there was a return to the military values that had characterised the tenth century, a time when emperors were generals, and the army was the cornerstone of Byzantium. Alexios himself was most comfortable in the outfit of a soldier, rather than the lavish vestments of the emperor, and he preferred a small group of intimates over the elaborate ceremonials that characterised the court in Constantinople.[56]

Alexios abandoned the complicated hierarchy that dictated who sat where while dining in the palace, establishing an altogether more modest and basic regime. The emperor frequently invited the least fortunate in society to share his table, dining with epileptics and reportedly being so eager to help them that he himself forgot to eat.[57] Even a contemporary who was otherwise almost uniformly hostile to Alexios commented that his attitude to the poor was both unusual and commendable. In addition, he 'never drank, and could not be accused of being a glutton'.[58] Rather than delegating affairs to bureaucrats, he made himself available to discuss matters of concern with his subjects, and even with foreigners; he would meet with anyone who wanted to see him personally, often staying up late into the night to do so.[59]

While the close control Alexios maintained over Byzantium was impressive, it was also suffocating. There was violent opposition to his style of leadership on the eve of the Crusade and, as we will see, this played a central role in the emperor's appeals to the papacy. The heavy emphasis on military affairs was oppressive and drained the empire's resources; art, architecture and literature stagnated during Alexios' reign. What little was produced in terms of visual culture was austere and sombre: a mural painted at the Great Palace of Blakhernai depicted the emperor at the time of the Last Judgement acting as a representative of Christ.[60] This was an immensely revealing representation of how Alexios saw himself: God's faithful servant at a time of darkness.

Apart from his coinage, we have only two images of the emperor, but one can get a sense of the impression Alexios made from Anna's idealised description of him in the *Alexiad*. He struck an imposing figure, even if he spoke with a lisp: 'when one saw the grim flash of his eyes as he sat down on the imperial throne, he reminded one of a fiery whirlwind, so overwhelming was the radiance that emanated from his bearing and his very presence. His dark eyebrows were curved, and beneath them the gaze of his eyes was both terrible and kind. A quick glance . . . [would] inspire in the beholder both dread and confidence. His broad shoulders, muscular arms and deep chest, all on a heroic scale, invariably commanded the wonder and delight of the people. He radiated beauty and grace and dignity and an unapproachable majesty.'[61]

This was the man who prompted the First Crusade, a seminal moment in the history and development of the medieval world. Yet with the repulse of the Normans and the comprehensive defeat of the Pechenegs, the fortunes of the Byzantine Empire appeared to be well on the mend. Why, then, by 1095, did Byzantium require outside help to take on the Turks?

3

Stability in the East

The Byzantine Empire was under great pressure when Alexios took the throne – threatened by the incursions of aggressive neighbours, weakened by a collapsing economy, and riven with political infighting. Looking back through the distorting prism of the First Crusade, it would seem natural to assume that the greatest of these dangers came from hostile Turkish expansion in the east. This was certainly the impression created by Anna Komnene; her testimony even suggested that Asia Minor had been essentially lost to the Turks before Alexios came to power. In fact, Asia Minor was relatively stable in the 1080s; indeed, the relationship between Byzantium and the Turks in the first part of Alexios' reign was generally robust and pragmatically positive. It was only in the early 1090s, in the years immediately before the beginning of the First Crusade, that there was a dramatic deterioration of Byzantium's position in the east. Conflict with the Muslim world, in other words, was by no means inevitable; it appears that the breakdown in relations between Christians and Muslims at the end of the eleventh century was the result of a spiralling political and military process, not the unavoidable conflict between two opposing cultures. It was, though, in the interests of Anna Komnene to create the opposite impression; and it is an impression that has lasted down through the centuries.

At the start of his reign the new emperor's attentions were focused squarely on the Normans and the Pechenegs. The Byzantine position in Asia Minor, on the other hand, was fairly resilient: there were many locations which had mounted stern resistance against the Turks in the decade following the battle of Manzikert, and they continued to hold out effectively after Alexios took the throne. In many cases, the defiance was the result of effective local leadership, rather than of the actions of Constantinople. The area around Trebizond on the north coast of Asia Minor, for example, was secured by Theodore Gabras, a scion of one of the town's most prominent families. Such was the ferocity of Gabras' defence of the surrounding region that his exploits and bravery were remembered with admiration by the Turks more than a hundred years later in a lyrical poem about their conquest of Asia Minor.[1] A substantial area around Amaseia, meanwhile, had been held extremely effectively in the 1070s by Roussel Balliol, a Norman initially in imperial service before declaring himself independent of Byzantium, frustrated by the lack of support he was being given by the government and inspired by the strong support of the local population which lionised him for the protection he provided.[2]

Commanders were holding out far into the eastern extremities of Anatolia, even into the Caucasus. Three sons of Mandales, 'Roman magnates' according to a Caucasian chronicler, were occupying strongpoints in the region of Kaisereia in 1080–1, presumably on behalf of the empire, rather than opportunistically for themselves.[3] Basil Apokapes held the important town of Edessa before Alexios' usurpation and after, to judge from lead seals issued in his name.[4] The appointment of a new governor of Mesopotamia by Alexios' predecessor in 1078 likewise provides an indication that there were significant Byzantine interests worth protecting hundreds of miles east of Constantinople.[5]

Some Byzantine commanders were actually flourishing in the eastern provinces – most notably Philaretos Braakhamios, a talented general whose career had suffered a serious setback after refusing to support Romanos IV Diogenes' successor, Michael VII Doukas, when he became emperor in 1071. As the empire imploded with one revolt after another in the 1070s, Philaretos wrested control of many towns, forts and territories and built up a substantial power base in the process. He continued to prosper after Alexios became emperor, and by the early 1080s held the important cities of Marash and Melitene as well as much of Cilicia, before becoming master of Edessa in 1083.[6]

The *Alexiad*'s sweeping – and damning – account of the situation in the east has shaped modern opinions about the situation in Asia Minor at the time of Alexios' seizure of power. A common consensus has emerged that the eastern provinces were overrun by the Turks in the early 1080s. There is also wide agreement, likewise based on Anna

Komnene's account, that there was a significant Byzantine recovery on the eve of the First Crusade which, taken together with the death of the sultan of Baghdad in 1092, provided an inviting and enviable opening for the empire to exploit in Asia Minor.[7] Yet commentary provided by the *Alexiad* needs to be treated cautiously for the author's aim in stressing the parlous state of the empire in 1081 was to underline Alexios' achievements, to emphasise that he saved Byzantium from the very brink of disaster. There was a darker motivation as well: to absolve the emperor of blame for a series of major disasters which occurred not before he took the throne, but afterwards – and which are cleverly concealed in Anna's history.

Yet even the *Alexiad* inadvertently reveals the strength of the empire's position in 1081. As the new emperor prepared to deal with the Norman invasion of Epirus he put together as large an army as he could, summoning men from all over the empire to gather in Constantinople. This included the withdrawal of men stationed in Asia Minor: Alexios 'realised that he must quickly recall all the *toparkhes* [senior officers] in the east, men who as governors of forts or towns were bravely resisting the Turks'. At once, the emperor gave orders that these commanders, in provinces like Paphlagonia and Cappadocia, secure their respective regions, 'leaving for that purpose enough soldiers, but with the rest they were to come to Constantinople, bringing with them as many able-bodied recruits as they could find'.[8] There were officers in other regions in Asia Minor as well who were also holding out against the Turks, and they too were ordered to send men to a new emperor preoccupied with preparing a large army to deal with the attack by the Normans.[9] This freeing-up of manpower in Asia Minor suggests that the Byzantine hold over the region was fairly robust.

In fact, there is little to suggest that the Turks posed a major problem in this period. There were bands of raiders who were a menace, attacking soft targets like Kyzikos, which were poorly defended and offered little resistance.[10] But even the presence of such opportunistic groups was not necessarily unwelcome: when one aristocrat came across a party of Turks while on his way to join Alexios and Isaac Komnenos during their rebellion, he did not engage them in combat but persuaded them to join him as mercenaries.[11]

Other evidence too presents a picture sharply at odds with the idea

that the Byzantine east had collapsed by the time of Alexios' usurpation. For example, Attaleia, an important trading post and naval base
on the south coast of Asia Minor, was raised in status to an archbishopric in the early 1080s, a sign that the town was not only still in
Byzantine hands but growing in importance.[12] Archaeological finds
reveal the existence of an extensive cast of bishops, judges and officials
holding positions in many provinces and towns in Asia Minor immediately before Alexios came to the throne as well as afterwards, which
demonstrates that the damage done by the Turks to the provincial
administration around this time was hardly extensive.[13]

In fact, the situation in the east improved significantly after Alexios
took power, with the return of stability to much of Asia Minor during
the first half of the 1080s. This was a major achievement, especially
in view of the fact that Alexios' regime had been so fragile at the
outset: there had been concerns about the loyalty of his own troops
during the entry to Constantinople in 1081, while some of his most
prominent supporters considered abandoning him soon after. His
failure to have his wife, Eirene, crowned empress alongside him
provoked a violent reaction from her powerful family, who bristled at
Alexios' attempt to show himself to be independent. Their menacing
warnings had the desired effect: Eirene was crowned a week later.[14]
In addition, Constantinople's high-ranking clergy had been demanding
a public apology – as well as penance – from Alexios for the behaviour
of his men after they rampaged through the capital during his coup.[15]
And as we have seen, the western flank of the Byzantine Empire was
in chaos in the early 1080s with a major Norman invasion of Epirus
under way and Pecheneg raids devastating the Balkans in the north.

When it came to Asia Minor the emperor was less concerned with
the Turks than with the more significant problem posed by this region
in the previous decade: uprisings by Byzantine aristocrats. The eastern
provinces were home to most of the major landowners in Byzantium,
and had proved a fertile breeding ground for insurrection since the
battle of Manzikert. The new emperor was anxious that another challenge did not emerge while he was away from Constantinople to fight
Normans and Pechenegs. In the very first weeks of his reign, therefore,
Alexios turned his attention to the east. According to the *Alexiad*, he
sent an expedition into Bithynia to drive back the Turks, personally
issuing detailed instructions which included advice on how to pull

oars through the water silently to retain the element of surprise and how to tell which rocky inlets the enemy might be hiding in, ready for ambush.[16]

To ensure the stability of this region, Alexios turned to a man whom he had dealt with before. Anxious not to entrust too much military power to a Byzantine aristocrat – mindful of the fact that he had himself wheeled the imperial army back on the capital when given similar responsibilities – Alexios sought to reach an agreement with an ally with a rather different profile. Sulayman was a Turkish chieftain who had made his way into Asia Minor in the 1070s in search of opportunity and fortune. He quickly found both, being hired by Constantinople to fight against rebel aristocrats on several occasions and being richly rewarded in the process.[17] Alexios first co-operated with him when the Turkish warlord sent men to help him put down an attempted coup in the western Balkans shortly before his own successful revolt. Turkish auxiliaries proved loyal, brave and highly effective, playing a decisive part in putting down rebellions against the emperor and even being responsible for capturing their leaders.[18]

The fact that Alexios relied on a Turk was, if anything, a positive advantage to the new ruler who was not secure in his position. Choosing Sulayman, someone who was not part of the Byzantine elite, to become the key military figure in Asia Minor was not without logic – even if it was unusual. But then Alexios was much more open-minded than his peers when it came to outsiders. Byzantines generally took a dim view of foreigners, regardless of where they came from, perceiving them as useful mercenaries, but also as uncouth, driven by lowly passions and motivated by money. This was not how Alexios Komnenos saw things. As he showed on countless occasions during his reign, Alexios was more than happy to entrust sensitive tasks to foreigners living in Byzantium. Indeed, one writer commented that the emperor liked nothing better than being surrounded by 'barbarians from captivity'.[19] It was a reputation that spread across Europe and was recorded as far away as Normandy.[20] Alexios felt comfortable with such people, men like him who were from military backgrounds and had come to Constantinople to find service. Ethnicity and religion were of little importance to him, perhaps the result of being brought up alongside Tatikios, the son of a Turk captured by his father, and who later became the emperor's most trusted confidant.[21]

After limited operations in Bithynia, therefore, Alexios approached Sulayman in the summer of 1081 and came to an agreement with him. Lavish gifts were presented by the emperor in return for setting a boundary at the river Drakon beyond which the Turks were not allowed to encroach. Sulayman was effectively appointed as the emperor's representative in western Asia Minor, with the remit not only to prevent incursions of his own men, but of all Turks in this region.[22] Additionally, Alexios received a commitment that military assistance would be provided as, where and when it was needed. When the emperor found himself overstretched near Larissa in 1083, struggling to relieve a Norman siege of the town, 'he called on [Sulayman] to supply forces with leaders of long experience. The request was answered without delay: 7,000 men were sent along with highly skilled officers.'[23] Turkish auxiliaries who fought alongside him against the Normans on other occasions in the early 1080s may likewise have been supplied by Sulayman.[24]

Alexios gained much from the agreement. It left him free to deal with the troubles in the western provinces being caused by Normans and Pechenegs. It also provided him with the security of knowing that he had not inadvertently provided a platform from which an ambitious Byzantine aristocrat might mount a challenge against his rule. Best of all, however, was the fact that Sulayman proved to be an outstanding ally.

For one thing, the truce agreed in 1081 was extremely effective. Turkish raids on Byzantine territory were brought to an immediate end, with the peace agreement diligently enforced by Sulayman. As a message from the sultan of Baghdad to the emperor reveals, the treaty concluded between Alexios and Sulayman remained intact until at least the middle of 1085 and possibly later still.[25] It provided the basis for stability in Asia Minor at a time when the empire was elsewhere teetering on the brink of collapse. Indeed, it appears that the agreement brought further benefits to the emperor that were not limited to western Asia Minor alone. A chronicler from the Caucasus noted that soon after terms were reached, the 'entire country of Cilicia' came under the control of 'a certain emir, Sulayman, son of Kutlumush'.[26] To judge from the comments of another author, writing in Syriac, this expansion of Sulayman's power was advantageous to Byzantium. 'In the year 475 [AD 1082]', he wrote, 'Sulayman departed from the territory of the Rhomaye [Byzantium] and went and captured the cities on the sea coast, namely Antarados and Tarsos.'[27] The nuance here is easy to miss: Sulayman was not attacking targets that were held by Byzantines; he was recovering towns which had fallen to the Turks. In other words, through the treaty concluded in 1081 Sulayman effectively became Alexios' agent, securing strategically important locations in Asia Minor as the emperor's representative.

Although the emperor's reliance on the Turks was inspired, it was not wholly unprecedented from the wider perspective of Byzantine foreign policy. As one tenth-century manual on the craft of diplomacy makes clear, setting neighbours off against one another and hiring warlords to attack unruly enemies was an accepted way of establishing and maintaining a favourable balance with the peoples outside the empire.[28] Alexios' use of Sulayman was bold; but it was not revolutionary.

There was, however, a price to pay: Nicaea. One of the most important towns in Asia Minor, Nicaea was enviably situated, defended by vast walls and fortifications, with a lake to the west side offering additional protection, as well as its own independent water supply. Its location made it the gateway to the rich river valleys of Lycia and Phrygia and the lush western and southern coasts, as well as into the Anatolian plateau. It was a vital node through which all communication flowed between Constantinople and the Byzantine east.

The circumstances of Nicaea's occupation by the Turks are murky. It is normally assumed that the town was lost during the failed uprising of Nikephoros Melissenos, which was contemporaneous with Alexios' own revolt against his predecessor in 1081. A member of one of Asia Minor's leading families, Melissenos won sweeping support as he moved towards Constantinople: 'The inhabitants of the towns recognised him as though he were emperor of the Romans and surrendered to him', wrote one author several decades later. 'He in turn placed them in the care of the Turks, with the result that all the towns of Asia, Phrygia and Galatia quickly came under the sway of the Turks; [Melissenos] then took Nicaea in Bithynia with a sizeable army, and from that location sought to take the empire of the Romans.'[29] It therefore seems that Melissenos passed Nicaea – as well as many other towns of Asia Minor – into Turkish hands. Melissenos made a convenient scapegoat, however, not least since he was to cause significant problems for Alexios later in his reign and would live out the rest of his life exiled in a monastery.[30] The blame attached to him is rather unconvincing: pinned too neatly by Alexios' son-in-law, Nikephoros Bryennios, whose history was commissioned by the emperor's wife.[31]

In fact, the more natural and logical explanation for the handover of Nicaea lies in the agreement reached between Sulayman and Alexios in 1081. Just as a new governor was sent out to Dyrrakhion after Alexios took power, therefore, the appointment of someone who could be trusted as the emperor's representative in Nicaea – and would not challenge for the throne – was an important step. The fact that a Byzantine was not immediately dispatched to the town after Alexios' usurpation suggests that other arrangements had been made to secure Nicaea – that is, to place it in the hands of Sulayman. It is not surprising that some accounts refer to the Turk as the governor of Nicaea.[32]

The decision to entrust Sulayman with Nicaea became a sensitive issue, though not because this policy backfired in the short term. The problem was that by the start of the 1090s Sulayman was dead and his successor Abu'l-Kasim proved to be a different proposition entirely. As a result, obscuring how and when Nicaea came to be occupied by the Turks became an important part of protecting the emperor's reputation. Yet the fact that the loss of Nicaea can be traced back to none other than the emperor Alexios I Komnenos completely undermines the *Alexiad*'s careful and repeated assertions that all of Asia Minor had been lost before Alexios took power.

The attempt to suppress the truth was made easier by the fact that although many histories were written in Byzantium in the eleventh and twelfth centuries, with only two exceptions, they either end at the point of Alexios' seizure of power or begin with the reign of his son and heir, John II.[33] Even after his death, it was difficult to write about Alexios, and for the most part, historians did not try. This stemmed in large part from deliberate efforts by the Komnenos family to control the image and reputation of the emperor as the founder of the dynasty.[34]

Nevertheless, Alexios' role could not be completely disguised, at least to well-informed westerners. The chronicler Albert of Aachen knew that Nicaea had been lost by Alexios, though he was not aware of the details; he was led to believe that it happened after the emperor had been tricked by the Turks.[35] When Ekkehard of Aura was told that the emperor had surrendered the town to the Turks, he was appalled, accusing Alexios of committing a most disgusting crime in handing over this jewel of Christianity. Ekkehard had, though, misunderstood the situation: he thought that Alexios had given away Nicaea some time after 1097, when in reality the emperor had placed it in the hands of the Turks in 1081.[36]

However, it was not in Nicaea or western Asia Minor where things began to go wrong but much further east – in Antioch. The consequences were devastating. Like Nicaea, Antioch was a vital location in the eastern half of Byzantium: a town of great economic significance, strategic value and prestige whose church was overseen by a patriarch and whose governor was one of the highest-ranking officials within the empire.[37] As with Nicaea, it was essential for Antioch to be controlled by a loyal lieutenant, someone who did not seek to take advantage of Alexios' preoccupations elsewhere to plot against him. As a commander who had proved himself time and again on the eastern frontier, Philaretos Braakhamios seemed to fit the bill. But Philaretos was an erratic and difficult figure. He was an excellent general, wrote one Byzantine historian who knew him, but he was also an impossible man who would not take orders from anyone.[38]

Alexios worked hard to woo Philaretos at the start of his reign, awarding him numerous titles and responsibilities.[39] But the emperor was not the only suitor: in the early 1080s, Philaretos also began to receive overtures from the Muslim world. His major fiefdom in eastern Asia attracted the attention of the Turks and Philaretos was eventually persuaded to abandon Byzantium and Christianity in around 1084 when he 'decided to join them and offered himself for circumcision, according to their custom. His son violently opposed this ridiculous impulse, but his good advice went unheeded.'[40] One author expressed his indignation rather more emphatically: 'the impious and wicked chief Philaretos, who was the very offspring of Satan . . . a precursor of the abominable Antichrist, and possessed by a demonical and extremely monstrous character . . . began to war against the Christian faithful, for he was a superficial Christian'.[41]

For Alexios this was catastrophic news. The prospect of Philaretos recognising the authority of the caliph and the sultan was worrying enough; the threat that, with Melitene, Edessa and Antioch under his control, he might also turn over important towns and provinces to the Turks provoked a serious crisis. Alexios reacted immediately, taking countermeasures to secure the towns and regions the rogue general controlled and transferring them into the hands of loyal supporters. A certain T'oros, or Theodore, whose court title of *kouropalates* indicates that he was a close retainer of the emperor, took control of Edessa.[42] His father-in-law, Gabriel, did the same in Melitene, being named governor of the town.[43] Castles, fortresses and other strongpoints in this region were also occupied by commanders loyal to the emperor.[44]

Yet it was to Sulayman that Alexios turned to secure Antioch. According to one source, the Turk moved quickly on the city in 1085, travelling via a 'secret route' to avoid detection, presumably shown to him by Byzantine guides. When he reached the city, he entered it with little ado and took control of it, harming no one and treating the inhabitants conspicuously well: 'Peace was re-established, everyone returning to his place unharmed.'[45] Arabic sources likewise comment on the kindness Sulayman showed to Antioch's inhabitants.[46]

The peaceful occupation of Antioch contrasts sharply with the experiences of western knights who tried to take the city just a few years later. Protected by fearsome natural and man-made defences, Antioch was all but impregnable. But Sulayman did not have to use force to take control: he was acting on behalf of the emperor and so the inhabitants of the city – the majority of them Greek-speaking Byzantines – were willing to let him in. The fact that Alexios seems to have made no attempt to counter either the threat of Philaretos' defection by sending his own troops or stop Sulayman's move on Antioch is revealing. This was another case of fruitful collaboration between the Turk and the Byzantine.

Later Arabic writers came to present Sulayman's occupation in glorious terms. In the words of one poet: 'You have conquered Byzantine Antioch which enmeshed Alexander in its toils / Your steeds have trampled her flanks, and, humbled, / The daughters of the pale face miscarry their unborn children.'[47] However, this was little more than poetic licence, designed to show Antioch as having a Muslim overlord. In fact, after taking the city, Sulayman showed his intentions and his loyalties by immediately suspending the tribute which Philaretos had been paying a local Turkish warlord. When warned that it was dangerous to act against the authority of the sultan, Sulayman responded angrily that he remained obedient to the ruler of Baghdad. In territories subject to the sultan, he replied, there was no question that he was loyal; by implication, therefore, what he did in Nicaea and Antioch – cities belonging to Byzantium – had no bearing on his obligations to the sultan.[48] Using the same logic, Sulayman set out from Antioch for Aleppo in the summer of 1085, which had been razed by the Byzantines a century earlier, demanding that its Turkish governor hand the city over to him. It was another town that Alexios was keen to recover.[49]

The emperor pinned too much hope on his ally, however. Local Turkish warlords soon recognised that Sulayman was overstretched, with limited resources to hold on to his new gains, let alone make new conquests. In the middle of 1085, shortly after Sulayman had taken Antioch, Tutush, the sultan's belligerent half-brother, marched on the city and drew him into battle. There was some dispute among contemporaries as to whether Sulayman committed suicide when it became obvious his army had been routed or was killed by an arrow which struck him in the face. Whatever the facts, Antioch was now in Tutush's hands.[50]

This was a major setback for Byzantium. It was also a disaster for Alexios. Focusing his attention on the threats to the western provinces in the early 1080s, the emperor had not campaigned once in Asia Minor, pinning his hopes on two dominant local figures, Sulayman and Philaretos. In a matter of weeks, this policy had unravelled catastrophically.

Things only got worse when reports were received in Constantinople that Abu'l-Kasim, the man whom Sulayman had left in charge of Nicaea, had launched a wave of raids on towns and villages in Bithynia. Other opportunistic Turks were also taking advantage of the situation to establish themselves in Asia Minor, seizing towns and fortresses which had previously been controlled by Sulayman.[51] Byzantine authority in the east was on the point of collapse.

The emperor was not alone in his concern about the sudden changes to the status of Antioch and Nicaea. The sultan of Baghdad, Malik-Shah, also grew alarmed about the situation: the rise in power of local warlords such as Abu'l-Kasim and Tutush threatened to destabilise the Turkish world as much as the Byzantine.[52] Like his father Alp

Arslan, Malik-Shah was careful to maintain control over his western frontier, often leading expeditions to assert himself over unruly regions which were not of immediate strategic importance to Baghdad but nevertheless vital to the personal power of the sultan. The Turks knew for themselves how important it was to keep an eye on developments in these borderlands; only a few decades earlier they had lingered on the eastern periphery of the caliphate before taking it over completely.

Around the middle of 1086, therefore, Malik-Shah sent envoys to Alexios bearing a letter noting the problems in western Asia Minor. Abu'l-Kasim had failed to respect the agreement which the sultan had made with Sulayman and which had remained intact for several years: 'I have heard, Emperor, of your troubles. I know that from the start of your reign you have met with many difficulties and that recently, after you had settled the Latin affairs [the Norman attacks of 1081–5], the [Pechenegs] were preparing to make war on you. The emir Abu'l-Kasim, too, having broken the treaty that Sulayman concluded with you, is ravaging Asia as far as Damalis itself . . . If it is your wish that Abu'l-Kasim should be driven from those districts [that he had attacked] and that Asia, together with Antioch, should be subject to you, send me your daughter as wife for the eldest of my sons. Thereafter nothing will stand in your way; it will be easy for you to accomplish everything with my aid, not only in the east, but even as far as Illyrikon and the entire west. Because of the forces I will send you, no one will resist you from now on.'[53] Malik-Shah also promised he would force the Turks to withdraw from the coastal regions and give the emperor his full support to recover all locations that had been lost by the empire.[54] Anna Komnene reported that the emperor was bemused by the marriage proposal: he burst out laughing and then muttered that the Devil himself must have put this idea into Malik-Shah's head. Nevertheless, Alexios did not dismiss it out of hand, sending a delegation to Baghdad to offer 'vain hopes' about a marriage tie.[55]

The Alexiad gives the impression that nothing came of negotiations. However, the discussions did in fact lead to a concrete agreement in the mid-1080s, as Anna Komnene herself reveals later in the text. Reporting on the emperor's preparations for a major battle with the Pechenegs, Anna states that among the men sent to his aid were Turks from the east, dispatched by the sultan in accordance with a treaty that had been agreed previously.[56]

The outline terms of this treaty can be unscrambled from other passages in the *Alexiad*. The author reports that her father had the good fortune to woo a Turkish envoy, who defected to Byzantium and handed back to the emperor many towns in Asia Minor in the mid-1080s. Yet the story is too good to be true. It appears what actually happened was that Malik-Shah agreed to expel Turks who had taken control of towns on the coast of Asia Minor and ordered that these locations be restored to Byzantium, with the Turks withdrawing from Sinope on the Black Sea coast, for example, even leaving the town's treasury behind untouched.[57] As a result, all over the region towns were surrendered to Byzantium; this was the result of high-level diplomacy, and not, as Anna Komnene suggests, sleight of hand and cunning on the part of the emperor.

Malik-Shah was well compensated for his crucial help: magnificent gifts were brought to the sultan by Greek envoys in the mid-1080s.[58] 'The rulers of Byzantium brought him tribute', reported an Arabic writer after the sultan's death, noting that Malik-Shah's name was renowned 'from the borders of China to the limits of Syria, and from the remotest lands of Islam in the north to the confines of Yemen'.[59] This hints at a clear demarcation of interest: while Asia Minor belonged to the Byzantine sphere of influence, areas further east were subject to the Turkish sultan.

The sultan's warnings to local emirs in Anatolia were followed up by aggressive action to impose his direct authority over warlords on the periphery of the Turkish world. A major expedition was dispatched deep into Asia Minor against Nicaea and its governor Abu'l-Kasim, whose raids on Byzantine territory had so troubled Alexios.[60] Malik-Shah also set out on campaign in person, marching into the Caucasus before turning south into Syria where he took Aleppo. After Antioch had surrendered to him, the sultan went down to the Mediterranean shore, dismounted and stepped into the sea, plunging his sword three times into the water with the words: 'Lo, God has allowed me to rule over the lands from the Persian Sea to this sea.'[61]

The sultan's capture of Antioch was likely the price to pay for his co-operation against Abu'l-Kasim and for the restoration of towns in Asia Minor. It is striking that Malik-Shah was welcomed by the Christian populations in many of the places he passed through at this time who saw his involvement in the region as a prerequisite for stability, acting as a restraint on local Turkish leaders. The sultan met with no resistance in the Caucasus, for example, where the grace and 'fatherly affection' with which he treated the local Christians did much to allay fears of what the direct overlordship of Baghdad might entail.[62] It helped too that Malik-Shah had a reputation for tolerance towards Christianity: around the start of 1074, soon after he became sultan in succession to his father, for example, he had sent a delegation to Constantinople with detailed enquiries about Christian doctrine, belief and practice.[63] In addition, during his campaign of 1086–7 he seemed to one observer to have come to impose his authority over his own subjects, and not over Christians;[64] although he entered Edessa and Melitene, he neither installed his own governors nor removed those who were holding the towns on behalf of the emperor.[65]

The emperor also took military action in 1086–7, re-establishing his authority over locations in the regions that did not surrender according to the sultan's instructions. Attacks emanating from Nicaea were brought to a stop following operations against Abu'l-Kasim. 'The raids were checked', noted Anna Komnene, 'and [Abu'l-Kasim] was constrained to seek terms of peace.'[66] Imperial troops were dispatched to recover Kyzikos and Apollonias and other locations in western Asia Minor that had been targeted by local Turkish leaders.[67] Kyzikos, which had fallen on the eve of Alexios' coup, was restored to imperial control around the middle of 1086 and placed under the command of Constantine Humbertopoulos, one of the emperor's closest supporters, until he was recalled to deal with yet another wave of Pecheneg attacks.[68]

Other locations were recovered after the promise of substantial rewards persuaded some Turkish commanders to take service with the emperor and to convert to Christianity.[69] The conversions were welcomed by clerics in Constantinople, who praised Alexios for his evangelism and his advancement of the true faith.[70] The emperor was happy to take the credit, but rather than being motivated by religious fervour, he was acting in line with classic diplomacy: offering imperial titles and financial rewards to leading Turks was an effective way of showing the benefits of co-operation with Byzantium. They were a small price to pay for recovering towns and regions that had been lost.

Consequently, in a speech by a senior cleric delivered in the presence of the emperor and his closest advisers on 6 January 1088, the

Feast of Epiphany, little mention was made of affairs in the east. In contrast to the western provinces which continued to suffer from the ravagings of the Pechenegs, this was no longer a region of major concern. After dwelling on the threat posed by the steppe nomads and commending Alexios on a peace treaty which had been concluded with the nomads shortly beforehand, Theophylact of Ohrid had nothing of note to say about Asia Minor. Alexios, pronounced the cleric, was fortunate to enjoy excellent relations with the Turks and above all with the sultan. Such was Malik-Shah's admiration for the emperor that he raised a toast in his honour whenever he heard mention of the emperor's name. Reports of the emperor's courage and glory, noted Theophylact approvingly, resounded throughout the world.[71]

This upbeat assessment of 1088 could not contrast more sharply with the bleak view of the empire's predicament in 1081 provided by Anna Komnene and long accepted by modern commentators. Stability, not collapse, marked the eastern provinces, even if occasional challenges required decisive action. The situation had been brought under control by the Byzantines – and there would have been no need to appeal to the Pope for help from abroad. In the late 1080s, there was no need for a Crusade.

4

The Collapse of Asia Minor

Apart from Nicaea itself where Abu'l-Kasim still held power, Byzantium retained control of many prime parts of the eastern provinces in the late 1080s, above all the crucial coastal regions, the fertile river valleys and the islands of the Aegean – that is to say the strategically sensitive locations that were critical for the empire's trade and communication networks. Evidence that many of these areas were thriving under Byzantine control can be found in the intense lobbying of the emperor's mother by monks on islands such as Leros and Patmos in 1088 and 1089. The monks were planning a considerable building programme and were hoping to secure valuable tax exemptions.[1]

The situation soon changed drastically. As we have seen, the threat posed by Pecheneg raids on the western provinces escalated sharply in 1090, with the random attacks of previous years replaced by the migration of the entire tribe deep into Thrace. The resulting pressure provided the perfect opportunity for Turkish warlords in the east to move against Byzantium. Abu'l-Kasim was one who did just that. Around the middle of 1090, he began preparations to attack Nikomedia, an important town north of Nicaea that lay barely fifty miles from Constantinople.[2]

Alexios took desperate steps to try to hold on to the town. Five hundred Flemish knights, sent by Robert, Count of Flanders, who had met Alexios on his way home from pilgrimage to Jerusalem at the end of 1089, were supposed to have been deployed against the Pechenegs.[3] When they arrived in Byzantium in the middle of the following year, they were instead immediately transferred across the Bosphorus to help reinforce Nikomedia. Their presence proved vital in the short term, but when the Flemish knights were recalled to face the Pechenegs at Lebounion in the spring of 1091,[4] one of the oldest and most famous

towns of Asia Minor, which had briefly served as the eastern capital
of the Roman empire in the third century, fell to Abu'l-Kasim.[5] The
loss of Nikomedia was a disaster for Byzantium and raised serious
questions about the empire's long-term ability to hold on to its eastern
provinces as a whole.

Fears about Byzantine prospects in Asia Minor were raised further
by the fact that others were also poised to exploit the problems facing
the empire. Danishmend, a charismatic Turkish warlord, launched
daring raids from eastern Asia Minor deep into Cappadocia and on
major towns such as Sebasteia and Kaisereia.[6] Then there was Çaka,
an ambitious Turk who established himself in Smyrna on the western
coast of Asia Minor and paid local shipbuilders to construct a fleet to
attack a range of targets close to his new base, including islands in
the Aegean.[7] If anything, this was as serious as the loss of Nikomedia,
for Çaka's fleet gave him the power to strike further afield. It also
allowed him to disrupt shipments from towns and islands along
the coast, which were destined for Constantinople. At a time when the
provisioning of the capital was already under pressure because of
the Pecheneg threat, this brought with it the prospect of shortages,
inflation and social unrest. Matters were made worse by a particularly
severe winter in 1090–1, the harshest in living memory, when so much
snow fell that many were trapped in their houses.[8]

A poem from around this period described how a woman from
one of the provinces in Asia Minor endured such deprivation that she
was forced to eat snake meat: 'Did you eat snakes whole or only in
parts? Did you cut off the tails and heads of creatures or did you eat
all their parts? How could you devour poisonous flesh full of poison
and not die at once?' Such were the consequences of a terrible winter,
severe famine, and the barbarian scourge.[9]

Efforts to deal with Çaka went spectacularly wrong. One local
governor fled without putting up any resistance at all, while a hastily
assembled force sent by the emperor to secure the western coast of
Asia Minor was a fiasco. Not only was the Byzantine fleet routed, but
Çaka managed to capture several imperial vessels in the process. This
only served to accelerate gains he made elsewhere.[10]

The building up of Çaka's fleet was a worrying development for
another reason. Constantinople was protected by formidable land
walls, ditches and heavily armed towers, but the Byzantines had a

particular anxiety about the prospect of attack on the capital by sea. A giant sea chain laid across the entrance to the Golden Horn gave some reassurance, though in practice this often did not prove effective. Seaborne assaults on the city, even by small numbers of raiders, triggered hysteria amongst the inhabitants, as had happened in the ninth and tenth centuries, when Viking and Russian raiders made surprise strikes on the suburbs, causing widespread panic. In Çaka's case, the fear was that the Turk might come to an accommodation with the Pechenegs and launch a joint assault on the city. In the spring of 1091, rumours began circulating that there had been exchanges between the nomads and Çaka, with the latter offering his support against Byzantium.[11]

The mood in the capital became dark and poisonous. In the presence of the emperor and his retinue in the spring of 1091, the patriarch of Antioch, John the Oxite, delivered a damning assessment of the empire's predicament. The contrast to the upbeat view provided by Theophylact barely three years earlier could not have been sharper. Khios had been lost, said the patriarch, as had Mitylene. All the islands in the Aegean had fallen, while Asia Minor was in complete turmoil; not a single fragment of the east remained.[12] The Pechenegs, meanwhile, had reached the walls of Constantinople, and Alexios' efforts to deal with them had proved singularly ineffective.[13] Reflecting on why the threats had become acute, John reached a stark conclusion: God had stopped protecting Byzantium. The lack of military success and the terrible hardships being endured were the fault of the emperor, declared the patriarch. Alexios had been an outstanding general before he became emperor but since then he had brought one defeat after another. By seizing the throne in 1081 he had angered God, who was now using pagans to punish Byzantium. Repentance was urgently required if things were to change.[14] This apocalyptic verdict is a stark indication of the scale of the problems affecting Byzantium at the start of the 1090s.

The rapid downturn in Asia Minor was viewed with horror by westerners living in Byzantium. 'The Turks allied themselves with many nations and invaded the rightful possessions of the empire of Constantinople', wrote one eyewitness from central France. 'Far and wide they ravaged cities and castles together with their settlements; churches were razed down to the ground. Of the clergymen and monks whom they captured, some were slaughtered while others were with unspeakable wickedness given up, priests and all, to their dire dominion and nuns – alas for the sorrow of it! – were subjected to their lusts. Like ravening wolves, they preyed pitilessly on the Christian people whom God's just judgement had handed over to them as they pleased.'[15]

News of the devastating collapse in Asia Minor spread quickly all over Europe. Stories of plunder and arson, kidnap and sexual violence were reported across France, for example, with gory accounts of brutality, disembowelling and decapitation recorded by monks in their chronicles.[16] Information of this kind was passed on by westerners who were living in or visiting Constantinople in the early 1090s, such as a monk from Canterbury, who had made a home for himself in the capital, or an awestruck traveller who described the sights of Constantinople and recounted the conversations he had with its inhabitants.[17]

Alexios himself was the source of some of the reports describing the horrors endured by Byzantines at the hands of the Turks. A letter sent by the emperor to Robert, Count of Flanders, gives a devastating picture of the situation in Asia Minor in 1090–1.[18] This correspondence has traditionally been viewed as a forgery, its contents discounted by generations of scholars on the grounds that Byzantium's eastern provinces had been lost by 1081 and that there was therefore no major change in conditions in the years immediately before the First Crusade. Thus the claims about the shocking reversals against the Turks have been regarded as wild, implausible, and with only a slender basis in fact. Scholars have forcefully argued that the letter is a fabrication to rally support against Byzantium at the start of the twelfth century after relations between Alexios and some of the senior figures who took part in the Crusade irretrievably collapsed.[19]

It is widely recognised, conversely, that a letter probably was sent by Alexios to the Count of Flanders in the early 1090s, given the relations between the two men. As such, it has been suggested that there was an original document sent from Constantinople that provided the base of the letter that survives – albeit translated, elaborated on and added to.[20] Certainly, the prose and language of the letter are unmistakably Latin, while the diplomatic and political thought are clearly western, rather than Byzantine in style.

However, this does not mean that the text is a falsification. As we have seen, there were many westerners living in Constantinople in the late eleventh century, including a number who were close to the emperor. As such, both the tone and ideas expressed in the letter could just as easily represent the hand of a foreigner writing in the imperial capital, as that of an author writing after the First Crusade. And in this respect, what is perhaps most striking about the letter is that almost everything it says tallies with the new picture of Asia Minor that can be established from other contemporary sources. The letter to Robert of Flanders also reports desecration of churches in the early 1090s that we know about from elsewhere: 'The holy places are desecrated and destroyed in countless ways and the threat of worse looms over them. Who cannot lament over these things? Who has no compassion when they hear of it? Who cannot be horrified? And who cannot turn to prayer?'[21] The letter contains accounts of the ferocity of the Turkish attacks which likewise find parallels with other sources from this period, albeit in more detail: 'Noble matrons and their daughters, robbed of everything, are violated, one after another, like animals. Some [of their attackers] shamelessly place virgins in front of their own mothers and force them to sing wicked and obscene songs until they have finished having their way with them . . . men of every age and description, boys, youths, old men, nobles, peasants and what is worse still and yet more distressing, clerics and monks and woe of unprecedented woes, even bishops are defiled with the sin of sodomy and it is now trumpeted abroad that one bishop has succumbed to this abominable sin.'[22]

It certainly made sense for Alexios to appeal to Flanders, having already received military support in the form of 500 knights shortly beforehand. Alexios hoped to attract further assistance from Count Robert, a man of similar character to himself – ascetic, pious and pragmatic. And while the desperate descriptions of the situation in the east have been dismissed by many as implausible, there is much to suggest that the letter genuinely reflects Byzantium's dire position. Even the downbeat statement that 'although I am emperor, I can find no remedy or suitable counsel, but am always fleeing in the face of the Pechenegs and the Turks', is not out of place at a time when one of the highest clerics in the empire could state publicly that God had abandoned Alexios.[23] The siege mentality that had begun to emerge in Constantinople strikes a closer chord with the letter than often presumed.

The recall of the Flemish garrison from Nikomedia may not have been solely responsible for the loss of the town to the Turks, but it certainly did not help. Soon after the defeat of the Pechenegs in 1091 a major effort was made to recover the town and to drive the Turks back from the areas closest to the capital. Assembling a substantial force, Alexios sent in an army which recovered territory as far as the Arm of St George, that is to say up to the Gulf of Nikomedia. Eventually the town itself was recaptured, with its conquerors immediately setting about restoring its defences to prevent it falling so easily in the future. A fortress was constructed opposite Nikomedia, designed in the first instance to provide additional protection for the town, but also built to act as a base from which to attack if it did fall to the Turks once again. In addition, grandiose work began on the creation of a giant ditch to act as a further barrier to defend Nikomedia. It was a sign of desperation and an indication of the limitations of Byzantine ambitions in Asia Minor in the early 1070s: rather than reconquest, attention was focused on retaining the few possessions still in imperial hands.[24]

A full six months were spent reinforcing the town. In the meantime, attempts were made to persuade its inhabitants to leave the 'caves and hollows of the earth' which they had escaped to during Abu'l-Kasim's attack and return to Nikomedia. Their reluctance to return would suggest that many thought that the Byzantine recovery may not be permanent.[25]

While Nikomedia had been recovered, the situation worsened on the western coast and the islands in the Aegean. Once again, the chronology provided by the Alexiad is untrustworthy. A corpus of documents relating to a monk named St Christodoulos reveals the true escalation of the threat posed by the Turks. Christodoulos was a magnetic character with friends in high places. Alexios' mother, Anna Dalassene, helped the monk secure land grants and tax exemptions for properties on the Aegean islands of Kos, Leros and Lipsos where Christodoulos had ambitious plans to build a series of monasteries. Anna's support was instrumental in convincing the emperor to give his personal approval for the establishment of the monastery of St John on the island of Patmos in 1088.[26]

At the start of the 1090s, however, physical survival – rather than grants or tax exemptions – had become the main concern for Christodoulos and the monks on these islands. Attacks by Turkish pirates and raiders forced them to take urgent steps to reinforce their settlements. On Patmos, Leros and Lipsos, small castles were built in an attempt to protect the communities, but it soon became clear that Christodoulos was fighting an uphill battle.[27] The monks fled, in fear of being captured by the Turks, and in the spring of 1092 Christodoulos himself gave up, escaping to Euboea where he died a year later. As a codicil to his will reveals, written shortly before his death, he was the last to leave Patmos; relentless attacks by 'Agarenes, pirates and Turks' had made life impossible.[28]

There was little improvement in the situation in the Aegean or the western coast of Asia Minor in the years that followed. Although Anna Komnene belittled Çaka, mocking him as a poseur who strutted about Smyrna wearing sandals styled on those of the emperor, and implying that he was easily and quickly dealt with, the truth was very different.[29] In 1094, Theodore Kastrisios, who had been appointed caretaker of the monastery of St John on Patmos following the death of Christodoulos, felt he had no option but to resign his position. He did so, he said, because he was unable to fulfil any of his duties: constant Turkish raids in the eastern Aegean meant that he could not even reach the island, let alone look after the monastery.[30]

The near total collapse of Asia Minor was rapid and spectacular. While the Pecheneg threat had played an important role in creating opportunities for individual Turkish leaders, such as Abu'l-Kasim and Çaka, it was the failure of Alexios' previous policy of forging local alliances that lay at the heart of the problems now facing Byzantium. In the past, Alexios had been able to win over Turkish warlords and had backed this up with an effective agreement with the sultan of Baghdad, who had his own interests in maintaining control over emirs on the periphery of the Seljuk world.

This alliance with Malik-Shah was still active in the spring of 1091, when Alexios complained that reinforcements sent to him by the sultan were being diverted and recruited by Çaka.[31] Malik-Shah was also perturbed by the dramatic shift in power, and in the summer of 1092, sent a major expedition under the command of one his most loyal officers, Buzan, deep into Asia Minor to teach Abu'l-Kasim a lesson. Although Buzan advanced decisively on Nicaea, he was unable to make an impression on the town's formidable defences and eventually withdrew.[32] Nevertheless, diplomatic exchanges between Constantinople and Baghdad were still ongoing in the autumn of that year, continuing to explore how the two rulers could best co-operate against Abu'l-Kasim and other renegades in the region.[33]

The death of Malik-Shah in November 1092 therefore served as a body blow for Alexios' policy in the east. In the months before he died, the sultan found his grip on power weakening as rivals in Baghdad jockeyed for position. In an attempt to consolidate his authority, Malik-Shah demoted many of his leading officers, which only stoked dissent further.[34] Antagonism focused on the sultan's vizier, the polymath Nizam al-Mulk, a powerful figure who had played a fundamental role in shaping the Seljuk world in the later eleventh century. Towards the end of 1092 he was disposed of, murdered by a secretive sect of fanatics known as the Assassins, if not on the direct instructions of the sultan, then at least with his knowledge, according to one well-informed source.[35] The death of Malik-Shah just a few weeks later – after eating contaminated meat – threw the Turkish world into turmoil, as uncertainty raged as to who amongst the sultan's immediate and extended family would succeed to the throne. The result was two years of almost constant civil war.[36]

Many scholars have argued that this upheaval within the Turkish Empire presented Alexios with the ideal opportunity to strengthen Byzantium's position in Asia Minor. In fact, the opposite was the case. Malik-Shah's death robbed the emperor of an invaluable ally at the worst possible moment. What is more, the problems over the succession meant there was a power vacuum in Anatolia which was quickly exploited by local Turkish warlords. This made things much more difficult for Alexios, who struggled to make an impression on the succession of Turkish leaders who were making the most of both their new-found freedom and the weakness of the Byzantine response.

By 1094, the situation was critical. At a church synod in Constantinople, attended by bishops from all over the empire, discussion turned to those with pastoral responsibilities in the east. Many were present in the capital not by choice but because they could not get back to their respective sees because of the Turks. Acknowledging the problems they faced, the emperor tartly noted that bishops from western regions had no such excuse, and ordered them to leave Constantinople and return to their duties.[37] Bishops from Anatolia, it was acknowledged, could not be expected to do the same, and furthermore needed financial support while they remained in the capital, cut off from their sees. A resolution was duly passed to this effect.[38]

The failure of Byzantine Asia Minor was universal: the collapse of the interior, together with the loss of the seaboard, meant that it was not possible to reach important locations such as Antioch either by land or by sea; John the Oxite, the patriarch of Antioch, was unable to travel to his see for several years.[39] Town after town fell into Turkish hands in the early 1090s. According to Michael the Syrian, whose twelfth-century chronicle is one of the few sources to focus on this period, Tarsos, Mopsuetia, Anazarbos and all the other towns of Cilicia were taken around 1094/5.[40] This corresponds with what the western knights found as they crossed Asia Minor not long afterwards. When they reached Plastencia, 'a town of great splendour and wealth', they found it besieged by the Turks, its inhabitants still holding out;[41] a nearby town, Coxon, was also still in Christian hands.[42]

The loss of the western coast of Asia Minor and of the rich river valleys of its hinterland was a catastrophe for Byzantium. Something had to be done urgently to reverse the series of setbacks and to lay a platform on which to build a later recovery; if not, it was likely that the eastern provinces would be lost forever. Attention turned to Nicaea, superbly fortified and controlling access to the interior as well as the land routes to the coast. Taking the city would be the key to any wider restoration of imperial control in the east; its retrieval now became the principal thrust of the emperor's strategy.

Making an impression on the city was not easy: a masterpiece of defensive fortification, it was all but impregnable. As one Latin chronicler observed: 'Nicaea has a very favourable site. It lies in the plain, yet is not far from the mountains, by which it is surrounded on almost every side . . . Next to the city, and extending to the west, is a very wide lake of great length . . . this is the best defence the city could have. A moat surrounds the walls on the other sides, and this is always full to overflowing by the influx of springs and streams.'[43]

Alexios knew that there was little prospect of taking the town by force.[44] Apart from anything else, the Byzantine military was already overstretched. As John the Oxite had noted, a decade of near constant campaigning against the Normans and the Pechenegs had worn out the imperial forces and inflicted many casualties.[45] In addition, the situation was still tense to the north of Constantinople. There was danger of an imminent attack on imperial territory from the Danube region by Cuman steppe nomads, while incursions by the Serbs across the north-western frontier were becoming increasingly troublesome.[46]

Raising a force sufficiently large to move on Nicaea was one problem. Another was trying to make an impression on its defences. Byzantine siege warfare lagged a long way behind the west, where techniques had developed rapidly during the eleventh century. And then there was the question of who should take charge of operations against the city. Given the failure of Alexios' policy in Asia Minor and the pressure on the empire as a whole, there was a real risk that a general in command of substantial resources might see an opportunity to try to take the throne for himself.

It was to Tatikios, his childhood friend, that Alexios turned, confident of his loyalty. In the middle of 1094, Tatikios arrived at Nicaea, supplied with instructions to engage any defender who dared make a sortie. He soon charged a group of 200 men who had come out to disperse the imperial force. This was the extent of his achievement, however: a morale boost, but of little tangible value. He achieved nothing more before withdrawing to Constantinople in haste after learning that a major Turkish expedition was closing in on Nicaea.[47] This had been sent by Barkyaruq, one of the sons of Malik-Shah, who had finally triumphed over his rivals in Baghdad having the *hutba* declared to proclaim him as ruler in February 1094.[48]

Barkyaruq's intervention was deeply disturbing for Alexios as it became clear that its aim was not just to stamp the new sultan's authority on emirs in Asia Minor, but to take possession of Nicaea. The emperor was not alone in his concern at the advance of the force under Bursuk, a particularly bloodthirsty commander: 'the inhabitants of [Nicaea], and indeed Abu'l-Kasim himself saw that their condition was really desperate – it was impossible to hold out against Bursuk any more'. They took a bold decision; according to the *Alexiad*, 'they got a message through to the emperor asking for help, saying that it was better to be called his slaves than to surrender to Bursuk. Without delay, the best available troops were sent [by the emperor] to their aid, with standards and silver-studded sceptres.'[49]

There was cool logic behind Alexios' decision to help the governor of Nicaea, even though he had been the cause of problems for Byzantium over many years: 'He calculated that providing help would bring about the ruin of Abu'l-Kasim', reported Anna Komnene. 'For when two enemies of the Roman Empire were fighting one another, it would pay him to support the weaker – not in order to make him more powerful, but to repel the one while taking the town from the other, a town that was not at the moment under Roman jurisdiction but would be incorporated in the Roman sphere by this means.'[50] Although Bursuk withdrew, frustrated by Nicaea's defences, the respite was brief: reports were soon received in the city that another massive expedition 'from the deep interior of the Turkish Empire' was on its way.[51] Abu'l-Kasim realised that it was only a matter of time before he was forced into submission; he was ready to listen to the emperor's proposals about the handover of Nicaea.

Constantinople regularly received diplomatic missions and high-ranking visitors from foreign shores. In the tenth century, a text known as The Book of Ceremonies had been compiled providing instructions how these were to be dealt with, with the relative importance of the country in question underpinning the lavishness of the reception.[52] The aim was to show the splendours of the capital and to underline the empire's cultural, political and spiritual superiority. Alexios now used this tried and tested technique with Abu'l-Kasim. When the Turk was invited to Constantinople later in 1094, the emperor laid on a specially tailored schedule designed to impress the emir and show him the benefits of co-operating with the empire.

Alexios personally oversaw the programme of events. He made sure Abu'l-Kasim was shown the main sites in the capital, singling out highly symbolic monuments such as the statues set up in honour of Roman emperors in celebration of great military victories. The Turk was taken horse racing and shown first-hand the prowess of Byzantium's finest charioteers, designed to make an impact on a man whose people's use of the horse was critical to their military success. He went hunting with the emperor and was taken to that most Roman of institutions, the baths. In short, Abu'l-Kasim was being lavishly entertained and assiduously courted.[53]

Alexios wanted a concrete agreement about Nicaea and the approach he took was one often used to deal with difficult neighbours: the award of a title and a fat stipend. The aim was to make the enemy recognise, even if only implicitly, the overlordship of the emperor – while buying him off at the same time. Before he returned to Nicaea, therefore, 'Alexios presented the Turk with more gifts, honoured him with the title of *sebastos*, confirmed their agreement in greater detail and sent him with every sign of courtesy back over the sea.'[54] The title *sebastos* was one of the very highest in the empire, which was normally only awarded to members of the ruling family and their closest intimates. Its bestowal on Abu'l-Kasim reveals that Alexios hoped to gain substantially as a result of the agreement reached in the capital. If the emperor's gamble was successful, it would restore the pivotal location in western Asia Minor to imperial hands, opening up the possibility of a wider recovery of this region. If unsuccessful, Alexios risked serious damage to his reputation for pinning his hopes on a man who had been a thorn in the empire's side for many years.

Disaster struck as soon as Abu'l-Kasim returned to Nicaea. The emir's discussions with the emperor did not meet with enthusiasm from other leading figures in the town. When reports started to circulate that Bursuk was again approaching with an even larger force, the governor of Nicaea was rounded on by a group of 200 leading Turks, keen to make a favourable impression on the new sultan. Seizing Abu'l-Kasim, they placed a noose made of bowstring around his neck and strangled him.[55]

The murder was a major blow to the emperor. Alexios reacted desperately, making contact with Abu'l-Kasim's brother, Buldagi, who had taken control of the city, and made him a direct offer. This time, there was no visit to Constantinople, no trips to the races, no awarding of titles, but the heart of the offer was the same. The emperor therefore made his proposal short and bold: he offered to buy Nicaea.[56]

Once more, however, things went against Alexios. With the Turks in Nicaea now in disarray, a new figure arrived on the scene. Kilidj Arslan made straight for the city after being released from prison in Baghdad in late 1094 or early 1095. As soon as he reached Nicaea, the Turks 'ran riot with joy', and handed control of the town over to him. This was not entirely surprising: he was, after all, the son of the late Sulayman.[57] His return to the family power base seems to have been engineered by the new regime of Barkyaruq, which clearly set great faith in him; and in the summer of 1097 he would command the massive army assembled to confront the Crusaders as they crossed Asia Minor.[58] His appointment to govern Nicaea on Barkyaruq's behalf was a shrewd choice, but it scuppered the emperor's chances of retaking this vital city and therefore stemming the collapse of the eastern provinces.

Byzantium's hold over its eastern provinces was slipping away fast. Those who reached Asia Minor in 1097 could not believe their eyes or hide the horror at what they saw when they got to Nikomedia: 'Oh, how many severed heads and bones of the dead lying on the plains did we then find beyond Nicomedia near that sea! In the preceding year, the Turks destroyed those who were ignorant of and new to the use of the arrow. Moved to compassion by this, we shed many tears there.'[59] A sign of how bad conditions were and how limited Byzantine ambitions had become, the road beyond Nikomedia was all but impassable by this time: 3,000 men with axes and swords had to be sent ahead to clear the way and to hack open a route to Nicaea.[60]

The lack of progress over Nicaea was mirrored by the string of setbacks on the coast, where Çaka continued to wreak havoc. Although Anna Komnene's account has persuaded most historians that the threat posed by the Turk had been contained in 1092, in fact the opposite was the case.[61] In the mid-1090s, exasperated by the ineffective and incompetent efforts to deal with Çaka, Alexios recalled his brother-in-law, John Doukas, from Dyrrakhion where he had been successfully shoring up the frontier against the Serbs for more than a decade. The earliest he could have been sent against Çaka was 1094.[62] This corresponds closely with observations from elsewhere that constant Turkish attacks in this region at that time made even basic travel impossible.[63]

A full report of the major expedition sent to oust Çaka and reconquer the coast is provided in the *Alexiad*, though this is dispersed across several books, giving the impression of multiple campaigns and sustained success.[64] In reality, there was one concerted effort to deal with Çaka which was spearheaded by John Doukas, who led Byzantine land forces, and another close relative of the emperor, Constantine Dalassenos, who took charge of the fleet. Operations began in the summer of 1097.

The aim of the expedition was clear. It was essential to secure the coast and to restore imperial authority to this region. The orders given to Doukas were uncompromising: he was to take back the islands that had fallen one after another to the Turks and to recover the towns and fortifications which had been lost. As we shall see, the primary target was Smyrna and its troublesome ruler Çaka.[65] In obvious contradiction to Anna Komnene's account, Çaka was still a major force in 1097. And as one Latin source therefore noted correctly, the entire maritime region of Asia Minor was under Turkish control when the Crusaders arrived there a few years later.[66] Nicaea remained elusive; and efforts against the coastal region had come to nothing. The situation facing Byzantium in the mid-1090s was not so much desperate as catastrophic.

5

On the Brink of Disaster

The deteriorating situation in Asia Minor was not the only problem Alexios Komnenos had to contend with. On the eve of the First Crusade, Constantinople itself imploded. The failure to make any progress against the Turks led to serious concerns about the emperor's judgement and his abilities. As further threats emerged, in the form of renewed nomad attacks deep into the Balkans and Serbian raids on the north-western frontier, Alexios' rule was in jeopardy. The situation became critical shortly before envoys were sent to the Pope in 1095, when the emperor was faced with a coup that was supported by almost the entire Byzantine elite: senior officers, senators, aristocrats and some of Alexios' closest intimates rose up against him, including many who had helped propel him to power. The spiral of disintegration that would lead Alexios to seek help from the west continued.

Pressure began to mount on the emperor in Constantinople as soon as the situation in Asia Minor began to worsen. After the first wave of Turkish successes in 1090–1, Alexios was already being roundly criticised in the capital. To John the Oxite, the patriarch of Antioch, the emperor had become a liability; endless wars in the 1080s had achieved nothing and military setbacks had brought great suffering.[1] And the patriarch's admonition fell on fertile ground. Dissatisfaction was widespread amongst those who were not part of the golden circle that Alexios had set up around him at the start of his reign. He was assiduous, reported one Byzantine commentator, in promoting members of his family, lavishing vast amounts of money on them: 'When it came to his relations or some of those who served him, [Alexios] distributed public funds by the cartload. They received fat yearly donations, and enjoyed such wealth that they could have at their service a retinue which was not appropriate to a private person but to emperors; they could have houses the size of cities, not distinct in their splendour from palaces.' The rest of the aristocracy, the author remarked sadly, was shown no such generosity.[2]

The favouritism shown by the emperor to members of his family was extensive. Nikephoros Melissenos, one of Alexios' brothers-in-law, was granted the tax revenues of the important city of Thessaloniki, while the emperor's brother Adrian was settled with the income of the peninsula of Kassandra in 1084.[3] A myriad of monastic establishments set up or endowed by members of the imperial family in this period, such as the church and monastery of the Saviour Pantepoptes established by Anna Dalassene, or the Kosmoteira monastery of the Mother of God founded by Alexios' son Isaac Komnenos, attest to substantial disposable wealth in the hands of those close to the emperor at a time of huge economic strain.[4]

Many of the most sensitive positions in Byzantium were handed over to close relatives of the emperor. The governorship of Dyrrakhion, one of the most important towns in the western half of the empire, was entrusted to two of the emperor's brothers-in-law, George Palaiologos and then John Doukas, before being placed in the hands of Alexios' eldest nephew.[5] Adrian and Nikephoros Komnenos, the emperor's two younger brothers, were appointed to senior commands in the army and the navy respectively. Their elder brother Isaac, meanwhile, became the main enforcer of policy in Byzantium, with special responsibility for stamping out dissent in Constantinople. Constantine Dalassenos, a cousin on the emperor's maternal side, was entrusted with the responsibility of recovering the town of Sinope from the Turks in the mid-1080s, before being put in command of the maritime operations against Çaka and coastal Asia Minor.[6] Others too were similarly awarded elevated titles and status in Alexios' Byzantium.[7]

The emperor's dependence on his family has shaped posterity's view of him. This concentration of power is seen as ushering in a new system of government in Byzantium, replacing a wide civil administration with a small interest group made up of the emperor's inner circle.[8] However, while it is tempting to see Alexios as basing his authority solely on his relatives and in-laws, in fact he drew support from a more strategically selected and considerably wider group than is usually assumed.

For example, there were many cousins, nephews, nieces and in-laws who did not find favour, position or high rank during the first decade and a half of Alexios' reign.[9] There were also many beneficiaries of the new regime who were not related to the emperor – Gregory Pakourianos, for example, who came from a distinguished family from Georgia and was appointed commander of the imperial army in 1081.[10] Constantine Opos, who was given important military responsibilities in the mid-1080s, likewise had no family link with the Komnenoi.[11] The most outstanding example was Leo Kephalas, governor of Larissa when the town was subjected to a horrific Norman siege in 1083, during which the inhabitants reportedly resorted to cannibalism.[12] He was later appointed commander of the town of Abydos in western Asia Minor at a time when the threat of the Turks was rising sharply. His ability and loyalty marked him out as a rising star under the Komnenoi. Throughout the 1080s, he was granted a series of villages and other lands, together with exemptions from taxation and eventually the right to pass these properties on to his heirs.[13]

Mixobarbaroi, 'half-caste' nomads who took service with the emperor and prospered, such as Monastras and Ouzas, also enjoyed Alexios' confidence. So did westerners like Constantine Humbertopoulos, nephew of the emperor's nemesis Robert Guiscard, and Peter Aliphas, who became a trusted lieutenant in spite of his role in the Norman attack of 1081–3, during which he nearly killed Alexios in combat.[14] In addition, the emperor personally oversaw the baptism of Turkish allies and their admission to the senate.[15]

It was not just the imperial family, therefore, who were beneficiaries of Komnenian government. There was a never-ending stream of supplicants, seeking preferential treatment, exemptions, rewards or favours from Alexios – men like Manuel Straboromanos who presented flowery eulogies to the emperor, extolling his virtues in detail, in an attempt to have lands which had been confiscated restored to him.[16] Not all petitioners were well received, however, and from time to time the pious emperor lost patience even with the monks who appeared in Constantinople to plead their cases: 'I want to slit their nostrils', he wrote to the patriarch Nicholas III, 'and then to send them home so that the rest of the monks will understand what the imperial view of things is.'[17]

What shaped Byzantium under Alexios was not the concentration of power into the hands of the Komnenoi and their supporters, but rather the iron grip which the emperor himself established over the apparatus of the state from the start of his reign. It was Alexios personally who took decisions, made appointments, gave promotions and rewards – or cast enemies into the wilderness. Such close control over every aspect of military, civilian and even ecclesiastical affairs was in sharp contrast to the rule of many of his predecessors. It was a strategy that allowed Alexios to shape Byzantium in his own image.

The promotion of those that the emperor was comfortable with – whether members of his family or outsiders – came at the expense of Byzantine aristocrats who found themselves excluded from positions of influence. The problems this caused were more acute than lost status. The bedrock of imperial society was the distribution of annual salaries to those with positions in Constantinople and the provinces. Funds were channelled from the centre to a wide group of officials in the civilian and military administrations, and changes to this system were a cause not just of resentment but of financial loss. In fact, it had been Alexios' predecessor, Nikephoros III Botaneiates, who first reduced the salaries paid out by the central government in an attempt to cut costs. Yet Alexios took things further, reducing and in many cases suspending payments altogether to reduce expenditure and bolster the precarious economy. These steps were bound to prove unpopular, as were the confiscations of property belonging to high-ranking officials accused of plotting against Alexios, which was used to boost the sparse imperial coffers. The emperor's policy of using debased coinage to pay for government expenditure while insisting on higher-value coins when it came to collecting tax, further aggravated the situation.[18]

Alexios took these steps because of the substantial costs of funding military operations against Byzantium's neighbours. Maintaining the army in the field almost continuously for more than a decade after 1081 was expensive in terms of salaries, equipment and provisioning. It was costly in indirect terms too, with the diversion of manpower from agricultural production resulting in lower yields, falling tax revenues and rising prices. The payment of tribute to the Pechenegs and to the sultan in the 1080s also required funding, as did other efforts to improve the empire's situation. An alliance with Henry IV of Germany against the Normans came at great expense: the Byzantines agreed to pay the enormous sum of 360,000 gold coins – with the stipulation that this was to be paid not in newly minted (and heavily debased) currency, but in coins of substantially higher quality.[19]

Desperate efforts were made to boost the state's income. In 1082, Alexios swore on oath that he would never again take treasures from the church, having expropriated high-value objects to fund his campaign against the Normans after they attacked Dyrrakhion. But three years later he again resorted to seizing precious ecclesiastical objects. The emperor was furiously criticised for breaking his promise, with attacks on his character led by the bishop of Chalcedon, a highly vocal and effective agitator, even if Anna Komnene dismissed him as 'incapable of expressing his ideas accurately and without ambiguity, because he was utterly devoid of any training in logic'.[20] Although Alexios managed to weather the controversy, his efforts to extract funds from the church for a third time at the start of the 1090s earned him a stinging rebuke from the patriarch of Antioch.[21]

Heavy increases in taxation were introduced to cover the mismatch between revenue and expenditure. According to one Byzantine commentator, officials were appointed to gather taxes by inventing debts that needed to be paid off. Failure to meet these phantom obligations was used as a pretext to confiscate property and to provide yet another shot in the arm for the imperial treasury.[22] These tax rises had devastating consequences. The increased obligations resulted in death, famine, depopulation and homelessness. In some cases, according to the patriarch of Antioch, it had caused people to join 'the barbarians who murder Christians, judging that servitude and life with them was more palatable than with us'.[23]

Even the monks on Mount Athos attracted the attention of an emperor desperate for funds. Athos was home to several monastic communities, and the monks had accumulated an impressive range of land and property and proved adept at gaining exemptions from taxes. The lands they owned were concentrated in one of the few regions of the empire that had not come under pressure from the Normans, Pechenegs or Turks. These territories were also amongst the few places where productivity had not declined in the late eleventh century, and in 1089 Alexios turned to them to raise money. Three charters record the introduction of a new charge, the *epibole*, which made fresh demands on landowners. Those who could not or would not pay immediately were penalised, amongst them the monastery of Iviron on Mount Athos, which had lands of almost 20,000 acres confiscated by the emperor.[24]

By the time the situation in Asia Minor started to deteriorate at the start of the 1090s, Alexios had run out of options. Debasement of the coinage had reached a nadir, while central government had been stripped to the barest bones to save money. To make matters worse, around the start of 1091, Crete and Cyprus, the two largest and most important islands in the eastern Mediterranean, rose up in revolt against the emperor and declared effective independence from Constantinople. This rebellion was the result of heavy overtaxation.[25] Raids on the north-western frontier likewise put yet more pressure on the embattled emperor – as well as stretching Byzantium's resources further still.[26]

At the start of 1092, Alexios reached a decision that was to have a major impact on the history of the eastern Mediterranean. During the Norman attacks of the 1080s, the emperor had worked closely with Venice, with Venetian ships patrolling the Adriatic to prevent Norman supplies crossing over from southern Italy to provision the invaders, in exchange for an upfront payment.[27] Alexios issued a series of grants to ensure further co-operation during the Norman assaults of 1081–5, which included the award of titles to the doge as well as an extension of Venetian authority in the Adriatic to include Dalmatia.[28]

Desperate to stimulate the empire's financial system, Alexios concluded that this could only be achieved with a major injection of foreign capital. In the spring of 1092, therefore, the emperor issued a grant giving a sweeping set of privileges and concessions to Venice.[29] The ruler of Venice had used the title of doge of Venice and Dalmatia and imperial *protosebastos* in the 1080s; after 1092, however, he was also granted jurisdiction over Croatia in a further enlargement of Venetian authority – an important concession from Constantinople. This was further reinforced by the doge being given the right to pass these new honours on to his successors.[30] In addition, the churches of Venice were to receive funds, with St Mark's singled out for particularly generous treatment to help pay for the major restoration works undertaken at the start of the 1090s in advance of its imminent reconsecration. Part of the quayside in Constantinople, stretching from the Gate of the Hebrews to the Vigla tower, was to be set aside for the exclusive use of Venetian traders, with provision for similar arrangements in a range of other ports in the empire, including Antioch, Laodikeia, Tarsos, Mamistra, Attaleia, Athens, Corinth, Thebes, Thessaloniki and Dyrrakhion.[31] This gave Venice a significant competitive edge over other Italian city-states in the eastern Mediterranean.

Yet Alexios' grant went further, as he offered unprecedented incentives to encourage Venetian traders to invest in Byzantium. For example, immunity was awarded to protect against claims made on the properties they were given.[32] All taxes on Venetian shipping and the goods they were transporting, imports and exports alike, were removed.[33] By not giving similar concessions to Amalfi, Pisa and Genoa – other Italian city-states with important trade links with the empire – the emperor provided Venice with a major competitive advantage and incentive to boost their investment in Byzantium. So significant was this development that the patriarch of Grado himself, the head of the church in Venice, journeyed to Constantinople in the spring of 1092, presumably to witness the signing of the trade privileges in person.[34]

Alexios' move was another one of his gambles. There was the risk that other Italian city-states might demand the same terms. There was also the question of how to cancel or modify the terms of this generous grant in the future, to which the emperor seems to have given little thought in 1092. More significant in the short term was that the advantage handed to Venice placed further pressure on Byzantine merchants, as the widening of margins for the Italians made them dangerously competitive to local traders.

It is difficult to quantify the impact of the grant, but it is no coincidence that shortly after awarding the trading concessions, Alexios undertook a complete overhaul of the Byzantine monetary system. In the summer of 1092, the *hyperpyron* (literally' 'refined gold'), a new high-value coin, was introduced alongside several lower denominations, fixed in value in relation to each other. Although the new coins appeared only in limited numbers to start with, the re-coinage was a prerequisite for international exchange, as a stable currency was essential for foreign trade. Reforming the tattered currency was also crucial for the recovery of the severely depleted economy which had been battered by successive debasements which left little clarity over what the coinage was actually worth. Whether or not it would resuscitate the empire's ailing aristocracy was another matter.

* * *

There had been remarkably little opposition to Alexios I Komnenos in the first decade of his reign. In spite of the difficulties posed by Byzantium's neighbours and the worsening economic situation, the emperor was not put under serious pressure in Constantinople. Criticism of Alexios after the fall of Dyrrakhion in 1082 did not turn into direct action against him, and nothing came of the rumours of plots against the emperor which circulated in the capital in the winter of 1083.[35] Nor did a disastrous expedition to the Danube region a few years later prompt rebellion, even though the emperor was wounded in battle and had to hide one of the empire's most revered relics, the cape of the Virgin Mary, in a bed of wild flowers to prevent it being captured by the Pechenegs.[36]

The passivity of the ruling elite in the 1080s is all the more striking when set against the disturbances of the previous decade, when the empire was racked by civil war as several magnates took turns to try to seize the throne. This apparent calm was partly caused by the sharp decline in the fortunes of the aristocracy during this period. The removal of salaries, the collapse of independent incomes from lands which had come under pressure from raids by Byzantium's neighbours, and the unstable financial system had significantly weakened the empire's elites. But the failure of the aristocracy to challenge Alexios was also the result of the new emperor's grip on the realm. Carefully targeted confiscations of property at the outset of his reign made it clear to potential rebels that dissent came at a high price. Those seen as a threat were dealt with ruthlessly; as the deposition of two patriarchs in the first three years of Alexios' reign showed, the new emperor would not tolerate signs of mutiny or disloyalty.

By the start of the 1090s, however, Alexios could do little to prevent his position coming into question. It was becoming increasingly apparent that Alexios had steered the empire backwards. Scarce resources had been all but exhausted, with tax burdens leading to rebellion in places like Crete and Cyprus that could evade the fading grasp of Constantinople. The grant to Venice had antagonised too many, with properties given to the Italian traders taken from private individuals and from churches who were not only deprived of compensation, but also the right of appeal.[37]

Yet nowhere were Alexios' limitations clearer than in Asia Minor, where the emperor's attempts to reverse Turkish advances had proved woeful. Attempts to recover the coast had failed completely and efforts against Nicaea had been embarrassingly ineffective. As Alexios' reign began to look like a disaster, minds inevitably turned to the alternatives.

Remarkably, the efforts to replace the emperor did not come from the most obvious sources – those who had lost status and position as a result of the Komnenoi coup in 1081, or landowners in Asia Minor whose properties had been lost to the Turks or were under threat. Nor did it come from those whose prospects had been dented by Alexios' predilection for promoting outsiders to important positions in Byzantium, as articulated darkly by one author offering advice to the emperor in this period: 'whenever you honour a stranger coming from the rabble [of foreigners] by naming him as *primikerios* or as a general', he wrote, 'what possible position can you give to a Roman which is worthy? You shall make him your enemy in every way'.[38] In fact, the bitterest opposition to the emperor came from those who had been his strongest supporters: his own family.

Matters reached a climax in the spring of 1094 when Alexios prepared a major expedition to reinforce the north-western frontier, following repeated Serbian incursions into Byzantine territory. This was the final straw. With Asia Minor in tatters, the decision to focus on an outlying area of limited strategic importance appeared to show a profound lack of judgement. It provided confirmation, if confirmation were needed, that the emperor needed to be replaced.

Reports of misgivings about Alexios reached the ears of his nephew John Komnenos, who had recently been appointed governor of Dyrrakhion following the recall of John Doukas. Yet rather than warn his uncle about the rumours, John presented himself as a possible successor. It was a position he had become used to in the 1080s when he had been offered as a suitable match for the daughter of Henry IV of Germany during discussions to seal the alliance against the Normans.[39] But the coronation of Alexios' eldest son, John II Komnenos, as co-emperor alongside his father in the autumn of 1092 dealt a blow to John's hopes of succession.[40] When the archbishop of Bulgaria, Theophylact, informed the emperor about his nephew's plot against him, John was summoned and put in his place by Alexios. But although the matter was swiftly resolved, the affair revealed that even some of his own family had come to believe that Alexios was living on borrowed time.[41]

John's ambitions were part of a wider movement in Byzantium and there were plenty of other candidates to challenge the emperor. One was Constantine Doukas, the son of Michael VII, a young man with an impeccable pedigree but a limp character, and prone to bouts of ill health. Alexios had watched him carefully after taking power, aware that he was a potential rival to the throne, and to secure his loyalty had arranged Constantine's betrothal to his eldest daughter, Anna Komnene, soon after she was born in December 1083.[42] If reports that spread throughout the empire and beyond are to be believed, this union was not going to produce an heir: Constantine had apparently been castrated by Nikephoros III Botaneiates in 1078.[43]

After Constantine showed little appetite for insurrection, attention fell on another man whose breeding was matched by his character. Nikephoros Diogenes was the son of Romanos IV, who had been humiliated at Manzikert in 1071. Along with his younger brother, Nikephoros had also been watched closely by Alexios as he grew up. The two boys were like lion cubs, says Anna Komnene, the emperor nurturing them as if they were his own children. He never had a bad word to say about them, and consistently looked to their best interests. Where others might have viewed the Diogenes boys with suspicion, reported Anna, Alexios chose to treat them with honour and affection. That, at least, is what the emperor's daughter says.[44]

Nikephoros now emerged as the strongest contender for the throne. Unlike Alexios, Nikephoros was 'porphyrogennetos' – meaning, literally, 'born in the purple', the designation given to all children of ruling emperors who were born in the porphyry chamber of the imperial palace. He also possessed strong personal qualities: natural charm, a magnetic character and good looks. Even Anna Komnene was impressed: 'He was physically strong and boasted that he rivalled the Giants; a broad-chested, blond man, a head taller than others of his generation. People who saw him playing polo on horseback, shooting an arrow or brandishing a spear at full gallop stood open-mouthed, almost rooted to the spot, thinking they were watching a genius never seen before.'[45]

As the emperor embarked on his campaign in the Balkans in the summer of 1094, Nikephoros decided to take the initiative. Resolving to murder Alexios in person rather than delegate the task, Nikephoros approached the imperial tent one evening with a sword concealed under his arm. But he could not seize the moment, put off, it was said, by a young girl fanning mosquitoes away from the sleeping emperor and the empress who was accompanying Alexios on campaign. Nikephoros was thwarted again soon after, when he was challenged by a guard who saw him carrying a weapon, despite being ostensibly on his way to bathe.[46]

Informed of this suspicious behaviour, Alexios asked his brother Adrian, the military commander in charge of the western armies, to intervene quietly, fearing that a public confrontation would further weaken his position. Yet Adrian knew more about Diogenes' plans than the emperor realised and returned claiming to have found out nothing about the supposed conspiracy.[47] The emperor now resorted to more blunt measures and after being arrested and tortured, Nikephoros confessed all.

When he discovered exactly who had been implicated in the conspiracy, Alexios was dumbfounded.[48] They included both the former empress Maria, ex-wife of Michael VII and Nikephoros III Botaneiates, who had once been so close to Alexios, and Michael Taronites, the husband of his sister Maria Komnene.[49] Nikephoros had also won the support of leading members of the senate, senior army officers and influential aristocrats.[50] They are not identified by name in the *Alexiad*, which provides the main account for this period, curtailing the list of conspirators in a diplomatic lacuna rather than recording the embarrassing extent of the plot. Nevertheless, it is possible to establish some of the conspiracy's leading supporters. Chief amongst them was Alexios' brother Adrian.

The commander of the empire's western armies was a prize asset for Nikephoros. The men were brothers-in-law through Adrian's marriage to Nikephoros' half-sister, and the fact that Adrian appears to have known the details of a previous attempt against the emperor suggests that he may have been involved.[51] But something else reveals that he was implicated in the plot against Alexios: after it was uncovered, he vanished.

Adrian played no role during the First Crusade, neither supervising contingents of westerners across Byzantine territory on their way towards Constantinople, nor receiving them in the capital when they arrived. When disputes and misunderstandings spilled over into violence and left the emperor with little option but to use force against the knights, Adrian was invisible, with others appointed to lead the counter-attacks of the imperial forces. He was not present at Nicaea before, during or after the siege of the town in 1097. In spite of his being the highest-ranked officer in the imperial army, it was not Adrian who was sent with imperial troops across Asia Minor to accompany and guide the Crusaders to Antioch. Not one of the many primary sources for the Crusade mentions his name or alludes to his existence. In fact, he had been disgraced; this was why he lived out his last years in a monastery, his name excised from imperial propaganda, and why his children were excluded from power in the twelfth century.[52]

Other leading figures also disappeared from view, a telling clue to their involvement in the plot. One was Nikephoros Melissenos: once Alexios' rival for power, Melissenos had turned into a sour figure, sniping at the emperor and openly stirring dissent.[53] Now he too was quietly removed.[54] The same was true for Nikephoros Komnenos, about whom very little is known, apart from the fact that he had been in charge of the imperial navy at some point before 1094.[55] He no longer held this post by the time of the Crusade, when it was occupied by Eustathios Kymineianos.[56] It was not just the Byzantine elite that had turned on Alexios therefore; his own family were deserting him.

Alexios' regime was under serious threat. The emperor moved quickly to conceal the true extent of the plot. A report was circulated that the conspiracy had been revealed to the emperor by Constantine Doukas. This simply was not true.[57] In a telling admission of just how far the emperor's stock had fallen, Alexios was forced to rely on lies to claim that he still enjoyed the confidence of leading figures in Byzantium. Public knowledge of the damaging involvement of the ex-empress Maria was also suppressed.[58] The *Alexiad* indicates that many leading figures as well as the rank and file of the army were implicated in the conspiracy.[59] The emperor's supporters, meanwhile, 'were now limited to a handful of men and his life was in danger'.[60]

The emperor called a crisis meeting of his loyal relatives by blood and marriage – 'those, that is, who were really devoted to him', according to Anna Komnene. Trying to take control of the situation, Alexios took a courageous decision: he announced that he wanted to hold a general assembly the next day so that he could address all those who were on campaign with him in person. As dawn broke the following morning, a procession accompanied Alexios to the imperial tent, where he took up position in front of the gathered troops. Resplendent on his golden throne, his cheeks burning red with anticipation, he faced the crowd. The tension was all but overwhelming.[61]

Men loyal to Alexios took position next to the throne, armed with spears and swords, while members of the Varangian guard formed a semicircle behind the emperor with their heavy iron axes slung over their shoulders. Alexios was dressed not in imperial robes, but in the modest clothing of a soldier, a statement rich with symbolism and intent. If he was about to be hacked to death, it was as a soldier that he would fall. The emperor's reign and the fate of the Byzantine Empire seemed to turn on this moment.

'You know that Diogenes has never suffered ill at my hands', Alexios began. 'It was not I who deprived his father of this empire, but someone else entirely. Nor have I been the cause of evil or pain of any sort as far as he is concerned.' Although he had always looked after Nikephoros, he had been consistently ungracious and above all selfish, said the emperor. Diogenes had repaid Alexios' kindness with treachery. He had been repeatedly forgiven for undermining the emperor and even being caught plotting to take power, he continued. 'Yet none of my favours has succeeded in altering his perfidy. Indeed, by way of gratitude, he sentenced me to death.'[62]

To the emperor's relief, his speech had an immediate impact on his audience, as men started to exclaim that they did not wish anyone to take Alexios' place. This reaction was not simply the result of well-chosen words, but also stemmed from a rising sense of panic as the crowd feared that the emperor's guard was about to embark on a mass slaughter of the assembled gathering. When Alexios then talked of forgiveness and offered an amnesty to all who were present on the basis that the main conspirators had been identified and would be punished separately, pandemonium broke out: 'A great clamour arose, such as none of those present had ever heard before and have never heard since, at least to judge from those who were there; some praised the emperor and marvelled at his kindness and forbearance, while others abused [the leaders of the conspiracy], insisting they should be punished by death.'[63]

The chief conspirators were spared the death sentence in spite of the seriousness of their crime but were disgraced and exiled; Nikephoros Diogenes and his fellow ringleader, Katakalon Kekaumenos, were blinded.[64] But Alexios was genuinely shocked that such strong opposition had been fomenting against him, and according to Anna Komnene, the conspiracy had a major impact on his mental and physical health.[65] Anna reports that anxiety would plague him later in his reign, causing him on some occasions to find it difficult to breathe.[66]

The setbacks in Asia Minor of the early 1090s had been at the heart of the efforts to depose Alexios, but it was the emperor's decision to take a major military force to review the north-western frontier and tackle Serbian raids that sparked fury with the disillusioned elite in Byzantium who felt their interests in the empire's heartlands were being deliberately ignored. Central to Alexios' success after taking the throne in 1081 had been his consolidation of power and his creation of a political system with himself at the heart of every appointment, every military expedition and every policy. This in turn was based on weakening the authority and influence of the aristocracy, which was achieved indirectly through the centrality of the emperor's own role, and directly through the reduction and removal of salaries. Heavy taxation, officious revenue gathering and politically motivated confiscations also served to reduce the fortunes of the ruling classes in Byzantium.

Such treatment of the empire's nobles had brought his reign to the brink of disaster. When he returned to Constantinople after the Diogenes conspiracy was uncovered in 1094, the emperor's first action was to purge the ruling class. Those who had held important responsibilities in the first part of his reign were replaced by a new generation, promoted en bloc. The new officials were chosen not on the basis of their family wealth, connections or political importance, but on a more direct criterion: complete loyalty to Alexios. Amongst the principal beneficiaries were men from the western provinces; in a major recalibration of the empire itself, this marked a decisive swing in the distribution of power from the old dynasties of the Byzantine aristocracy of Anatolia to a new set of up-and-coming families from Thrace.

Others too sprang to prominence. Manuel Boutoumites appeared on record for the first time in the aftermath of the Diogenes revolt, rising from obscurity to hold some of the most sensitive responsibilities in Byzantium; he would play a major role during the First Crusade. Eumathios Philokales, a man so tough that one holy man felt he would not even be saved by prayer, was plucked from the backwaters of the Peloponnese and appointed governor of Cyprus once Alexios' authority on the island had finally been restored.[67] Others, like Niketas Karykes and Eustatios Kymineianos also found themselves promoted to leading positions in the wake of the attempted coup.[68] Then there was Nikephoros Bryennios, hand-picked by the emperor to replace Constantine Doukas as fiancé to Anna Komnene.[69]

The sweeping changes of 1094 saw foreigners rise even higher than they had before. Peter Aliphas, the Norman who took service a decade earlier, became increasingly relied upon by the emperor.[70] The imperial navy was placed under the command of Landulph, whose name suggests he was of Lombard origin, and the first non-Byzantine to take charge of the imperial fleet.[71] The ever-reliable Tatikios, meanwhile, was pushed to the very top of the army; he too would be given one of the most sensitive and important tasks during the First Crusade.[72]

Very few leading officials survived the reshuffle. George Palaiologos and John Doukas still had roles to play, the former zealously promoting the emperor's best interests during his negotiations with the Crusaders, and the other spearheading the recovery of western Asia Minor,[73] together with Constantine Dalassenos.[74] But the clearing out of the old guard carried risks. There were real dangers in removing in one fell swoop all those who had lent their backing to Diogenes or who had shown other signs of discontent. As a result, it seems that at least in some cases, removals were phased. Nikephoros Melissenos, for example, was still active some months after the conspiracy, serving on campaign against Cuman steppe nomads in the spring of 1095 where he was closely watched by newly promoted senior commanders before quietly slipping from view.[75]

In spite of all his efforts, Alexios' hold on power remained precarious. This became even more pronounced at the start of 1095 when news was received that Togortak, a ferocious Cuman chieftain, had crossed the Danube and was attacking imperial territory. The Cumans were accompanied by a man claiming to be Leo Diogenes, one of the sons of the emperor Romanos IV, seeking to capitalise on the discontent in Byzantium and on the headway made by Nikephoros Diogenes, his 'brother'. Leading the Cumans to Adrianople in Thrace, he subjected this important town to a lengthy siege while nomads caused havoc elsewhere in the Balkans.[76] Although eventually the Cumans returned to the Danube, Byzantium's crisis was continuing unabated.

The most urgent problem, however, remained the reconquest of Asia Minor, and particularly the recovery of Nicaea. Alexios' previous efforts to take the town by ruse, by buying it or by trying to harass its defences had come to nothing.[77] There was only one solution left: a sustained siege. Yet this required a substantial body of men, ideally made up of those with experience in attacking large fortified targets. There was one obvious source for the manpower and technology that Alexios needed.

6

The Call from the East

The decades prior to the First Crusade had witnessed the emergence of a heightened sense of Christian solidarity, of a shared Christian history and destiny that united east and west. This was largely the result of increased movement of people and ideas across Europe, but it was also deliberately cultivated by Byzantine propaganda.

There had of course always been interaction between east and west, but with the Byzantine Empire eager to attract western knights to Constantinople, this exchange had become increasingly institutionalised in the eleventh century. There was even a recruitment bureau in London where those seeking fame and fortune had their appetites whetted, with Byzantine officials assuring those who wanted to venture east that they would be well looked after in Constantinople.[1] A range of interpreters were kept on hand in the imperial capital to greet those who had come to serve the emperor.[2]

It seems that at times, it was a struggle in the west to stop adventurous young men from leaving home. A letter written in the late eleventh century by Anselm, abbot of the influential monastery of Bec in Normandy and later archbishop of Canterbury, to a young Norman knight named William indicates that it was common knowledge that tempting rewards were on offer in Byzantium. Do not be taken in by lucrative promises, advised Anselm; follow instead the true destiny and design that God had in mind for you and become a monk. Perhaps William followed this advice; but it is likely that he did not: as the same letter reveals, his brother had already gone to Constantinople and William would be following in his footsteps.[3]

This steady flow of knights was widely welcomed in Byzantium, even before Alexios took the throne. Unlike the Byzantine imperial armies which remained largely an infantry force, western warfare had evolved a strong emphasis on cavalry. Technological advances in western armour meant that the knight, mounted on a heavy charger, was formidable on the battlefield. Tactical developments reinforced this advantage: the western cavalry were at their most effective when holding a battle line, both when advancing and in defence.[4] Their discipline made them redoubtable in the face of fast-moving enemies like the Pechenegs and the Turks, whose aim in battle was to split the enemy and then pick off elements that had been separated from the main force.

But not everyone in Constantinople was happy about the arrival of these ambitious outsiders from the west. The resentment towards Hervé Frangopoulos (literally, 'son of a Frank'), who proved extremely successful in thwarting Turkish raids in Asia Minor in the 1050s and was rewarded by the emperor with generous land grants and a high-ranking title, was so strong that he ended up at the bottom of the Mediterranean with a stone around his neck.[5] Robert Crispin was another westerner whose accomplishments stoked envy among the Byzantine aristocracy: he met his end not on the battlefield fighting the Turks, but after taking poison administered by jealous rivals in Constantinople. That, at least, was the rumour that swirled around Europe at the time.[6]

As the situation in Asia Minor deteriorated towards the end of the eleventh century, Alexios began to look more keenly for help from outside the empire. Contemporaries from all over Europe started to note increasingly anxious calls for assistance emanating from Constantinople in the 1090s. Ekkehard of Aura recorded that embassies and letters 'seen even by ourselves' were sent out by Alexios to recruit help in the face of serious trouble in 'Cappadocia and throughout Romania and Syria'.[7] According to another well-informed chronicler: 'At last an emperor in Constantinople, named Alexius, was trembling at the constant incursions of the heathens and at the diminishment of his kingdom in great part, and he sent envoys to France with letters to stir up the princes so that they would come to the aid of . . . imperilled Greece.'[8]

Correspondence of this kind was also received by Robert, Count of Flanders. Every day and without interruption, came reports from the emperor, countless Christians were being killed; boys and old men, nobles and peasants, clergymen and monks were suffering the terrible sin of sodomy at the hands of the Turks; others were being forcibly circumcised, while aristocratic ladies and their daughters were being raped with impunity. The most holy empire of the Greek Christians, stated Alexios, was being oppressed from all sides by pagans.[9]

These shocking tales of Turkish violence and Christian suffering provoked outrage in the west. In the early 1090s, when Nikomedia came under attack, Alexios' appeals became more urgent. The emperor 'sent envoys everywhere with letters, heavy with lamentation and full of weeping, begging with tears for the aid of the entire Christian people' to appeal for help against the barbarians who were desecrating baptismal fonts and razing churches to the ground. As we have seen, a western force was raised as a result by Robert of Flanders, finally enabling the recovery of the town and of the land as far as the Arm of St George, extending into the Gulf of Nikomedia.[10]

News of the empire's collapse spread across Europe, brought by embassies made up of 'holy men'.[11] According to one chronicler it became widely known that Christians in the east, 'that is to say the Greeks and Armenians', were facing 'extensive and terrible persecution at the hands of the Turks throughout Cappadocia, Romania [Byzantium] and Syria'.[12] Other reports were more specific: the Turks had 'invaded Palestine, Jerusalem and the Holy Sepulchre and captured Armenia, Syria and the part of Greece that extends almost to the sea which is called the Arm of St George', wrote one contemporary.[13] It was also known in the west that the landed gentry had suffered greatly from the loss of their estates.[14]

Up-to-date and extremely accurate information about the plight of Byzantium had spread so extensively that when Urban II stood before the assembled crowd at Clermont in the winter of 1095, he hardly needed to introduce the subject. 'You must hasten to carry aid to your brethren dwelling in the East', reported one version of the speech, 'who need your help for which they have often entreated. For the Turks, a Persian people, have attacked them, as many of you already know, and have advanced as far into Roman territory as that part of the Mediterranean which is called the Arm of St George. They have seized more and more of the lands of the Christians, have already defeated them seven times in as many battles, killed or captured many people, have destroyed churches, and have devastated the kingdom of God.'[15] The widespread knowledge of the downturn in the east owed much to the letters that Alexios had sent out and the efforts that he had made to solicit support for his empire in the 1090s.

Information did not just arrive in the west through official lines of communication. Some of the news from Asia Minor was brought back by travellers and pilgrims who had journeyed to Constantinople or Jerusalem at the end of the eleventh century. Men like Robert of Flanders saw for themselves the position Byzantium was in when he travelled home from the Holy Land in 1089. William of Apulia, writing in southern Italy at the end of the eleventh century, had also heard of the attacks on churches and of the persecution of the Christians but believed that the crisis was the result of the Byzantine emperor having become too close to the Turks, hoping to use them to bolster his own position.[16] Given Alexios' alliances with Sulayman and especially Malik-Shah, there was substance to such views. Yet the assessment that the emperor was to blame for the dire situation shows that the flow of news from the east could not be exclusively controlled by the imperial court.

However, despite visitors to Constantinople and the Holy Land bringing home with them their own stories, the consistency of their reports shows how efficiently, on the whole, information was being managed from the centre. Their content, tone and message were near identical: churches in the east were being destroyed; Christians, especially the clergy, were subject to terrible persecution; Asia Minor had collapsed, with the Turks reaching as far as the Arm of St George; military assistance was urgently required in Byzantium. The narrative was so universal because so much of the information was emanating from the emperor.

One particular element common to many of the reports was the worsening situation in Jerusalem itself. Conditions seem to have become increasingly precarious in Palestine and in the Holy City towards the end of the eleventh century. Although the Turks initially displayed considerable tolerance to non-Muslim communities in this region, the capture of Jerusalem from the Fatimids of Cairo in the 1070s sharpened tensions between the Sunni Turks and Shia Fatimids. A major Fatimid expedition against the coastal region was able to make important gains in 1089, while the death of a leading Turkish commander in battle in 1091 inflamed anxieties futher still. These were taken out on the local population.[17] Reports stressed that there were forced conversions of Greek and Armenian Christians in Antioch, and sharp rises in taxes and obligations for Christians living in Jerusalem were accompanied by persecution.[18] Jews too were targeted. A major synagogue in Jerusalem was burnt down in 1077, just one example of the harassment recorded in this period.[19]

Although recent research has questioned how difficult conditions for non-Muslims became in the 1070s and 1080s, Arabic sources also recorded tensions in Jerusalem, Antioch and the Holy Land immediately before the Crusade.[20] One twelfth-century Arabic commentator from Aleppo noted that 'the people of the Syrian ports prevented Frankish and Byzantine pilgrims from crossing to Jerusalem. Those who survived spread the news about that to their country. So they prepared themselves for military invasion.'[21] Another writer speculated that the conspicuous mistreatment of the Christians in Antioch by the newly appointed governor, Yaghi-Siyan, was bound to provoke a reaction.[22]

As a result it had become more difficult for western pilgrims to visit the Holy City. Jerusalem had seen a massive increase in pilgrimage across the tenth and eleventh centuries, spurred on by increasing material wealth, intellectual curiosity and the greater openness to travel that brought about a general contraction of the early medieval world.[23] But pilgrim traffic now slowed dramatically as a result of the rise in violence in Asia Minor and the Levant. Shocking stories about the holy places were widely circulated and it was reported that pilgrims were subjected to torture and violence and forced to pay ransoms to the oppressive Turks.[24] Peter the Hermit, a charismatic preacher, told an extensive and horrified audience about the ill-treatment he had supposedly experienced on a harrowing journey to Jerusalem.[25] Not everybody was put off, however. Roger of Foix persisted in making arrangements to go to the Holy City in the spring of 1095, returning a year later to reclaim his lands in southern France.[26] Another knight from Normandy completed the pilgrimage not long after, celebrating his safe return by endowing the abbey of Jumièges.[27] But they were the minority; as one chronicler put it, such were the circumstances in the 1090s that few dared even to set off on the journey.[28]

This growing concern about Jerusalem in western Europe was exploited by Alexios. With many westerners living in Constantinople at the end of the eleventh century, including several at the very highest ranks of imperial service, the emperor well understood the significance and emotive lure of the Holy City. It was for this reason that in 1083 he called on Euthymios, patriarch of Jerusalem, to witness his peace agreement with Bohemond, 'that terrible Frank', after the first Norman attack on Byzantium had finally been curtailed by the emperor. The patriarch's presence was intended to demonstrate that the invasion of the empire was a matter of concern to one of the most important figures in Christendom.[29]

Another example comes from the interpolation to a contemporary Slavonic text. At the beginning of 1091, envoys arrived at the court of King Zvonimir of Croatia, sent by the emperor Alexios and Pope Urban II in the wake of the budding alliance between the Latin and Greek churches that had been forged in Constantinople eighteen months earlier. The envoys described to Zvonimir's court how Jerusalem and the holy places had fallen to pagans, who were destroying and desecrating these sacred sites. 'We ask and beseech you, our brother Zvonimir, most pious king of the Christians', they pleaded, 'to help us for the love of Christ and of the holy church.'[30]

Alexios' controversial letter to Robert of Flanders in the early 1090s also seems to have made deliberate use of Jerusalem to elicit a response from the west. If the kingdom of the Christians fell to the Turks, the emperor warned, the Lord's Sepulchre would be lost forever.[31] This twinning of the fate of the Byzantine capital and the Holy City found its way into the chronicles of early-twelfth-century Europe. 'Disturbing news has emerged from Jerusalem and the city of Constantinople', wrote Robert the Monk, 'the race of the Persians, a foreign people and a people rejected by God . . . has invaded the lands of the Christians, depopulated them by slaughter and plunder and arson, kidnapped some of the Christians and carried them off to their own lands.'[32] It was a message that could be traced back to the emperor in Constantinople.

Alexios' championing of Jerusalem was a shrewd move, bound to provoke a reaction among the Christian knighthood of Europe which had become increasingly attuned to the ideals of piety and service. The introduction of sanctions by the church for fighting on Sundays, feast and holy days, helped instil in western knights a Christian ethos that transcended mere fighting and military conquest.[33] Although there was a marked difference between rhetoric and practice – demands like those of Ivo of Chartres that anyone who engaged in violence between sundown on Wednesdays and sunrise on Mondays should be excommunicated were undoubtedly ambitious – the attempts of the church to intervene in secular life were striking and clearly made an impact on society.[34]

In this context, news of the distress in the east had a particular resonance. With interest in Jerusalem already at almost obsessive levels at the end of the eleventh century, reports about the threat to Christians and to the Holy Land sat neatly alongside the rising fears of an imminent apocalypse. Floods, famine, meteor showers and eclipses all seemed to point to the conclusion that the end of the world was nigh.[35] The Pope's calls to the defence of the church therefore gave the western knighthood a new *raison d'être*. The promise of spiritual reward for those prepared to go to the aid of the faithful in the east was a seductive rallying call. Alexios' call for help lit a touchpaper in Europe.

Alexios' elision of Constantinople and Jerusalem, and his presentation of himself as championing the interests of the Holy City as much as his own empire, certainly made an impact on contemporaries in southern Italy. One chronicle, attributed to Lupus Protospatharius, reported that the reason knights from western Europe set off in the mid-1090s was so that 'with the aid of the emperor Alexius in fighting the pagans, they might reach the Holy Sepulchre in Jerusalem'.[36] Gilbert of Mons likewise noted the attention drawn to the plight of the Holy City by envoys sent from Constantinople.[37] One later author had no doubts that Alexios utilised the problems in Jerusalem to his own advantage. 'He realised he would have to call on the Italians as allies, and to do so with considerable cunning', wrote Theodore Skutariotes in the thirteenth century. The emperor realised that he could take advantage of the popularity Jerusalem enjoyed in western Europe: 'That is the reason why many of them, numbering thousands and tens of thousands, having crossed the Ionian Sea, rapidly reached Constantinople.'[38]

In short, Alexios knew how to pull the emotional triggers of western Christians. He also played on the rapidly growing obsession with relics, where any object relating to Christ's life, however banal and improbable – including his milk teeth and bread he had once chewed on as a baby – had spiritual significance.[39] The emperor actively stimulated this demand in the years before the First Crusade. An otherwise unremarkable account of the life of Bishop Pibo of Toul reveals that the bishop had brought a part of the Holy Cross back to Germany with him on his return from pilgrimage in 1086. The bishop had not found this by chance: it had been given to him personally by the emperor. Little wonder that Alexios was described by Pibo as 'the most glorious emperor of the Greeks, who loved him most dearly'.[40]

Other beneficiaries of Alexios' relic diplomacy included Henry IV of Germany, who was sent religious treasures to win his support against the Normans in the early 1080s. He was given 'a gold pectoral cross set with pearls and a reliquary inlaid with gold containing fragments of various saints, identified in each case by a small label'.[41] According to two German authors, other items included vases and jugs that were very likely to have come from the collections expropriated by Alexios from the churches of Byzantium not long before.[42]

When Peter the Venerable writes that the emperor enriched a great many chapels and churches north of the Alps, he can only refer to the relics and holy objects Alexios dispatched to far-distant regions. Although Peter, abbot of the great monastery of Cluny, does not specify which gifts he himself received from Alexios, or when he received them, his emphatic approval suggests that Alexios had been sending items of genuine significance: truly he was 'great in name and deed'.[43]

It is not surprising that the letter from Alexios to Robert of Flanders drew attention to Constantinople's collection of relics, which included the most holy and significant objects relating to Christ's life, such as the pillar to which Jesus was bound before being submitted to the scourge, as well as the lash itself; the scarlet robe in which Christ was arrayed; the crown of thorns; garments from the Crucifixion, as well as most of the Holy Cross and the nails that had fastened him to it; linen cloths from the tomb; the twelve baskets with remainders of the five loaves and two fish which had fed the 5,000; and relics and bones belonging to any number of the Apostles, martyrs and prophets.[44] Guibert of Nogent, who had read the letter and provided a summary of its contents, noted the claim that the head of John the Baptist, including his hair and his beard, were in Constantinople – something that surprised him since he had been under the impression that John's head was preserved in the church treasury at Angers. 'Now we are certain', he wrote wryly, 'that two John the Baptists did not exist, nor did one man have two heads, for that would be impious.'[45] He promised he would investigate the matter further.

Alexios was particularly creative in his use of various sections of the Holy Cross as his appeals for help gathered pace in the mid-1090s. The Cross was the relic most closely associated with Constantinople after being brought to the capital during the reign of the emperor Constantine in the fourth century. The flurry of altars and churches blessed by Pope Urban II in central France in 1095–6 suggests that Alexios may have given the pontiff pieces of the Cross as powerful tools to help galvanise support for the military expedition.[46]

Influential western visitors to Constantinople were judiciously shown the relics held in the capital. A monk from Kent who visited in the early 1090s fortuitously met a friend from home serving in Alexios' bodyguard and was allowed into the emperor's private chapel. Access was normally strictly controlled. The fact that the monk was allowed in and then given relics belonging to St Andrew, which he took back to Rochester cathedral, suggests that the emperor was monitoring diplomatic channels to win the goodwill of westerners.[47]

Alexios' shrewd ability to decipher what mattered to westerners extended to the language he used when communicating with leading figures in Europe. Contact with Henry IV in the early 1080s, for example, was couched in terms of Christian solidarity and religious obligation. Henry and Alexios had to co-operate against the Norman leader, Robert Guiscard, wrote the Byzantine emperor, 'so that the wickedness of this enemy both of God and of Christians will be punished – murderer and criminal . . . You and I can be friends as Christians, brought more closely together as kinsmen; thus deriving strength from one another, we shall be formidable to our enemies and with God's help invincible.'[48]

His communication with the great Benedictine monastery of Montecassino in Italy was no less carefully judged. Thanking the abbot for a letter expressing warm regards and wishing for great favours from Almighty God, Alexios replied that 'through His compassion and His grace He has honoured and exalted my empire. However, not only because I have nothing of good in me, but because I sin above all men, I pray daily that His compassion and patience be sent to sustain my weakness. But you, filled with goodness and virtue, judge me, sinner that I am, a good man.'[49] Alexios was keen to show his humility and underscore his personal piety and devotion: it was calculated to impress a monk at the head of an order based on strict rules of obedience and self-restraint.

It seems clear, therefore, that Alexios knew how to appeal to western-ers. In this he was undoubtedly drawing on his experiences with men such as Peter Aliphas, the Norman who took imperial service in the 1080s, and Goibert, a monk from Marmoutier who became a close confidant of the emperor and his inner circle shortly before the First Crusade. The emperor deliberately used the lure of Jerusalem to draw military support to Byzantium, and to cast the empire's troubles and its political interests in terms of Christian obligation.

In his appeal, Alexios could be encouraged by the success of his earlier pleas for help. The letters he sent out after Nikomedia fell to Abu'l-Kasim in the early 1090s, for example, had yielded immediate results, with western knights joining him to drive back the Turks 'with God's assistance'.[50] But as the situation deteriorated in Byzantium, the emperor required more formidable assistance. Alexios therefore care-fully targeted his appeals to those who had responded enthusiastically in the past. Most promising was Robert of Flanders. Alexios knew Count Robert personally from meeting him at the end of 1089 and had benefited from the 500 knights that Robert had dispatched to Constantinople soon after. It was no surprise, then, that Flanders was heavily canvassed by the emperor in the 1090s even after Count Robert's death in 1093. When Pope Urban II wrote to 'all the faithful' of this region in 1095, he noted that they needed no introduction to the problems in the east: 'Your brotherhood, we believe, has long since learned from many sources that a barbaric fury has disastrously attacked and laid waste the churches of God and the regions of the Orient.'[51] The Pope was right – people in Flanders who were particu-larly well informed about the situation in the east included Count Robert's heir, Robert II of Flanders, and his wife, Clementia, who in a charter issued in 1097 noted with sadness that the Persians had occupied the church of Jerusalem and had destroyed the Christian religion in every direction.[52]

The emperor sought to capitalise on his relations with Count Robert I to recruit other nobles.[53] Deliberately widening his appeals for help, his letter to Flanders was addressed not only to the count, but 'to all the princes of the realm and all lovers of the Christian faith, laypeople and clerics alike'.[54] As Guibert of Nogent astutely noted, the emperor 'did not approach him because he thought that Robert was extremely wealthy and capable of raising a large force . . . but because he realised that if a man of such power went on such a journey, he would attract many of our people, who would support him if only for the sake of a new experience'.[55]

But the person on whom Alexios most focused his attention was Pope Urban II. Here too the emperor could draw on a personal relationship – and here too he would have been encouraged by the help he had previously received from the pontiff. Around the end of 1090, Alexios had sent a delegation to Urban to ask for help against both the Pechenegs and the Turks: 'The Lord Pope was in Campania and was addressed with due reverence by all Catholics, that is to say, by the emperor of Constantinople', wrote one contemporary historian.[56] Even though Urban was in an extremely weak position himself at the time – which was why he was found in Campania, rather than Rome – he agreed to send a force to the east.[57] Knowing that his message to the pope would be circulated more widely, Alexios assured Urban that he would personally do all he could to provide whatever assistance was necessary to those who came to support him, whether by land or sea.[58] The precariousness of the Pope's own position meant there was little more Urban could do to help Alexios at the time, but as the situation in Italy and Germany began to change in the mid-1090s, Urban would capitalise both on the developments in the west and on the threats in the east – of which Alexios regularly informed him – in a rhetorical and political tour de force.[59]

And there had been an even more important precedent. In fact, in his appeal to Urban, Alexios was deliberately emulating the previous attempt by one of his predecessors to come to almost exactly the same arrangement with an earlier pope. In the summer of 1073, Emperor Michael VII had sent a small delegation to Rome with a written proposal to forge an alliance with Pope Gregory VII, following Byzantium's collapse in southern Italy and the increased threat posed by Turks in Asia Minor. The Pope, also worried by the rise in Norman power, replied enthusiastically, thanking the emperor for his letter which was 'filled with the pleasantness of your love and with the no

small devotion that you show to the Roman church'.[60] Recognising
that this offered the opportunity to mend the rift with the Orthodox
Church while also strengthening his own position in Italy, the Pope
leapt into action.

Gregory was much taken with the idea of recruiting a military
force to defend Constantinople: he could cast himself as a defender
of all Christians, and in so doing galvanise support that could also be
targeted against Robert Guiscard and the Normans. Over the course
of the following months, the Pope sent letters to leaders all over
Europe, setting out his message. In February 1074, for example, he
wrote to Count William of Burgundy, asking him to send men to
Constantinople 'to bring aid to Christians who are grievously afflicted
by the most frequent ravagings of the Saracens and who are avidly
imploring us to extend them our helping hand' – though first they
should help defend papal territories from Norman attacks.[61]

The following month, the Pope sent a letter sent to 'all who are
willing to defend the Christian faith', which contained a stark warning.
'A race of pagans has strongly prevailed against the Christian empire',
Gregory wrote, 'and with pitiable cruelty has already almost up to
the walls of the city of Constantinople laid waste and with tyrannical
violence has seized everything; it has slaughtered like cattle many
thousands of Christians.' It was not enough to grieve for those who
were suffering, the Pope declared; 'we beseech you and by the authority
of blessed Peter the prince of apostles we urge you to bring reinforcements to your brothers'.[62]

Gregory continued to canvas support for a military expedition to
reinforce Byzantium against the Turks throughout the year. Further
letters sent in 1074 pointed out that 'I have sought to stir up Christians
everywhere and to incite them to this purpose: that they should
seek . . . to lay down their life for their brothers' by defending
Christians who were being 'slaughtered daily like cattle'.[63] The Devil
himself was behind this suffering, he said; those wishing 'to defend
the Christian faith and to serve the heavenly King' should show themselves now to be the sons of God and prepare to cross to Constantinople.[64]

As it happened, nothing came of Gregory's plans – though not for
lack of interest; the Pope's powerful messages struck a nerve with
some of the leading figures in the west. William, Duke of Aquitaine
and Count of Poitou, for example, indicated that he was prepared to

march in the service of St Peter against the enemies of Christ.[65] Others, like the Countess of Tuscany, Beatrice, and Godfrey of Bouillon were also prepared to rally to the cause.[66] The problem was that at the same time as negotiating with Gregory, the Byzantines had also sounded out Robert Guiscard, reaching terms with the Norman leader in the middle of 1074.[67] This not only left the Pope exposed in Italy, it also compromised the prospect of a union between the Eastern and Western churches, which had been at the basis of his appeals to the knighthood of Europe. Gregory was forced to make an embarrassing climbdown. There was no need for William of Poitou to concern himself any more with the proposed eastern expedition, he wrote, 'for rumour has it that, in parts beyond the sea, by God's mercy the Christians have far repelled the savagery of the pagans, and we are still awaiting the guidance of divine providence about what more we ought to do'.[68] In fact, there had been no major military successes in Asia Minor in 1074, and nothing to support the Pope's suggestion that the situation had dramatically improved. Gregory was simply trying to back down as gently and diplomatically as possible.

By 1095, when Alexios dispatched envoys to the Pope activating the same channel as his predecessor, two crucial things had changed. First, the situation in Constantinople itself had degenerated beyond recognition. Whereas the appeals to Gregory VII were exploratory and partly an attempt by Byzantium to retain a foothold in the politics of Italy, Alexios' call to Pope Urban II was one of pure desperation. The delegation that found Urban in March 1095 in the town of Piacenza, where he was presiding over a church council, delivered a stark message: 'An embassy of the emperor of Constantinople came to the synod and implored his lordship the Pope and all the faithful of Christ to bring assistance against the heathen for the defence of this holy church, which had now been nearly annihilated in that region by the infidels who had conquered as far as the walls of Constantinople.'[69] Unlike two decades earlier, this time there was real substance to the picture painted of the Turkish advances in Asia Minor and of the impotent response of the Byzantine Empire. In fact, things were even more perilous than Alexios' ambassadors let on; they seem to have made no mention of the emperor's vulnerability as the result of the Diogenes conspiracy of 1094. Now Byzantium was truly teetering on the brink of disaster.

The second difference was that while Pope Gregory VII had much to gain from promoting himself as the champion of all Christians, the stakes for Urban II in the mid-1090s were much higher. Facing powerful enemies and a rival pope, Urban had far greater incentives than his predecessor to promote the unity of the churches and to position himself as the man who could bring an end to discord. And the timing was perfect. Just as Byzantium disintegrated and Alexios appealed for help, the political situation in Italy dramatically changed, following the high-profile defections of Henry IV's wife and son to the Pope. This energised Urban and, in the process, threw an extraordinary lifeline to the emperor.

The Pope immediately recognised the opening. He had already been intending to visit France in order to take advantage of the sharp improvement in his position. He reacted quickly and decisively to the appeals from the emperor's envoys at Piacenza: 'Our Lord Pope called on many to perform this service, to promise by oaths to betake themselves [to Jerusalem] by God's will and to bring the emperor the most faithful assistance against the heathen to the limits of their ability.'[70] Rather than sending out letters that talked about the principles of an expedition without providing detail, structure or purpose, Urban decided to devise and put in place personally an expedition to transform the eastern Mediterranean. He was single-minded in his purpose. As one chronicler reported, 'when he heard that the interior part of Romania had been occupied by the Turks and the Christians subdued by a ferociously destructive invasion, Urban, greatly moved by compassionate piety and by the prompting of God's love, crossed the mountains and descended into Gaul and caused a council to be assembled in Auvergne at Clermont'.[71]

This was to be the moment at which the Pope's grand scheme would be announced. Much now depended on the pontiff's stamina and his ability to engage with leaders and communities across France to mobilise a force to come to the help of Byzantium.

7

The Response of the West

The Crusade drew on passion, religious fervour and a desire for adventure. Many of its participants were certainly intoxicated by Urban's compelling insistence on Christian duty and the promise of salvation, and the speed and enthusiasm with which the Crusade began can easily be read as the surging of a great, spontaneous uprising. But the Crusade was also elaborately orchestrated: the rhetoric used to rouse the west was carefully weighted to attract the right kind of Crusader – whether in terms of military or social clout – and arrangements were made, as far as possible, to regulate and provision the stream of fighters who made their way towards the Holy Land. To understand the spectacular unleashing of Christian forces, therefore, the risky calculations behind it need to be appreciated. Urban's words were carefully chosen to speak to his western audience but his appeal was shaped by an agenda that was to a large extent set by Alexios in Constantinople. Urban was walking a difficult path: rousing mass enthusiasm to raise an efficient, controllable military force that could meet very particular Byzantine military objectives. The mobilisation of the west is a story of extraordinary political and logistical intricacy – it was a balancing act of such complexity that it was, ultimately, impossible to control.

Urban arrived in southern France in July 1095, and spent the next months laying the groundwork for the expedition. As he moved around the country meeting influential figures, the Pope articulated his aims forcefully and repeatedly: to drive back the Turks and, in doing so, to liberate both the Christian population in the east and the city of Jerusalem. But there was very limited discussion of the expedition's structure, its objectives, or its organisation – let alone what the 'liberation' of the east actually meant in practical terms.[1]

In some ways, the fact that Urban's appeals before, at and after the Council of Clermont were so vague goes some way to explaining the strength of the response. Joining the armed pilgrimage to Jerusalem was presented as an issue of faith rather than a blueprint for a military campaign. The knights who flocked to take part were driven by an enthusiasm to do God's work or, in many cases, to repent for their sins. But there was also a strong political reason why the logistics were put to one side: these were to be dealt with by the emperor in Constantinople. Alexios had called for military muscle to help against the Turks, and he, surely, would be responsible for planning the expedition and taking care of the practicalities.

Energised by his dramatic change in fortunes in Italy, Urban set out to identify and recruit leading figures whose participation would encourage others to take part. Over the course of the summer of 1095, he travelled to meet them individually. He went to see Adhemar of Monteil, the influential and well-connected bishop of Le Puy, who jumped at the chance of making the journey to Jerusalem. Urban also met Eudes of Burgundy and the powerful Hugh, archbishop of Lyons, during a punishing itinerary through southern France, where he visited Valence, Le Puy, Saint-Gilles and Nîmes in quick succession before moving north.[2]

Urban then made contact with Raymond, Count of Toulouse, who controlled a vast sweep of land stretching across southern France and Provence. He came from a family well disposed to the papacy, but also with a strong connection to Jerusalem. Raymond's elder brother, William, had made a pilgrimage to Jerusalem and died there in the early 1090s, either unable to get home or having decided to live his last days in the Holy City.[3] No less devout, Raymond funded a cohort of priests to perform a Mass and say prayers for him every day, and he ensured that a candle was kept lit by the statue of the Virgin Mary in the church of Le Puy as long as he was alive.[4] Raymond was one of the first figures Gregory VII had turned to for help after the Council of Brixen in 1080, when the election of an antipope threatened to split the church.[5]

Urban knew that Raymond's involvement was vital. His participation would show that the campaign had the backing of a major sponsor; which could then be used to spur other leading magnates into taking part in the expedition. It was a tactic that had much in common with Alexios' rationale for communicating with Robert of Flanders, hoping that Robert's example would inspire others to provide help. The Count of Toulouse's positive response to Urban was, therefore, a significant boost. And it was reassuring for another reason: the more alliances Urban could build that bolstered his image as the protector of the faithful, the stronger it made his position as leader of the church as a whole.

In the middle of October 1095, the Pope reached the mighty abbey of Cluny, where he had once been prior, pausing for a week and consecrating the high altar of the huge new abbey church that was under construction.[6] By this time, word had already spread and excitement about the expedition to Jerusalem was building.[7] It was here that the Pope announced that he had an important message to deliver to the faithful at the Council of Clermont. He encouraged participants such as the bishop of Cambrai and the archbishop of Rheims to bring with them 'all the most eminent men, the more powerful princes' from their dioceses.[8]

The Council of Clermont took place in November 1095, and concluded with Urban's speech which painted a terrifying picture of the situation in Asia Minor. Terrifying though the report given by the Pope was, it was also painfully accurate, as his listeners would have been aware from other news they had received from the east. The Greek Empire had been dismembered, the Pope correctly reported; the Turks had conquered a swathe of territory so vast that it took fully two months to cross. Urban begged his listeners to act: 'So let all feuds between you cease, quarrels fall silent, battles end and the conflicts of all disagreements fall to rest. Set out on the road to the Holy Sepulchre and deliver that land from a wicked race.'[9] Those who were willing to do so were enjoined to weave an image of the Cross, in silk, gold or more simple material, into their clothes, to show that they were God's soldiers, doing His will.[10]

As soon as the Pope had finished, the bishop of Le Puy, 'a man of the highest nobility, went up to [Urban] with a smiling face and on bended knee, begged and beseeched his permission and blessing to make the journey'.[11] Le Puy's importance was underlined when the Pope wrote to the faithful of Flanders not long after that he had 'appointed in [his] place as leader of the journey and labour, our dearest son, Adhemar, bishop of Le Puy'.[12] The day after Urban's speech, envoys arrived from the Count of Toulouse, declaring Raymond's willingness to take part in the expedition.[13] This high-profile support had all been carefully engineered in advance, to get the initiative off to a flying start.

Urban's speech at Clermont created shock waves across Europe, as news of an impending armed pilgrimage that would seek to journey to Jerusalem travelled rapidly. Interest was fanned by energetic clergy like Robert of Arbrissel who was told to preach in the Loire valley, where there was no shortage of attentive well-heeled aristocrats;[14] Jarento, abbot of Sainte-Bénigne of Dijon, was likewise sent to recruit suitable figures, heading first to Normandy and then to England.[15] Areas like the Limousin in France turned into hives of activity, with the Crusade message being spread with great enthusiasm and efficiency.[16]

The clergy everywhere disseminated the Pope's message, under strict instructions to report only his exact words and not to embroider them. But the main brunt of galvanising support fell on Urban himself.[17] In the months that followed his initial call to arms, the Pope remained in France, moving from community to community. He stayed on the move in 1095 and 1096, persuading, cajoling and exhorting the faithful. He gave addresses at Limoges around Christmas, and at Angers and at Le Mans in the spring of 1096, before heading south to Bordeaux, Toulouse and Montpellier, and addressing another church council in Nîmes in July. As the Pope moved from town to town, from one church foundation to another, local chroniclers were left in little doubt about the purpose of his visit. As one writer put it, Urban reached Le Mans in order to 'preach the journey to Jerusalem and came to these parts for the sake of this preaching'.[18] A grant to one church in Marcigny was dated to the year 'when Pope Urban came to Aquitaine and moved the army of Christians to repress the ferocity of the pagans in the east'.[19] The whole world was stirring, straining to march to Jerusalem.[20]

Letters were sent out to the places that Urban could not visit in person. He did not travel to Flanders, for example, no doubt because this was a region that had already been successfully cultivated by Alexios in the 1090s. Nevertheless, he sent a letter to the princes, clergy and people of Flanders explaining his efforts to secure help for Christians who were being persecuted. As they already knew well, the barbarians in the east were causing immense destruction. 'Grieving at the scale of this disaster, and moved by pious concern', Urban wrote, 'we have been visiting the regions of Gaul and devoting ourselves to urging the princes of this land as well as their subjects to free the churches of the East. We have solemnly enjoined on them at the Council of the Auvergne the importance of this undertaking, in preparation for the remission of their sins.'[21]

The idea that participation in the expedition would be rewarded by the forgiveness of sins was designed to widen the appeal of the Crusade even further. Whereas previous calls to arms by Gregory VII, and for that matter by Alexios I himself, had talked of the obligations that Christians had towards each other and of the solidarity they ought to show in times of need, what the Pope was offering was altogether more powerful. Those who took part were not just doing their duty, they were earning salvation.

Urban consistently reiterated the spiritual rewards on offer. Writing to his supporters in Bologna, the Pope noted that he was delighted to learn that many wanted to join the expedition to Jerusalem. 'You should also know', he went on, 'that if any of you make the journey, not for the desire of worldly goods, but for the salvation of your souls and the liberation of the church, you will be relieved of the penance for all your sins, for which you shall be judged to have made a full and perfect confession.'[22] Joining the expedition to Jerusalem would also benefit those who had specific sins to atone for. According to one chronicle, Urban suggested to 'certain French princes who could not perform a fitting penance for innumerable offences committed against their own people' that taking the oath and making the journey was a suitable act of contrition, which would bring profound spiritual rewards.[23]

'If anyone dies in expedition for the love of God and of his brothers', Urban wrote in a letter to the counts of Besalú, Empurias, Roussillon and Cerdana, 'let him not doubt that he will assuredly find indulgence of his sins and will participate in eternal life, through the merciful compassion of our God.'[24] Yet it took time for this concept of martyrdom and salvation to be fully accepted by the Crusaders. It seems to be only later in the campaign that the idea became established, possibly as a result of the profound suffering that the Crusader army experienced, especially at Antioch in 1098, which served to intensify a belief in spiritual rewards for those who paid the ultimate price for defending their faith.[25] Important though these incentives were, however, they are rarely mentioned in the sources that outline why particular individuals decided to take part in the expedition. Guy and Geoffrey of Signes, two brothers from Provence, simply stated that they were making arrangements to journey east in order 'to wipe out the wickedness of the pagans and the excessive madness because of which countless Christians have already been oppressed, taken prisoner or killed with barbaric fury'.[26]

Urban's rhetorical cocktail of Christian suffering, spiritual reward and the destination of Jerusalem was intoxicating. And he had another powerful tool. As the Pope moved around France, he consecrated the altars of many churches, such as the Church of the Trinity in Vendôme and the abbey churches at Marmoutier and Moissac, a large number of which were given parts of the Holy Cross.[27] There was no more emotive relic connected to the liberation of Jerusalem; not for nothing did those participating in the expedition take the way of the Cross (hence 'Crusade') and indeed marked their clothes with this symbol.[28]

More pertinently, it was well known that pieces of the Cross were kept in Constantinople and had been used as an important instrument of imperial diplomatic policy from the fourth century, when Constantine the Great gave precious fragments to the Sessorian Palace in Rome. The Holy Cross was the great prize of Byzantium's international diplomacy.[29] So while it is not impossible that Urban was distributing fragments already held in the papal treasuries, it is more plausible that the relics, so closely associated with Constantinople, were provided by Alexios.

This high-profile channelling of significant relics contributed to the excitement sweeping through France, with the Pope, meanwhile, tirelessly 'exhorting our people to go to Jerusalem in order to hunt the pagans who had occupied this city and all the lands of the Christians as far as Constantinople'.[30] Other resources were perhaps also being used to galvanise support, as in the case of a document recording the destruction of the Church of the Holy Sepulchre at the start of the eleventh century whose intention was not just to inflame anger about Jerusalem, but specifically to link the Muslims to Christian suffering.[31] That the expedition was to provide military support to Byzantium was not always clearly articulated; the lure and name of Jerusalem was much more enthralling to the Pope's audience than mission detail.

Knights scrambled to make the necessary preparations. Achard of Montmerle was one who promptly did so, coming to an arrangement with the monastery of Cluny by placing a charge over his lands in return for 'the sum of 2,000 [gold coins] and four mules'. Reckoning that he needed additional means to make the long journey to Jerusalem, Achard declared that if he died or decided not to return, 'rightful and hereditary possession in perpetuity' would pass to Cluny and 'its eminent men'. The funds were being raised, noted the agreement, 'because I wish to be fully armed and join the magnificent expedition of the Christian people seeking to fight their way to Jerusalem for God'.[32]

Many others took similar steps in 1095 and 1096, taking out loans in return for mortgages against their land and property. The sources leave no doubt that Jerusalem was the main attraction, with almost every individual who signed a charter in this period expressing their desire to travel to the place where Christ walked on earth.[33] The prospect of finding repentance in the process was clearly also powerful, as in the case of two brothers from central Burgundy who 'were going with the others on the expedition to Jerusalem in order to remit their sins'.[34]

Some sought to repent before they set out. Hugh Brochard, a knight from Tournus in Burgundy, sought absolution for the many wrongs he had committed, not least seizing land from the church of St Philibert, an act he now recognised as unjustified and sinful.[35] His contrition was spurred by the realisation that it was wrong for a sinner who had transgressed against the church to march in its defence, with a cross stitched into his tunic or marked on his forehead.[36]

Yet in some cases, efforts were made to actively prevent knights from joining the march east. Pons, Peter and Bernard, three particularly troublesome knights from Mézenc who had relentlessly terrorised the parishioners of the monastery of Le Chaffre in the Auvergne, were initially thwarted in their desire to take part in the expeditions. Public renunciations of their past violence did not convince the local monks, who referred the brothers to the bishops of Le Mende and Le Puy for a ruling as to whether they should be allowed to participate in the expedition. As the bishops listened to the accusations against the three men, they found themselves 'astonished by their cruelty; but they absolved them on account of the fact that they were going on the expedition to Jerusalem and their apparent contrition'.[37] Few would have been sad to see them go. Nevertheless, the fact that the church was trying to control who took part in the expedition and who did not, was an indication of its growing assertiveness and ambition.

Another reason for the consolidation of the power of the church was that it provided the necessary funds for those travelling east. Pilgrimage, armed or otherwise, was expensive. Travelling long distances involved heavy costs in food, transport, equipment and arms, which were magnified when a whole retinue of men had to be supported. As we have seen in the case of Achard of Montmerle, the church was the obvious place to turn to, for monasteries, bishoprics and parishes were often well endowed and able to provide the necessary liquidity. As a substantial landowner the church was a natural lender and an obvious buyer. Thus, when Godfrey of Bouillon, who was to become the first king of Jerusalem after its capture in 1099, set about raising funds for the journey, it was to the church that he turned. He sold his claim to the county of Verdun and the castles of Mosay, Stenay and Montfaucon-en-Argonne to Richier, bishop of Verdun. Other lands and possessions, meanwhile, were sold to the convent of Nivelles. An additional 1,500 marks came from the bishop of Liège, given to Godfrey as a loan. Converting illiquid land holdings into cash, Godfrey was able to raise a very substantial sum of money.[38] Robert, Duke of Normandy and son of William the Conqueror, borrowed the enormous sum of 10,000 marks from his younger brother, the English king William Rufus. This meant that Robert did not have to sell ducal lands or borrow from a third party to raise the necessary cash for the Crusade.[39]

Despite the expense, dangers and complicated arrangements involved, the popular response to the Pope's call was all but overwhelming. Men from all over France prepared to head for the east, with major contingents forming under the command of Robert of Normandy, his brother-in-law, Stephen of Blois, and Raymond of Toulouse. Substantial forces were also gathered by Godfrey of Bouillon and his brother Baldwin, as well as by Robert II, Count of Flanders, who had succeeded his father in 1093.

Other important figures committed to join the expedition. One was Hugh of Vermandois, brother of Philip I, king of France, apparently persuaded by a dramatic lunar eclipse at the start of 1096 during which the moon turned blood red, which he interpreted as a sign that he should join the campaign.[40] Philip himself was not welcome. His excommunication in 1095 on the grounds of adultery had been confirmed at Clermont, after he had abandoned his wife for being too fat and taken up with the comely Bertrada of Montfort – a woman about whom, apparently, no man had a good word to say, apart from when it came to her looks.[41] As excitement about the expedition grew, Philip's subjects clamoured for him to resolve his position. The king convened a special meeting of his nobles to discuss his options, and by the summer of 1096 he was offering to give up Bertrada to regain Urban's favour. It was a clear sign that the Pope's bid to become the leading authority in western Europe was proving successful.[42] Although Philip did not take part in the Crusade, his brother Hugh willingly participated and provided a representative of the house of France to the expedition – another boost to the Pope's plans.

Bohemond, the son of Robert Guiscard, was another stellar recruit. According to the anonymous author of the *Gesta Francorum*, Bohemond first heard about the expedition when he was besieging Amalfi in 1096 and noticed men passing on their way towards the ports of southern Italy shouting '*Deus vult! Deus vult!*' The author reports that 'Bohemond was inspired by the Holy Ghost, and ordered the most valuable cloak which he had to be cut up forthwith and made into crosses; most of the knights who were with him at the siege [of Amalfi] began to join him at once.'[43] Bohemond and his men formed an impressive force: 'What human eye could bear the glitter of their breastplates, helmets, shields or lances in brilliant sunshine?'[44]

Yet Bohemond's actions were not quite as spontaneous (or plausible) as this report would suggest: instructions to a certain William Flammengus, Bohemond's right-hand man in Bari, to make a series of land sales in early 1096, suggest that like many others, Bohemond had already liberated funds to take part in the expedition.[45] The speed with which he abandoned the siege of Amalfi, raised his men and set out east also indicates that arrangements had been made in advance and were not the result of a sudden decision on the Norman's part.

Bohemond was an aggressive character with a formidable physique and strong ideas about everything ranging from battle tactics to his

hairstyle: he did not grow his hair to his shoulders like other westerners, but insisted on wearing it just above the ear.[46] He was an
outstanding commander, but as his attack on Byzantium in 1082–3
revealed, he was also prone to egocentricity and laziness – apparently
sitting eating grapes with friends on a riverbank while his army
attacked imperial forces at Larissa.[47] From the Pope's point of view,
however, it was important that at least one leading Norman from
southern Italy took part in the expedition. It was difficult to recruit
others: Roger of Sicily was shrewd enough to realise that a campaign
against Muslims in the east could cause difficulties in his territory,
which was home to a sizeable Muslim community.[48] Roger Borsa,
who succeeded to the dukedom of Apulia in 1085, appears to have
had no interest in taking part. His older half-brother, Bohemond,
who had been outmanoeuvred on the death of their father Robert
Guiscard, jumped at the chance of adventure in the east.

In many ways, Urban's plan was brilliantly executed: key individuals
willing to join the expedition were targeted so that their participation
would act as a catalyst for others. As a result, the Pope inspired a mass
movement of knights. Enormous effort went into disseminating the
call to arms and making the necessary arrangements to translate the
massive response into action. But some aspects of Urban's plans were
still vague. The question of the leadership of the expedition was
confused, with several figures under the impression that they were
commander-in-chief of the massed Crusader army. To start with at
least, Urban regarded the bishop of Le Puy as his representative to
lead the expedition.[49] Others, though, thought of themselves in this
role. Raymond of Toulouse, for one, referred to himself as the leader
of the Christian knights setting out to capture Jerusalem.[50] Hugh of
Vermandois also had a high estimation of his own status and carried
with him a papal banner, suggesting that he was Urban's representative on the expedition.[51] Some considered Stephen of Blois to be the
'head and leader of the council of the whole army';[52] he himself
certainly thought this was the case, writing back to his wife Adela,
daughter of William the Conqueror, that his fellow princes had chosen
him to be commander of the entire force.[53]

In reality, the leadership evolved during the course of the difficult
journey east. And while there is something to be said for the idea that
Urban hedged his bets, avoiding to disabuse the competing egos of

some of Europe's most powerful men of their belief that they were his representatives, there was another reason why the issue of overall leadership was not addressed decisively by the Pope: the westerners would come under the command of Alexios I Komnenos when they arrived in Byzantium. Urban, for reasons of tact and strategy, may have been chary about making it explicit, but the truth was that the Byzantine emperor was overseeing operations.

Similarly, while the overarching aims of the Crusade were clear enough – defending the Christian Church in the east, driving back the pagan Turks, and finally reaching Jerusalem – the precise military objectives were left obscure. There was no talk of conquering or occupying the Holy City, let alone holding it in the future. There was no clear plan, for example, of what they would do when they reached Jerusalem. Nor were there any details about which towns, regions and provinces were to be targeted in their fight against the Turks. Again, the explanation for this lay in Constantinople. It was Alexios who was to set the strategic goals: Nicaea, Tarsos, Antioch and other important towns that had fallen to the Turks were the Byzantine priorities – and, at least to start with, these targets would be accepted by the Crusaders when they arrived in Constantinople. In the meantime, the military plans were of secondary importance, and limited significance, to the politically minded Pope.

The emperor's vision was also fundamental in shaping the recruitment process for the Crusade. Alexios needed military support, rather than goodwill. He needed to attract individuals with fighting experience to take on the Turks, and, accordingly, this was relentlessly stressed by the Pope. As one contemporary cleric emphasised: 'I am in a position to know, as one who heard with his own ears the words of the Lord Pope Urban, when he at once urged laymen to make the pilgrimage to Jerusalem and at the same time, prohibited monks from doing so.'[54] He forbade 'those unsuited to battle' to take part in the expedition, says another chronicler, 'because such pilgrims are more of a hindrance than a help, a burden rather than of any practical use'.[55]

Amid 'the popular and great arousal of the Christian people', as one document refers to it, the Pope had to make strenuous efforts to exclude all whose participation would be obstructive.[56] He was explicit about this when he wrote to the monks of the monastery of Vallombrosa in Tuscany in the autumn of 1096: 'We have heard that some of you want to set out with the knights who are making for Jerusalem with the good intention of liberating Christianity. This is the right kind of sacrifice, but it is planned by the wrong kind of person. For we were stimulating the minds of the knights to go on this expedition, since they might be able to restrain the savagery of the Saracens and restore the Christians to their former freedom.'[57] He said much the same thing when he wrote to the inhabitants of Bologna shortly before this.[58]

Senior clergy reinforced the message, although not without difficulty. The bishop of Toulouse had to work hard to dissuade Emerias of Alteias, a woman of considerable wealth, from joining the expedition. She was so determined that she had already 'raised the cross on her right shoulder', and taken a vow to reach Jerusalem. Very reluctantly she agreed not to make the journey – but only after the bishop made great efforts to convince her that the establishment of a hospice for the poor would be both a more welcome and appropriate gesture.[59]

Giving Alexios an effective fighting force was important. So too was forming an idea of its size. Logistical arrangements had to be to put in place in Constantinople to receive large numbers of men in a short period of time, and central planning was required to work out how to welcome, provision and guide the westerners as they arrived in Byzantium. This was presumably one reason why the Pope insisted from the very outset that anyone wishing to join the expedition was required to take an oath. At Piacenza, after listening to the Byzantine envoys, 'Our Lord Pope called upon many to perform this service, to promise by oaths to journey there by God's will and to bring the emperor the most faithful assistance against the heathen to the limits of their power.'[60] This was restated emphatically at Clermont, where Urban emphasised the requirement to declare formally the intention to participate.[61] Conversely, those who thought about changing their minds were threatened with terrible consequences, warned that they were turning their back on God: 'anyone who seeks to turn back having taken the vow shall place the cross on his back between his shoulders . . . and is not worthy of me [cf. Matthew 10:38]'.[62]

There is no evidence to suggest that a formal record was being kept to note how many individuals were preparing to take the cross, and it is unclear if it would have been possible to keep such a tally anyway. Nevertheless, it quickly became obvious that very substantial numbers indeed were committing themselves to taking part. In this respect, then, it was significant that it was Urban himself who was so central to the recruitment of knights in France. On several occasions, the Pope could be found personally taking the oaths of men who were to join the expedition.[63] And each time he met leading magnates or preached the Crusade – in places like Limoges, Angers and Le Mans, and in Tours, Nîmes and elsewhere – he could form an idea that huge numbers were clamouring to take part, even if these were difficult to quantify.

The ambitious and optimistic Pope and the beleaguered emperor in Constantinople both hoped for a substantial response to the calls to arms; but neither can have anticipated its extraordinary scale. The Pope's efforts to follow developments in Spain in the late 1080s and early 1090s had led him to offer incentives not dissimilar to those given to the would-be Crusaders; but this had not provoked a surge in knights heading into the Iberian peninsula.[64] The factors that inflamed Europe and opened the floodgates for the First Crusade, by contrast, were Jerusalem on the one hand, and the recognition that reports of the sudden collapse in the east – principally in Asia Minor – were accurate and a real cause for concern, on the other.

News of the numbers preparing to take part in the expedition, even if only rough estimates, evidently found their way back to Alexios, for the emperor set about preparing accordingly. That the Crusaders were successfully provisioned as they marched across Byzantine territory in several large contingents points tellingly to the fact that measures had been carefully put in place by the emperor. Necessary arrangements had been made at the entry points to the empire and along the principal routes leading towards Constantinople.

In part, this was itself possible because a clear time frame for the expedition had been established at the beginning. The Pope had set a fixed departure date of 15 August – the primary holy day of the summer, the Feast of the Assumption. While this was partly intended to impose a structure on the forthcoming journey, it was also designed to allow a co-ordinated response in Byzantium. And with a departure date in the summer, a good nine months after Urban's speech at Clermont, there was time to stockpile the foodstuffs that would be required to support the westerners on their arrival.

Nowhere was this more important than at Kibotos. This site was identified in advance by Alexios as the holding point for the western knights as they converged into a single force and prepared to assault Nicaea. A complex infrastructure was put in place in anticipation of the many thousands who were due to arrive: food stores, supplies and merchants were all made ready for a massive influx of men and horses.[65] A Latin monastery may well also have been founded immediately before their arrival to cater for spiritual needs – and also to underline Alexios' own openness to the Roman rite.[66]

There were other aspects of the expedition that needed careful thought. Preparations were made in Constantinople as to how best to police the vast number of westerners as they arrived in the east: 'The emperor summoned certain leaders of the Roman forces and sent them to the area around Dyrrakhion and Avlona with instructions to receive the voyagers kindly and to supply them abundantly with provisions gathered from all along their route; they were to watch them carefully and shadow their movements, so that if they saw them making raids or running off to plunder the neighbouring districts, they could check them by light skirmishes. These officers were accompanied by interpreters who understood the Latin language; their duty was to quell any incipient trouble that might arise.'[67]

Steps were taken to ensure easy passage across imperial territory. When Godfrey of Bouillon reached the frontier, he was issued with a special licence to acquire provisions from markets which appear to have been closed to the local population.[68] This meant that food was readily available along the way, a step designed to prevent a large armed force being dangerously antagonised by provisioning shortages and also to allow food prices to be fixed centrally. Price inflation would therefore be controlled, preventing local traders from exploiting supply imbalances.

Alexios also ordered that generous amounts of money be given to the westerners as they arrived in Byzantium. This was done in part to win the goodwill of men coming into contact with the empire for the first time. But, as one sharp commentator pointed out, it was also smart economics: all the funds paid out by the emperor found their way back into the imperial coffers, as the money was spent on goods sold by the emperor's agents.[69]

This pattern of closed markets and imperial largesse was reproduced across the Byzantine western provinces, along the two principal routes to Constantinople. When he reached the town of Naissos in the Balkans in the autumn of 1096, Godfrey was delighted to receive corn, barley, wine and oil, as well as many game animals as a personal gift from the emperor. A licence was again given to his men, allowing them to buy provisions and also to sell whatever they wished. Godfrey's force spent several days there 'in great plenty and enjoyment'.[70] The efficiency of the provisioning put in place by Alexios is revealed by the fact that Bohemond was so well supplied when he crossed difficult terrain through Epirus, Macedonia and Thrace that his stocks of wine and corn actually increased.[71]

A key issue that required thought was the route taken by the Crusaders. The principal leaders made their way to Constantinople with their various contingents under separate steam. Some, like Godfrey of Bouillon, passed through Germany and central Europe, making for Byzantium via the land route which took them through the Balkans and then on to the capital. Others, however, travelled the length of Italy, embarking on ships in Apulia before crossing over to Epirus and then following the Via Egnatia, the road linking Old and New Rome. Robert of Flanders, Hugh of Vermandois, Stephen of Blois and Robert of Normandy all took this route, as did Bohemond and the small contingent of Normans from southern Italy. Although there is little direct evidence to link the magnates' choice of route to Alexios, the intervals at which these contingents travelled seem too convenient and perfect to be coincidental. The gaps between their arrival minimised the strain on Byzantium's resources and infra-structure, and as such it is reasonable to assume they were deliberately co-ordinated.

One case in particular points to the emperor's involvement in planning the first stages of the expedition and suggests that he was playing an active role even before the Crusaders reached the empire's frontiers. As we have seen, Raymond of Toulouse was one of the first magnates that the Pope had turned to. His wealth, status and the support he had previously given to the papacy made him a powerful natural ally. The count had a difficult journey to Byzantium, travelling through Slavonia – 'a forsaken land, both inaccessible and mountainous where for three weeks we saw neither wild beasts nor birds', according to one man who accompanied him. This was hostile territory, where Raymond's men were regularly attacked and killed. Thick fog, dense forests and rugged mountains made it difficult to protect the force as it made its way south. The count responded with reprisals against the local population, blinding some, cutting the feet off others and mutilating the faces of more to serve as a stern deterrent.[72] So difficult was the journey that Raymond's chaplain only made sense of the travails by concluding that God was using the strength and suffering of the Crusaders to inspire 'brutish pagan men' to turn from their sinfulness and thus be spared from doom.[73]

In fact, the Count of Toulouse took this route for good reason: to bring to heel Constantine Bodin, the Serbian ruler whose attacks on Byzantium on the eve of the Crusade had done much to increase pressure on the emperor and whose contacts with the antipope had aggravated Urban. That so important a figure as Raymond passed through the remote coastal area of Zeta indicates how precisely the First Crusade had been planned in advance. The fact that Raymond went down the Dalmatian coast was a clear sign the emperor and the Pope had worked together. While the arrival of manpower was designed in the first instance to take Nicaea and to root out the Turks in western Asia Minor, Alexios was alert to other regions where he could also benefit. The Count of Toulouse, a man close to the Pope, was therefore chosen as a trusted figure who could take an unusual and difficult route so as to impress on Bodin the errors of his ways. Little wonder, then, that the latter became aggressive when he did so, setting his men to attack Raymond as an agent of the emperor and a threat to Serbian independence.[74] Nevertheless, there was to be no further disruption on the empire's north-western frontier for decades afterwards. It was an early indication that Alexios had much to gain from the expedition to Jerusalem.

In the second half of 1096, vast numbers of men were on the move, heading for Constantinople, the first stop on the way east. Estimates now suggest that as many as 80,000 may have taken part in the First Crusade.[75] Never before had there been such a large, organised movement of people over such a long distance and over such a short period. This presented problems to the participants, who were drawn from many parts of western Europe. 'Therefore since such a multitude came from all western countries,' wrote Fulcher of Chartres, 'little by little and day by day the army grew while on the march from a numberless host into a group of armies. You could see a countless number from many lands and of many languages.'[76] The same author later goes on to list the rich tapestry of people on the expedition: 'Who ever heard of such a mixture of languages in one army? There were Franks, Flemings, Frisians, Gauls, Allobroges, Lotharingians, Alemanni, Bavarians, Normans, English, Scots, Aquitanians, Italians, Dacians, Apulians, Iberians, Bretons, Greeks and Armenians. If any Breton or Teuton wished to question me, I could neither reply nor understand.'[77]

The expedition promised to be a demonstration of Christian solidarity, a unique occasion where church schism, regional identity, secular and ecclesiastical squabbles counted for nothing. But this was above all a crowning moment in the collaboration between Rome and Constantinople and a great cause for optimism. The union of the churches seemed to be within grasp when the Council of Bari in 1098 and that of Rome the following year attempted to resolve those issues that had strained relations between east and west for decades. If things turned out well, with the help of the westerners Byzantium would finally make headway against the Turks in Asia Minor. And those taking part in the expedition were eager to reach the Holy City. There was great anticipation as the First Crusade got under way.

But while there was an enormous amount to be gained from the Crusade, Alexios and Urban were also taking a huge risk: in unleashing the Crusade they were creating a movement that they could not necessarily control. Anna Komnene's account of the start of the Crusade provides a jolting reminder of this dilemma. The emperor, she writes, was disturbed by reports that countless armies from the west were heading for Byzantium:[78] 'full of enthusiasm and ardour they thronged every highway, and with these warriors came a host of civilians, outnumbering the sand of the seashore or the stars of heaven, carrying palms and bearing crosses on their shoulders. There were women and children too, who had left their own countries. Like tributaries joining a river from all directions, they streamed towards us in full force'.[79] This was not the disciplined and effective fighting force the emperor had expected. Had something gone wrong?

8

To the Imperial City

Alexios and Urban had played a dangerous game. The violent passions stoked up by the crusading propaganda were not easy to control; for all the logistical planning and nuanced political calculations, the raw enthusiasm for the Crusade was overwhelming. As tales of Muslim oppression and news of the expedition spread, it became impossible to control the message: Urban II was not the only charismatic figure who was preaching the Crusade in 1095–6. Peter the Hermit, a preacher from Amiens in northern France, capitalised on the excitement and the furore about the suffering of Christians in the east to unleash a People's Crusade – the dangerously chaotic force described by Anna Komnene. As the western forces moved towards the great imperial city of Constantinople, Alexios needed to assert his authority. His reaction to the People's Crusade, and the network of allegiances and relationships that were forged with the vanguard of the expedition proper, were to shape the future of crusading.

Contemporaries described Peter as 'a famous hermit, held in great esteem by the lay people, and in fact venerated above priests and abbots for his religious observance because he ate neither bread nor meat – though this did not stop him enjoying wine and all other kinds of food whilst seeking a reputation for abstinence in the midst of pleasures'.[1] Walking barefoot, Peter was a persuasive teacher travelling around the Rhineland, a region neglected by the Pope, who did not try to look for support in lands that were subject to Henry IV.[2] Peter spread horrific tales about conditions in the east, sometimes telling his rapt audiences that he had suffered personally at the hands of the Turks during a recent pilgrimage to Jerusalem. Although it seems unlikely that he had ever been to the Holy Land, he claimed that he had met the Pope on his way home, and also that he brought with him appeals from the patriarch of Jerusalem. Like Urban, he found that his calls to action fell on fertile ground.[3]

Unlike the Pope, however, his appeals had no structure. Where Urban planned matters carefully – seeking out powerful magnates who would bring substantial contingents with them, limiting participation to those with military experience and insisting on oaths to formalise inclusion in the expedition – Peter did nothing of the sort. There was no set date for departure; nor was there a selection or screening process of who should or should not make the journey. The result was a free-for-all. As one commentator put it, 'in response to [Peter's] constant urging and calling, firstly bishops, abbots, clerics, monks; then the most noble laymen, princes of different domains, and all the common people, as many sinful as pious men, adulterers, murderers, thieves, perjurers and robbers; that is to say every sort of people of Christian faith, indeed even the female sex, led by repentance, all flocked joyfully to this expedition'.[4]

At the start of 1096, groups of knights began to set off from the Rhineland, accompanied by clerics, the elderly, women and children; it was this first tide that became known as the People's Crusade. Recent scholarship has sought to rebalance this impression of utter chaos, emphasising the competence of some of those who took part, and pointing out that the motley collection gathered by Peter the Hermit did include some minor aristocrats and independent knights.[5] Nevertheless, not only did this scheme to journey to the Holy Land lack the approval of the church, it was markedly different from the detailed plans put into place by Urban and Alexios.

With no significant leadership, chaos ensued. Those inspired by Peter set off at their own pace, oblivious to or disregarding the official departure date set by the Pope. Whipped into a frenzy of excitement about the journey, with vivid stories of atrocities in the east ringing in their ears, and apocalyptic prophecies haunting and spurring them on at the same time, it was not long before they found their first victims: 'Whether by a judgement of the Lord, or by some error of mind, they rose in a spirit of cruelty against the Jewish people scattered throughout these cities and slaughtered them without mercy . . . asserting it to be the beginning of their expedition and their duty against the enemies of the Christian faith.'[6]

Horrific massacres accompanied the progress of the People's

Crusade as it passed through Germany; the Jewish populations in Cologne and Mainz became the victims of breathtaking violence. So shocking was the terror unleashed that in some cases, people took their own lives: 'The Jews, seeing how the Christian enemy were rising up against them and their little children and were sparing none of any age, even turned upon themselves and their companions, on children, women, mothers and sisters and they all killed each other. Mothers with children at the breast – how horrible to relate – would cut their children with knives, would stab others, preferring that they should die thus at their hands, rather than be killed by the weapons of the uncircumcised.' In other locations, such as in Regensburg, the Jews were at least spared death; but they were driven into the river Danube where they were forcibly baptised.[7]

The anti-Semitism spread. When Godfrey of Bouillon set out in the summer of 1096, he vowed to eradicate the Jews; he was only stopped from doing so after being warned by Henry IV that no hostile steps should be taken against anyone in his realm without his explicit authority. Such was the revulsion towards Godfrey that one Jewish contemporary prayed that his bones be ground to dust.[8] This surge in anti-Semitism as a result of the Crusade was not confined to the Rhineland; there were also cases of violence in France threatening to turn into wholescale massacres of Jewish communities.[9]

Many contemporaries were appalled. One writer noted that those involved in the persecution of the Jews were threatened with excommunication and with serious punishment by the leading magnates – though neither seems to have had any effect.[10] These German thugs, wrote Guibert of Nogent, represented the very worst of society; they were the faeces of the peoples of Europe.[11]

This view was echoed in Constantinople. Alexios had asked for, and was expecting, experienced fighting men to arrive in Byzantium towards the end of 1096, in accordance with the timetable set out by the Pope. He was startled not just by the fact that the first waves to reach the empire arrived months too early; it was also apparent that many of those who had come were completely incapable of taking on the Turks, let alone mounting a siege of the towns of Asia Minor. It is hardly surprising that, in the words of Anna Komnene, 'he dreaded their arrival'.[12]

As the many groups making up the People's Crusade approached

Constantinople, anxiety grew. Appalling acts of violence were committed as the first of the armed pilgrims neared the Byzantine frontier in the spring of 1096. The commander of the Hungarian army, a distinguished figure with dazzling snow-white hair, was beheaded after being sent by the king to escort the pilgrims safely across his territory.[13] The cocktail of religious fervour, excitement and ill discipline proved even more volatile when the first elements reached Belgrade, the empire's westernmost entry point on the Danube. Caught off guard, the Byzantine authorities struggled to deal with the situation. The sale of provisions was banned outright by imperial officials so supplies could be hastily rationalised. This provoked an immediate reaction from the westerners who went on the rampage, sacking the surroundings of Belgrade in anger. Calm was finally restored, but only after the Byzantine garrison secured the town by using force against the rioters. Once enough provisions had been organised, a market was opened up which appeased the jumpy would-be Crusaders.[14]

A more effective response had been organised by the time Peter the Hermit himself arrived at the Byzantine frontier at the end of May 1096. Leo Nikerites, a man promoted in the wake of the Diogenes conspiracy, treated the contingent with diligence and care: according to one account, Peter the Hermit and those travelling with him received everything they asked for – all their requests were to be granted, as long as they behaved well.[15] Nevertheless, frequent trouble accompanied the various strands of the People's Crusade as it snaked towards Constantinople. Towns in Byzantium's western provinces were regularly assaulted and the local populations attacked. In an attempt to contain the damage, markets were established exclusively for the Crusaders along the main road and escorts appointed to accompany the westerners, with orders to deal with troublemakers and stragglers by force if necessary. The arrival of Peter the Hermit in Constantinople was reportedly preceded by a plague of locusts that ravaged all the vines in Byzantium.[16] This was widely seen to be an omen of the impending swarm of westerners about to reach the capital.

Anna Komnene's account of the emperor's misgivings as the first waves of Crusaders approached Constantinople is usually interpreted as an attempt to absolve him of responsibility for an expedition which would have damaging consequences for relations between Byzantium and the west. However, it is difficult to see how Alexios can have been anything other than deeply dismayed by the appearance of Peter and his followers in Constantinople. The emperor's concerns, already heightened by reports brought back by his scouts, only grew when the vanguard of the People's Crusade arrived in the capital. Even Latin sources note that their behaviour was appalling: 'Those Christians behaved abominably, sacking and burning the palaces of the city and stealing the lead from the roofs of the churches and selling it back to the Greeks so that the emperor was angry and ordered them to cross the Hellespont. After they had crossed they did not cease from their misdeeds, and they burned and laid waste both houses and churches.'[17]

In the past, the emperor had dealt with sizeable groups of westerners, such as the 500 knights from Flanders, with little difficulty. But his first experiences with the Crusaders were harrowing. Having made them cross over to Asia Minor to minimise the threat to Constantinople itself, the emperor expected them to wait for other contingents before moving against the Turks. Yet such was their enthusiasm and misplaced confidence that they set out for Nicaea at once, sparing no one they met on the way. According to the *Alexiad*, they acted 'with horrible cruelty to the whole population; babies were hacked to pieces, impaled on wooden spits and roasted over a fire; old people were subjected to every kind of torture'.[18] Western sources are equally damning. It was not just the Turks who were brutalised, says the anonymous author of the *Gesta Francorum*; vicious crimes were also committed against Christians. There was no escaping the cruel irony that having set out to defend the Christian east from pagan oppression, the participants of the People's Crusade were ransacking and destroying churches in northern Asia Minor.[19]

Spurred on by the conviction that they enjoyed divine protection, one group advanced on Xerigordos, a small but well-fortified castle east of Nicaea. They took it without difficulty, slaughtering its Turkish inhabitants. Yet the ambition and single-mindedness of the Crusaders to take on anyone in their way, coupled with a lack of any clear plan, soon turned out to have catastrophic consequences. It was not long before the euphoria in Xerigordos was replaced by panic as a large Turkish force closed in to recover the fort.

The situation soon became desperate: 'Our men were so terribly afflicted by thirst that they bled their horses and asses and drank their blood; others let their belts and clothes into a sewer and squeezed out the liquid into their mouths; others urinated into one another's cupped hands and drank; others dug up the damp earth and lay down on their backs, piling the earth upon their chests because they were so dry with thirst.'²⁰ When the westerners surrendered, they were met with little mercy. The Turks marched through the camp murdering clerics, monks and infants. Young girls and nuns were carried off to Nicaea, as were clothes, pack animals, horses and tents. Young men were forcibly converted to Islam, relinquishing the Christian faith that had inspired them to head east in the first place.²¹ Those who refused suffered horrible deaths: they were tied to posts and used as target practice by the Turks.²²

The Turks now advanced on Kibotos, storming the camp set up by Alexios. People were slaughtered in their beds and the tents set on fire; those who did not flee into the mountains or jump into the sea were burnt alive. Conversion to Islam or death were again the options offered to those taken prisoner. Rainald, one of the leaders of the People's Crusade's foray into Asia Minor, chose the former, concluding that it was better to submit than to be murdered.²³ Others met their fates decisively. A priest found celebrating Mass was decapitated in front of the altar; 'what a fortunate martyrdom for that fortunate priest', exclaimed one chronicler, 'who was given the body of Our Lord Jesus Christ as a guide up to Heaven!'²⁴ So many were reportedly killed in the first contact with the Turks at Xerigordos, Kibotos and elsewhere that the mass of bones of the fallen were heaped up in huge piles. They were then crushed by the Turks to make mortar for filling cracks in the walls of fortifications: thus the bones of the first wave of knights seeking to fight their way to Jerusalem were used to obstruct the men following after them.²⁵

The catastrophic failure of the People's Crusade by the end of October 1096 was a significant setback for Alexios. It threw into question his whole policy of seeking help from outside Byzantium; it even looked as if it might prove counterproductive, adding to the difficulties the empire was facing. According to Anna Komnene, Peter the Hermit, who was discussing logistics with Alexios in Constantinople, took a tough view of events. The men who had been killed at Xerigordos and elsewhere deserved their fate, he said; they were brigands and robbers who had been disobedient and followed their whims. This was why they had not been given the chance to worship at the tomb of the Lord in Jerusalem.[26] Other contemporaries took a different view. Poor discipline, bad planning and overexcitement can exact the most terrible price, mused Guibert of Nogent; perhaps if this expedition had been led by a king, things might have turned out differently. The disasters had taken place 'because death comes to meet the undisciplined, and the man who cannot control himself does not survive long'.[27]

The *Gesta Francorum*, a text that circulated widely across Europe immediately after the First Crusade and formed the basis of many other chronicles of the expedition to Jerusalem, reported that 'when the emperor heard that the Turks had inflicted such a defeat on our men, he rejoiced greatly'. Alexios then 'gave orders for the survivors to be brought back over the Hellespont. When they had crossed over, he had them completely disarmed.'[28] Although this account was partly shaped by the intensely negative image of the emperor that emerged after the Crusade, it was also clear that Alexios had not been pleased with the first arrivals. He now had to prepare for the arrival of the First Crusade proper.

Managing the expectations of ambitious and powerful magnates arriving in Byzantium presented a set of complex political demands. Hugh of Vermandois, the brother of the king of France, sent ahead ambassadors to the governor of Dyrrakhion with a message for Alexios in the summer of 1096, setting out how he expected to be received: 'Know, Emperor, that I am the King of Kings, the greatest of all beneath the heavens. It is fitting that I should be met on my arrival and received with the pomp and ceremony appropriate to my noble birth.'[29] This was followed, not long after, by a message no less grand: 'Be it known, *doux* [the Byzantine governor], that our Lord Hugh is almost here. He brings with him from Rome the golden standard of St Peter. Understand, moreover, that he is supreme commander of the Frankish army. See to it then that he is accorded a reception worthy of rank, and yourself prepare to meet him.'[30]

Hugh's eventual arrival in Constantinople was disappointing – though not because of the failure of the Byzantines to welcome him in sufficient style. In fact, he was shipwrecked after sailing into a heavy storm as he crossed from southern Italy, and was washed up on the shores of Epirus, separated from his possessions, as well as from much of his force, who were lost at sea. Retrieved and quickly brought to Dyrrakhion, Hugh was promptly spirited to Constantinople by Manuel Boutoumites, who was rapidly emerging as a key lieutenant, so that Alexios could placate him.[31] As the *Alexiad* wearily puts it, 'the episode concerning Hugh was just the start of it'.[32]

Hugh of Vermandois was one of the first members of the Crusade proper to reach Constantinople, arriving at the end of October 1096.[33] Godfrey of Bouillon and his brother Baldwin reached the capital around the same time.[34] Robert of Flanders was not far behind, setting sail from Apulia in December.[35] Stephen of Blois and Robert of Normandy, who were travelling together, must have set out later than the others, for they were only ready to cross from Italy in early April 1097.[36] By then Bohemond had reached Constantinople, while Raymond of Toulouse was around a hundred kilometres away.[37]

The journeys across Byzantine territory by the aristocrats recruited by the Pope and the emperor were generally pacific, though marked by occasional misunderstandings. Some were the result of overeagerness. When the contingent led by Richard of the Principate crossed over to Epirus, his lookouts mistook the Byzantine fleet for pirates, prompting the order for battle to be given. A volley of crossbow bolts was fired from the Crusaders' ships, one of which struck the Byzantine commander, Marianos Maurokatakalon, on the helmet, while another went straight through his shield and body armour, lodging in his arm. A priest accompanying the western knights then became involved in the attack, seizing a bow and shooting arrows as fast as he could, before grabbing a sling and launching a large stone, which knocked Marianos out cold. As the officer was getting back on his feet after regaining consciousness, he was struck on the cheek by a barley cake which the priest was now throwing after running out of other missiles.[38]

There were other mishaps on the way. The bishop of Le Puy was attacked as he paused to rest during the long march across Macedonia. Robbed of his mule and his gold, and beaten severely about the head, Adhemar escaped a worse fate as his attackers argued about money, alerting the bishop's travelling companions who arrived in the nick of time to save his life.[39]

Where things went wrong, Alexios was often held responsible, even though attacks like these were the work of opportunistic locals rather than imperial agents. As we shall see, subsequent events led to a highly coloured and negative picture of the emperor, with the effect that the Latin accounts are quick to focus on anything that could vilify Alexios. In this context, the silence of various sources about conditions during the march to Constantinople is remarkable. Not one of them comments on shortages of supply, which indicates that successful arrangements had been put in place to meet the needs of the expedition. This was no fluke: high-ranking officials were sent out by the emperor to meet the various contingents, with instructions to guide them safely to the capital. 'Whenever we passed by any of their cities', wrote one eyewitness, 'this man [sent by Alexios] used to tell the people of the land to bring us provisions.'[40] Considerable planning and careful execution had gone into establishing, maintaining and provisioning markets along the arteries leading to the capital.

Escorts were assigned to the Crusaders to accompany them along the most efficient routes and to keep them moving and out of trouble. They were generally very successful in doing so, although one force was particularly rowdy. Bohemond and his men regularly left the main road to Constantinople to rustle livestock and other goods, and on one occasion set fire to a fort filled with what they deemed to be 'heretics'.[41] They also moved at a markedly slower speed than the other groups, suggesting that they took a dim view of the admonitions of the emperor's agents.[42] Their behaviour sharply improved on the arrival of an imperial guide, who prevented a proposed attack on a castle 'filled with good things', and convinced Bohemond to order that property plundered by his men be restored to the local population.[43]

As the Crusaders neared Constantinople, Alexios took further steps to make a positive impression on the most important leaders, sending personal messages that stressed the generous reception they were to receive in the capital and underlining his friendship with them. He affirmed ties of solidarity, extending the hand of brotherhood and even presenting himself as a father figure.[44] Yet contact between the western leaders was monitored carefully by the emperor to prevent contingents linking up before they reached Constantinople.[45] While he was concerned mass arrival would put a strain on provisioning arrangements, there was also the more pertinent danger of an attack on the capital. Alexios took steps, therefore, to ensure that communications were regularly intercepted.[46] He also sought to prevent trouble by inviting the various leaders to advance and meet him ahead of their forces. Hugh of Vermandois and Bohemond were brought swiftly to the capital, well ahead of their armies.[47] The same would have been true of others whose journeys are recorded in less detail, such as Stephen of Blois and Robert of Flanders.

Raymond of Toulouse was reluctant to meet the emperor on his own: the count understood that travelling ahead without his men would weaken his position in any negotiations.[48] His suspicions were well placed, for Alexios did indeed have an ulterior motive for meeting these prominent men one by one. He needed them to confirm their loyalty.

Alexios was a generous host, receiving the western leaders lavishly. In the summer of 1097, Stephen of Blois wrote to his wife Adela, daughter of William the Conqueror, reporting excitedly on his treatment in the imperial capital. The emperor showered gifts on all the leaders, he wrote, and took personal care to ensure supplies reached the western knights. 'It seems to me that in our times, no other prince has had a character distinguished by such complete integrity. Your father, my love, gave many great presents, but he was almost nothing in comparison with this man. Writing these few words about him, so that you will have some idea of what sort of person he is, has given me pleasure.'[49]

Stephen's letter reveals the level of attention paid to him by Alexios, who entertained him in the palace for ten days, giving him many gifts and asking Stephen to send his son to Constantinople so he could be honoured in a 'great and distinguished manner'. The effect was that Stephen looked at the emperor not only as an excellent man and a generous benefactor, but 'as a father'.[50]

Stephen's letter pre-dates the later collapse of relations between the emperor and the Crusaders, but even many of those writing later comment upon Alexios' largesse. According to Fulcher of Chartres who took part in the Crusade, the emperor gave out large quantities of coins, as well as highly prized silk garments.[51] Another eyewitness, scornful of Alexios' generosity and mocking his credulity, stated that the westerners were encouraged to ask for anything they liked, including gold, silver, gems and cloaks.[52] Even if it is not true that the emperor agreed to every request, it says much about his desire to win personal support from the expedition's leaders that his generosity was perceived to be boundless.

The sources also agree that the most prominent Crusaders met with Alexios in person. This approach was a radical departure for a Byzantine sovereign. Foreign dignitaries visiting Constantinople were usually kept at a distance from the emperor. Princess Olga, a leading member of the ruling house of Kiev, was invited only to take dessert with the emperor when she came to the capital in the mid-tenth century,[53] while an ambassador sent by the German emperor around the same time was kept waiting for days for an audience with the Byzantine sovereign.[54]

In the tenth century, admittance to the ruler's presence was an elaborate affair. As one eyewitness recalled: 'in front of the emperor's throne there stood a certain tree of gilt bronze, whose branches, similarly gilt bronze, were filled with birds of different sizes which emitted the songs of the different birds corresponding to their species . . . Lions of immense size (though it was unclear if they were of wood or brass, they certainly were coated in gold) seemed to guard [the emperor], and, striking the ground with their tails, they emitted a roar with mouths open and tongues flickering. Leaning on the shoulders of two eunuchs, I was led into this space, before the emperor's presence.' At this point, a mechanical device raised the throne towards the ceiling, taking the sovereign out of speaking distance from the foreign visitor.[55]

In his dealings with the Crusaders, Alexios opted for a style that would have astonished and appalled his predecessors. The emperor adopted an informal approach, designed to put the western leaders at ease. Indeed, some thought that Alexios was going too far; at one reception a particularly confident knight sat down on the imperial throne, left empty as the emperor mingled with his guests. After being reprimanded by a fellow knight he called the emperor names under his breath. 'What a peasant!' he reportedly said. When these comments were translated Alexios responded with grace, merely warning the knights of the stark dangers that lay ahead at the hands of the Turks.[56]

The best example of Alexios' dealings with the western leaders and of the lengths he went in order to win their support is his relationship with Bohemond. Bohemond was a highly charismatic figure, capable of inspiring strong feelings of loyalty among the Crusaders. Extremely attractive, he was clean-shaven – unusual in a world where warriors tended to be bearded.[57] According to Anna Komnene, he was a man 'unlike any other, whether Greek or barbarian, who was seen in those days on Roman soil. The sight of him inspired admiration, the mention of his name terror.' He certainly had charm, though this was 'somewhat dimmed by the alarm his person as a whole inspired' – according to the *Alexiad*, 'even his laugh sounded like a threat to others'. He was to go on to become Byzantium's and Alexios' nemesis.

The two men had fought each other tooth and nail in the early 1080s, and knew each other's strengths and weaknesses. As he rode into Constantinople, Bohemond cannot have known what to expect, and when he was ushered straight into the emperor's presence, the two men were soon talking about the past. 'I was indeed an enemy and foe then', Bohemond purportedly said, 'but now I come of my own free will as Your Majesty's friend.' Alexios did not push matters too far at the first meeting. 'You are tired now from your journey', he replied. 'Go away and rest. Tomorrow we can discuss matters at length.'[58]

Special arrangements had been made for the emperor's former enemy. 'Bohemond went off to the Kosmidion where an apartment had been made ready for him and a rich table was laid full of delicacies and food of all kinds. The cooks also brought in red meat and poultry, all uncooked. "The food, as you see, has been prepared by us in our customary way," they said, "but if that does not suit you, here is raw meat which can be cooked in whatever way you like."'[59] Alexios was not wrong to think that Bohemond would be suspicious: the Norman did not touch the food – although he insisted that his companions help themselves. Asked the next day why he had not eaten anything, his reply was unequivocal: 'I was afraid he might arrange to kill me by putting a dose of poison in the food.'[60]

Alexios was generous with gifts and arranged Bohemond's quarters so that he would find that 'clothes, gold and silver coins and objects of lower value [had] filled the place so completely that it was impossible for anyone to walk in it. He ordered the man deputed to show Bohemond the riches to open the doors suddenly. Bohemond was amazed at the sight . . . "All this", said the man, "is yours today – a present from the emperor."'[61]

The emperor's extravagant generosity extended to the lower ranks of the Crusader army. Stephen of Blois reported that Alexios' 'presents are making the lives of the knights easier, and his banquets are reinvigorating the poor'.[62] Every week, four envoys were sent to Godfrey of Bouillon, and presumably to other magnates too, weighed down with gold coins intended for the rank and file.[63]

Yet despite the care Alexios took in welcoming the Crusaders, things did not always go according to plan. The situation became uncomfortably tense following Godfrey of Bouillon's arrival near Constantinople shortly before Christmas 1096. Despite repeated requests, the Duke of Lorraine refused to cross over the Bosphorus, plunging the emperor into 'an ocean of worry', as he was deeply concerned about the presence of a substantial body of experienced knights in close proximity to his capital.[64] When Alexios' efforts to encourage and cajole Godfrey to cross over had little effect, he resorted to more direct methods. A heavily armed squad was dispatched under the command of his son-in-law, Nikephoros Bryennios, with orders to use force to move Godfrey and his men away from the city to their designated quarters on the eastern side of the Bosphorus.[65]

It was not long before the Byzantine troops and Godfrey's men engaged. 'Roaring like a lion', the duke himself killed seven members of the imperial force, while Bryennios' unerring aim as an archer marked him out as an equal to Apollo himself – at least in his wife's eyes. The significance of the encounter, however, lay less in the prowess of those who fought and more in the fact that Alexios had to resort to force to make the Crusaders obey his instructions.[66]

To start with, these efforts to dislodge Godfrey had little effect. His men ransacked the grandest properties on the outskirts of Constantinople, causing extensive damage to the city and its citizens.[67] When the military response did not work, Alexios decided to withdraw supplies and he 'removed barley and fish from sale, then bread to eat, so that the duke would be forced in this way to agree to see the emperor'.[68] This was a bold move, which risked escalating the situation. But it worked. Godfrey backed down and agreed to meet with the emperor in person after Alexios offered his eldest son, still not ten years old, as a hostage in yet another attempt to win over the duke.[69]

Godfrey and his followers arrived for their meeting splendidly attired, in ermine and marten robes lavishly fringed with purple and gold – clothing that was symbolic of their power and status.[70] Terms were finally agreed between the two sides, with Godfrey consenting that his men be transported across the Bosphorus to join up with the other knights at the designated holding camp near Kibotos. In return, he was rewarded with heaps of gold and silver, purple robes, mules and horses.[71] Alexios got what he wanted. While largesse, bribery and brute force had failed, the withholding of supplies served to underline that Alexios held the upper hand in his relations with the Crusaders. As one westerner noted candidly, 'it was essential that all establish friendship with the emperor, since without his aid and counsel we could not easily make the journey, nor could those who were to follow us by the same route'.[72] Stopping provisions was an effective way of driving the message home.[73]

The use of force was a last resort; in most cases, the handling of affairs by the imperial administration in 1096–7 was remarkably successful and the arrival of the western knights was managed calmly and smoothly. This was partly due to the attention and generosity that the emperor showed to the expedition's leaders. But other, more practical steps helped minimise the threat to the capital. For example, access into the city itself was strictly controlled and westerners were only allowed through the forbidding walls in small groups. According to one source, only five or six people per hour were let into the city.[74]

Alexios' priority was to get knights to cross the Bosphorus to Kibotos, where arrangements had been put in place to receive and supply large numbers of men. This was a matter of urgency, as the emperor's efforts against Godfrey of Bouillon showed. As we have seen, when the Crusaders approached Constantinople, a sense of foreboding had spread through the city. Some speculated that the expedition's real target was not Jerusalem but the Byzantine capital itself. The Crusaders, wrote Anna Komnene, were 'of one mind and in order to fulfil their dream of taking Constantinople, they adopted a common policy, which I have often referred to before: to all appearances they were on pilgrimage to Jerusalem; in reality, they planned to dethrone the emperor and seize the capital'.[75] This view was not just confined to Byzantines, who tended to be suspicious of the hidden agendas of foreigners. Other observers, like Michael the Syrian, writing on the periphery of the empire, also believed that the Crusaders had not only skirmished with the Byzantines but had launched an outright assault on Constantinople.[76]

The fears of the capital's inhabitants were heightened by the attacks of Godfrey of Bouillon. Anxiety was greatest among those closest to the emperor. Alexios' few remaining allies in Constantinople believed that hostile factions within the city would take advantage of the arrival of the Crusaders to rise up against the emperor. Some wanted to settle scores going back to seizure of power by the Komnenoi, and there were also more recent grievances in the wake of the Diogenes conspiracy. According to the *Alexiad*, at one point the emperor's followers rushed to the palace to mount a desperate last stand against the disaffected inhabitants of the city, whom they expected to rise at any moment. The emperor was urged to put on his armour and prepare for a fight to the death, but Alexios remained impassively on his throne in an admirable display of theatrical sangfroid.[77]

Rumours of plots to overthrow Alexios continued to circulate both inside Constantinople and beyond its walls. Mysterious strangers approached at least one of the western leaders when he reached the capital, warning that the emperor was devious and wily, and urging him not to trust Alexios' promises and flattery.[78] Add to this suspicions about the Crusaders and their intentions, and moving the Crusaders on to Kibotos was essential for the security of Alexios' regime.[79] The presence of large numbers of armed men so close to Constantinople was dangerous in itself; but there was the additional concern that those in the city might look for help from the newly arrived cohorts, or simply take advantage of the edgy situation, to make a move against the emperor.

Alexios had considered this in advance. Although he had brought all the principal western leaders to Constantinople ahead of their men to entertain them and win their goodwill, he also sought to bind them to him formally. One way he did so was by adopting them as his sons. This was an old tradition whereby Byzantine emperors established a spiritual and paternal relationship with foreign magnates. The Crusaders did not seem to have thought this strange; it was the emperor's custom to adopt high-ranking foreigners, wrote one chronicler, and the leaders were happy to acquiesce.[80] Another simply noted without comment that Alexios adopted all the western leaders as his sons.[81] But sensitive to the fact that adoption was a uniquely Byzantine custom, Alexios reinforced the bond with the main leaders in terms that they would certainly understand: Bohemond, Godfrey, Raymond of Toulouse, Hugh of Vermandois, Robert of Normandy, Robert of Flanders and Stephen of Blois were all asked to swear an oath of fealty to the emperor.

Fealty was a key element in the feudal structure and well established in western Europe by the time of the First Crusade. It created a relationship with specific legal implications between a vassal on the one hand, and a master on the other.[82] Paying homage, the vassal committed to serve his lord and not harm him by swearing an oath over the Bible or another suitable religious object, such as a sacred relic, in front of a cleric. It was this loyalty that Alexios Komnenos sought to extract from the visiting Crusaders. As Anna Komnene later put it, the emperor was asking each leader to become his 'anthropos lizios' – his liegeman.[83]

When this request was put to the more important aristocrats on the expedition, some objected strongly to any suggestion that they – leaders in their own lands – should pay obeisance to any man at all, let alone to Alexios, to whom they owed no obligation or duty. The objections were vociferous: 'This our leaders flatly refused to do, and they said "Truly, this is unworthy of us, and it seems unjust that we should swear to him any oath at all."'[84] Complaints were not unanimous, though: Hugh of Vermandois, Stephen of Blois and others were willing to swear loyalty to the emperor. This was perhaps because they had been so well looked after in Constantinople, but there would also have been an element of pragmatism, given that they needed the help and support of the emperor to make it to Jerusalem. As one eyewitness reported, 'To these, then, the emperor himself offered as many coins and silken garments as he pleased; also some horses and some money, which they needed to complete such a great journey.'[85] This was acknowledged by the author of the Gesta Francorum who, consistently hostile to Alexios and Byzantium, struggled to understand why oaths were given by the expedition's leaders. 'Why did such brave and determined knights do a thing like this? It must have been because they were driven by desperate need.'[86]

Bohemond, meanwhile, had his eye on a bigger prize, suggesting to Alexios that he should be appointed to lead the imperial army in the east – a position that presumably still lay vacant following the disgrace of Adrian Komnenos, the military's previous commander-in-chief.[87] With everything to gain from the expedition and little to lose, Bohemond from the outset sought to position himself as the emperor's right-hand man; he was quick to see that there were serious opportunities if he played his hand well.[88]

When agreement was finally reached with Godfrey of Bouillon after the fighting over the winter of 1096-7, part of the settlement was that the duke would take the oath to Alexios as others had already done. When he did so, 'he received generous amounts of money, and he was invited to share Alexios' hearth and table and was entertained at a magnificent banquet . . . The emperor then gave orders that plentiful supplies should be made available for his men.'[89]

The oaths had two separate and distinct purposes for Alexios. The first was the long-term aim of ensuring that all future gains made by the western knights across Asia Minor would revert to him in due course. But there was a short-term goal too: to safeguard his own position in Constantinople as the Crusaders gathered in Byzantium. The latter lay behind the compromise reached with Raymond of Toulouse, who rebuffed Alexios' demand for homage point-blank: 'Raymond responded that he had not taken the Cross to pay allegiance to another lord, or to be in the service of any other than the One for whom he had abandoned his native land and his paternal goods.'[90]

For a time, the count's refusal to take the pledge threatened to destabilise the expedition, both by delaying its progress and also because other leaders had already given commitments to the emperor. Robert of Flanders, Godfrey of Bouillon and Bohemond, all of whom had sworn the oath, urged Raymond to do the same, to little avail. Eventually, a compromise was reached: 'At this juncture, following consultation with his men, the count swore that neither he nor those in his service would harm the emperor's life or deprive him of his possessions.' He continued to insist, however, that he would not pay homage 'because of the peril to his rights'.[91] The fact that Alexios was prepared to accept this compromise reveals his primary concern: with the Crusader camp outside the city walls, the emperor required reassurance that his life and position was not under threat.

With Bohemond too Alexios was prepared to be flexible and accommodating. The Norman agreed to become the emperor's vassal in return for a specific agreement: 'the emperor said that if he willingly took the oath to him, he would give him, in return, land in extent from Antioch fifteen days' journey, and eight in width. And [Alexios] swore to him that if he loyally observed the oath, he would never pass beyond his own land.'⁹² Yet the value of this concession was negligible; if anything, it was to the empire's advantage. Encouraging Bohemond to take over lands that were beyond the empire's traditional frontiers could result in the creation of a buffer zone between Byzantium and the Turks. From the Norman's point of view, he would use the massive Crusader army for his own gains; this was particularly attractive given his limited prospects in southern Italy where his half-brother and his uncle held sway. It was, in other words, an agreement from which both men stood to gain.

Bohemond was so pleased by the prospect of carving out a realm for himself that he intervened on Alexios' behalf during the latter's negotiations with Raymond of Toulouse. It was Bohemond who cajoled and eventually even threatened the most powerful member of the expedition, telling Raymond that if he continued to refuse to take the oath, he would take direct action against him personally.⁹³ This endeared Bohemond to the rank and file of the entire expedition, who saw the disagreements between the leaders as distractions from the matter in hand of taking on the Turks in Asia Minor. Bohemond therefore took the credit for keeping the momentum of the Crusade going. It also endeared him to Alexios, who came to see his former rival as a valuable ally, someone with common sense and a common touch – in short, someone he could rely on.

Although the emperor had immediate concerns in 1096–7, as the Crusaders arrived in Byzantium, he also had an eye on long-term strategy when formalising his relations with the expedition's leaders. He was particularly concerned about what would happen to towns and regions that were to be taken by the westerners as they crossed Asia Minor. This issue was addressed explicitly in the oaths that were made in Constantinople. Godfrey of Bouillon, along with other leading western knights, 'came to the emperor and swore on oath that what-ever towns, lands or forts he might in future subdue that had in the first place belonged to the Roman Empire, would be handed over to the officer appointed by the emperor for this very purpose'.⁹⁴

Reports of this arrangement quickly spread well beyond Byzantium, becoming widely known in the Muslim world. Well-informed commentators writing in Baghdad and Damascus knew the outline of the terms that had been concluded in the imperial capital. One wrote that when the Crusaders arrived in Byzantium, 'the Franks, on their first appearance had made a covenant with the king of the Greeks, and had promised him that they would deliver over to him the first city that they captured'.[95] Another focused on the determination and resolve shown by Alexios to get what he had wanted: 'the Byzantine emperor refused them passage through his territory. He said, "I will not allow you to cross into the lands of Islam until you swear to me that you will surrender Antioch to me."'[96]

Latin sources noted not only the commitments given by the western leaders but also those offered in return by Alexios. 'The emperor', wrote the author of the Gesta Francorum, 'for his part guaranteed good faith and security to all our men, and swore also to come with us, bringing an army and a navy, and faithfully to supply us with provisions both by land and sea, and to take care to restore all those things which had been lost. Moreover, he promised he would not cause or permit anyone to trouble or vex our pilgrims on the way to the Holy Sepulchre.'[97]

In the coming years much was to turn on who fulfilled their obligations, with accusations of breaches levelled by both sides. But one thing was clear: Alexios perfectly understood the concept of fealty and acted like a western ruler, couching his requests for homage in language the knights were familiar with. Whether the emperor also recognised that these mutual commitments could be unpicked in difficult circumstances is another matter.

As the author of the Gesta Francorum was quick to point out, responsibilities cut both ways. When the Crusaders arrived in Constantinople, it was assumed that the emperor would be taking personal command of the expedition. After all, as the Crusaders converged at Kibotos, Alexios was behaving as their commander-in-chief, bestowing gifts, providing accommodation and food, co-ordinating their movements and advising on suitable tactics to use against the Turks. With his demand for oaths, furthermore, he had positioned himself as the central figure in the expedition.

This put Alexios in a difficult situation. He had called for help from the west because he urgently needed men to assist with a major reconquest of Asia Minor, after the advances of the Turks and the

BYZANTIUM IN CRISIS

Alp Arslan and Romanos IV after the battle of Manzikert.

BYZANTIUM'S GLORY

(*Above*) Christ and the Virgin Mary flanked by the emperors Constantine and Justinian. Mosaic in the south vestibule of Hagia Sophia, late tenth century.

(*Facing page, above*) Reliquary for wood from the True Cross, *c*.950.

(*Facing page, below*) The walls of Constantinople, first built by the emperor Theodosius in the fifth century.

THE CALL FROM THE EAST

(*Above*) The hope of Byzantium: Emperor Alexios I Komnenos.

(*Below*) Coin issued by Alexios, depicting Christ giving a blessing (*left*)
and the emperor himself (*right*).

THE RESPONSE FROM THE WEST

(*Above*) Pope Urban II arrives at the council of Clermont.

(*Below*) Emperor Alexios receives Peter the Hermit.

THE EXPEDITION TO
THE HOLY LAND

(*Left*) The Crusaders
at Nicaea, 1097.

(*Below*) The siege of
Antioch, 1097–8.

(*Above*) Crusaders massacring the inhabitants
of Antioch, 1098.

(*Below*) The siege of Jerusalem, 1099.

LIBERATING THE HOLY CITY

The looting of Jerusalem, 1099.

associated rebellion of the empire's aristocracy had left him dangerously exposed. His ability to play an active role in the campaign
was therefore limited, as Anna Komnene acknowledged: 'the
emperor would have liked to accompany the expedition against
the godless Turks, but abandoned the project after carefully
weighing the arguments for and against: he noted that the Roman
army was hopelessly outnumbered by the enormous host of the
Franks; he knew from long experience, too, how untrustworthy
the Latins were'. Alexios was also concerned about revolt breaking
out in Constantinople in his absence. 'So this was why the emperor
decided against joining the enterprise at that time', wrote Anna.
'However, even if his presence was unwise, he realised the necessity
of giving as much aid to the Kelts as if he were actually with
them.'[98]

There was no need for the emperor to declare his hand just yet.
He was able to accompany the Crusaders into Asia Minor and to take
the lead in the initial operations. But he had presumably yet to decide
what would happen if and when the expedition proved successful and
started to make serious headway against the Turks. But by the late
spring of 1097, things were going well for the emperor. He had successfully negotiated agreements with all the western leaders and had been
careful to promise to help the expedition; nevertheless, whatever the
western knights might have expected, he had at no stage indicated
explicitly that he would lead them in person to Jerusalem. Their future
relationship would depend largely on how successful the knights were.
Alexios thus watched intently as the Crusader army advanced towards
the first major target: Nicaea.

9

First Encounters with the Enemy

The Crusaders' advance into Asia Minor was a story of victories and near-disasters, high violence and clashing egos. Alexios, forced by political instability to remain at the heart of the empire rather than venture out on expedition, sought to manage the campaign from afar. It was a high-risk approach, but, for the first year or so of the Crusade, a triumphant one.

The size of the force that assembled at Kibotos in the spring of 1097, numbering in the tens of thousands, was astonishing; the challenge of keeping them supplied was enormous. The slickly run operation at Kibotos impressed Stephen of Blois, who wrote to his wife describing the extraordinary amount of food and supplies that the Crusaders found waiting for them.[1] Others too commented on the abundance of goods in the town, as well as the presence of a huge number of merchants selling wheat, wine, oil, cheese and other essentials to the westerners.[2]

As in the Balkans, the price of these commodities was not left to market forces or to the whims of sharp traders. Even when the very first westerners reached Kibotos, reported one author, goods were supplied not only in large volume, but at fixed prices as a result of centralised imperial control.[3] The plentiful provisioning kept morale high amongst the Crusader force; it also further boosted the emperor's high standing amongst the western army. Regular distributions of money to the rank and file likewise produced a swell of goodwill and gratitude that left the assembled force determined to advance on the enemy at Nicaea.[4] Alexios built on this enthusiasm, promising gold, silver, horses and more besides if the Turks were defeated and the town captured.[5]

The Crusaders set off for Nicaea in the early summer of 1097, reaching the town in May. As soon as camp was set outside the imposing walls, the westerners tried to take the town by storm. This took Alexios aback; he had concluded long ago that it could not be taken by force.[6] Indeed, he had sought military help from the west in the first place precisely because of the failure of his own efforts on Nicaea in the early 1090s. Now his assumption that the only way to capture Nicaea was through a lengthy siege, supported by substantial manpower, was immediately challenged by the Crusaders.

Rather than set up a perimeter and slowly tighten the noose round the town, the knights made a quick assessment of Nicaea's fortifications and straightaway set about probing its defences and attempting to breach the walls. They began their assault before some of the principal leaders had even reached the town; Robert of Normandy and Stephen of Blois arrived to find that the attack was already under way.[7]

Although enthusiastic, the westerners' initial efforts made little impression. According to one Crusader, Nicaea had been enclosed with such lofty walls that its inhabitants feared neither the attack of enemies, nor the force of any machine. As we have seen, the town was also perfectly positioned and well protected by natural terrain, including a substantial lake to the west.[8] To overcome the defences, the knights designed and built stone-throwing machines which, while not capable of seriously damaging the vast fortifications, were intended to provide cover so sappers could get close enough to the walls to start compromising them from below. A team under the supervision of Raymond of Toulouse soon managed to collapse a section of the defences, raising spirits in the Crusader camp and startling the Turkish garrison. It was only by working furiously through the night that the defenders were able to mend the damage that had been done.[9]

The Crusaders persisted despite sustaining early casualties. One leading knight, Baldwin of Calderun, had his neck broken by the blow of a stone hurled from the parapets as he led a charge against the town's gates. Other prominent figures were also struck, including Baldwin of Ghent, who was mortally wounded by a fine shot from the battlements. Disease also began to take its toll: the young and courageous Guy of Possesse came down with fever and died soon after.[10]

Those inside Nicaea held important strategic advantages over the attackers. The view from the towering battlements and walls enabled them to see what the Crusaders were doing and prepare accordingly.

They could also easily fire projectiles and arrows or drop objects down on to the exposed men below. And the Turks protecting Nicaea were resourceful: burning oil, grease and pitch were all used against those who came within touching distance of the walls.[11] Furthermore, the Turks knew that the Crusaders had been gathering at Kibotos since the summer of 1096, and they had spent months stockpiling the supplies they would need to withstand a lengthy siege. They seemed so confident that they would not be forced to surrender that Nicaea's governor, Kilidj Arslan, was not even in the town during the siege but elsewhere in Asia Minor.[12] Like Alexios, Nicaea's defenders felt that there was little chance that the town would be taken by assault.

They demonstrated their confidence by treating those they killed conspicuously badly. One knight from Robert of Normandy's contingent found himself isolated in an attack and was picked off by the town's defenders. After he had been killed, a device with sharp, iron claws attached to a chain was lowered over the walls, which clasped the corpse and dragged it back up over the battlements. The cadaver was then hung from a noose and suspended naked over the side of the walls for all to see. The message was clear: it was a waste of men, time and energy trying to take Nicaea.[13]

The Crusaders matched like with like. A detachment of Turks sent to relieve the garrison at Nicaea was defeated and its men all decapitated, their severed heads fixed to the end of spears that the westerners paraded to the town's inhabitants. As Anna Komnene noted, this was done 'so that the barbarians would recognise from a distance what had happened and being frightened by this defeat at their first encounter would not be so eager for battle in the future'.[14]

The knights stepped up pressure on the town. Siege warfare was an area where western European technology had evolved rapidly in the eleventh century. The Normans of southern Italy in particular had mastered the art of attacking heavily fortified towns and storming them, rather than slowly strangling them into submission. Their rapid conquests of Apulia, Calabria and Sicily in the 1050s and 1060s owed much to the innovation that they brought to siege craft and to the inventiveness they showed when dealing with well-defended fortresses. Thus the construction of siege engines, designed to test Nicaea's defences, had started as soon as the first knights approached the city.

Attention was focused on one section of the walls in particular, which was protected by the Gonatas tower. The tower had suffered damage during a rebellion a century earlier and was already leaning. The expedition's leaders immediately recognised it as the weakest point in the town's defences.[15] Raymond of Toulouse oversaw the design of a special siege engine to use against the tower, a circular contraption covered with thick leather hides to protect those working within it. After it was pushed against the wall, sappers with iron tools worked at its foot, digging out stones from the base of the tower and replacing them with wooden beams which were then set on fire. Although the Gonatas tower did not immediately collapse, the Crusaders' work produced a visible deterioration in the wall. It also provoked panic within Nicaea.[16]

Alexios sought to take advantage of the growing anxiety among the Turks. The emperor had taken up an advanced position at Pelekanos, from which he could monitor and direct proceedings. As the first assaults on Nicaea began, Manuel Boutoumites secretly entered the town to try to negotiate a settlement, reminding its inhabitants of the generosity the emperor had shown to Turks in the past and warning of the consequences should the Crusaders breach the town's defences. Manuel produced written guarantees of how they would be treated if the city was surrendered immediately.[17]

The Turks rejected this overture, confident of the strength of Nicaea's defences. In addition, they were also receiving reports that an enormous army was on its way to relieve the town. Indeed, in the early stages of the siege, it was the Crusaders who had reason to be anxious. Spies found in the westerners' camp, pretending to be Christian pilgrims, revealed under torture that the garrison in Nicaea was communicating freely with the outside world and that a large Turkish force was heading for the town.[18] The sight of supplies being brought into the town across the Ascanian Lake to the west underlined the need to take decisive action, rather than hope a long siege would bring about surrender.

Controlling operations carefully, Alexios gave the order for ships to be transported overland from the Gulf of Nikomedia to blockade the lake, while ordering the assault on the town to be stepped up. Byzantine archers were deployed close to the walls and ordered to provide such heavy covering fire that the Turks were unable to raise their heads over the battlements. Imperial forces, accompanied by trumpets and drums, launched into war cries, giving the impression that a heavy

attack was under way. The sight of a wave of imperial military standards advancing in the distance suggested the imminent arrival of yet
more men to attack the town.[19]

Alexios' plan was to present a picture of overwhelming military
superiority and to seek the surrender of Nicaea on his terms. Once
again, Manuel Boutoumites was secretly dispatched into the town,
taking with him a *chrysobull*, a document signed by the emperor in
gold letters, setting out terms. These included an amnesty, as well as
liberal gifts of money, 'extended to all the barbarians in Nicaea without
exception'.[20] This time the emperor's initiative and cunning convinced
the Turks to surrender.

This was a major coup for Alexios – and the vindication of his
ambitious policy of seeking help from the west. Nevertheless, the
situation had to be handled delicately. Fearing that the western knights
would not be satisfied by a brokered truce, the emperor gave the order
to stage an 'attack' on the walls. The aim was to give the impression
that it was the Byzantines who breached the defences and successfully
took the town, rather than the Crusaders.

On 19 June 1097, while the western army, still unaware of the deal
that had been struck, continued its assaults on the town's fortifications,
Byzantine soldiers scaled the walls on the lake side of Nicaea, climbed
on to the battlements, and set up the imperial standards above the
town. To the sounds of trumpets and horns, the fall of Nicaea and
its capture by the forces of the emperor Alexios I Komnenos was
announced from the walls of the city.[21]

The fall of Nicaea sent shock waves through the Muslim world. As
one contemporary writing in Damascus described it: 'There began to
arrive a succession of reports that the armies of the Franks had
appeared from the direction of the sea of Constantinople with forces
not to be reckoned for multitude . . . as reports grew and spread from
mouth to mouth far and wide, the people grew anxious and disturbed
in mind.'[22] The use of Turkish tombstones to rebuild an area of
Nicaea's walls that had suffered damage during the siege cannot have
helped calm nerves about what the implications of the massive western
expedition might be elsewhere in Asia Minor.[23]

The town's capture caused a stir closer to home as well. For the
Crusaders, it was proof that the expedition to Jerusalem enjoyed divine

blessing. As it became clear that the town had fallen, cries of 'Glory to Thee, O God!' went up inside and outside the walls, shouted in both Latin and in Greek.[24] Nicaea's capture revealed that the knights were doing the work of the Lord; it was a success they would refer back to when the odds ran sharply against them at later stages in the expedition. There was no such thing as an impregnable target for a force marching under God's protection.

For Alexios, the recovery of Nicaea had been one of his primary goals. Yet the ambition, speed and determination shown by the western knights had been remarkable. The town's capture in June 1097 was therefore a comprehensive vindication of the emperor's decision to call for military assistance from the west. For Alexios this was an unmitigated triumph.

The fact that Nicaea passed into Byzantine hands with little bloodshed also presented future opportunities for the emperor: he would be able to present himself as friend and protector of the Turks who could save them from slaughter at the hands of the knights. This intention was reinforced by the emperor's treatment of the Turkish inhabitants of Nicaea: having been offered imperial service and generous gifts, all were allowed to go on their way unharmed.[25] The Crusaders were also well rewarded: gold, silver and precious robes were given to the expedition's leaders, while the lower ranks received copper coins to celebrate the fall of the city.[26]

Not everyone was impressed by the emperor's largesse, however. Misgivings began to be articulated about Alexios' role and about why the emperor should be benefiting from western strength and skill. A leading cleric on the expedition wrote to Manasses II, archbishop of Rheims, some months later, noting that 'the princes of the army hastened to meet the emperor who had come to express his gratitude to them. After receiving gifts from him of priceless value, they returned, some feeling kindly towards him, others not.'[27] Ironically, it was Alexios' generosity that caused some of this bitterness. The knights had set out from western Europe to do God's will and to some, to be financially rewarded by the Byzantines seemed inappropriate.

Alexios' decision to raise the matter of the oaths once again at Nicaea caused further discontent. Anna Komnene's claim that her father wanted all those who had previously made commitments to reconfirm them in June 1097 seems unconvincing and is not supported by Latin sources.[28] In fact, it was those knights who had not already sworn allegiance that Alexios was seeking to pin down after the fall of Nicaea. Some prominent leaders had escaped his attention in Constantinople. Some, like Tancred, the nephew of Bohemond, had quietly avoided paying homage to the emperor, which he regarded as a yoke of bondage according to his twelfth-century biographer.[29] When, after the capture of Nicaea, Tancred too was pressed to take the oath, he protested violently – at least, that is, until he named his price: the same payments as had been given to the other leaders plus some additional incentives. When one Byzantine senior officer lunged at him for his insolence, the two men had to be pulled apart. Once again, it was Bohemond who smoothed things over, persuading Tancred to take the oath.[30]

Alexios' efforts to strengthen his personal authority over the expedition after the fall of Nicaea stemmed from his decision not to join the march across Asia Minor in person – at least not for the time being. Although the emperor had advanced to Nicaea to oversee and witness the fall of the town, he was reluctant to venture deeper into Anatolia. Mindful of the dangers of leaving the capital after the problems he had experienced on the eve of the Crusade, he instead chose an experienced and trusted general to lead the western army east. The obvious choice was the emperor's childhood friend Tatikios. Gnarled and experienced, Tatikios had long proved his loyalty to Alexios, especially during the denouement of the Diogenes conspiracy. He had a slit nose, which he covered with a gold proboscis – likely the result of his loyalty to the emperor during the fierce infighting of the mid-1090s.[31] Tatikios was appointed to command the force that was to lead the Crusaders across Asia Minor, and to take possession of any towns captured on the route to Jerusalem.[32]

Alexios' reluctance to take part in the expedition was understandable given the crisis in Byzantium on the eve of the Crusade. The emperor had told Raymond of Toulouse that he could not lead the knights to Jerusalem because 'he feared that the Alemanni, Hungarians and Cumans and other savage peoples would ravage his empire if he made the journey with the pilgrims'.[33] These were real dangers: the Cuman attack in the spring of 1095 had stretched Byzantium to breaking point, leaving the emperor unable to take direct action, having to stage an elaborate ceremony in Hagia Sophia where he placed two tablets on the altar – one saying he should march against the nomads, the other that he should not; the rest was left up to God.[34]

In 1097, therefore, the threats to the empire from within and without meant that the risks were simply too high for Alexios to contemplate taking the lead in person. As we shall see, a year later, when desperate reports from Antioch reached Alexios, begging him to head east to relieve the embattled Crusade force which was by that time on the edge of annihilation, there was little the emperor could do to help. The weakness of his position at the time of his appeals to the west underpinned the First Crusade. Nevertheless, Alexios still retained control of the expedition in 1097; although some of the knights agitated to press straight on with their journey after the fall of Nicaea, it was only when the emperor gave his permission to depart that the Crusaders got on their way at the end of June.[35]

Meanwhile the emperor stayed in northern Asia Minor, monitoring Byzantine attempts to recover the western coast and river valleys of the subcontinent. As soon as Nicaea was secure, Alexios equipped a force and placed it under the command of John Doukas and Constantine Dalassenos, with orders to move on Çaka's base at Smyrna. From there, they were to retake the other towns on the coast that had fallen to the Turks before turning inland, with Doukas marching up the Maiander valley, while in a flanking movement, Dalassenos was to head north to Abydos. The aim was to recover a substantial swathe of territory in western Asia Minor.[36]

The emperor's initiative was supported by the route taken by Tatikios when he set out from Nicaea to lead the Crusaders east at the end of June 1097. Rather than follow the most direct route across central Anatolia, the Byzantine commander led the massive army as far south as Antioch-in-Pisidia. This was done to maximise the Byzantine military presence across the coast and its hinterland as John Doukas' campaign got under way.[37] The idea was to persuade the Turks to surrender on the grounds that they might be otherwise subjected to a massive assault.

To further impress the Turks, Doukas took with him Çaka's daughter, who had been taken prisoner at Nicaea. She was brought to prove that the town had fallen, and to show that her father's power was waning. The fact that she was treated well by the Byzantines clearly demonstrated to Çaka's faltering followers the benefits of co-operating with the emperor.[38]

The Byzantine campaign that began in the summer of 1097 was spectacularly successful. Smyrna, Ephesus and all the towns on the coast were recovered. Philadelphia, Sardis, Laodikeia, Khoma and Lampe were then taken by force or surrendered as Doukas advanced. By the summer of 1098, the coast and the key nodes of the interior were once again back in imperial hands. Byzantine governors were quickly appointed in the locations that had been regained. All those given such positions – men like Kaspax, Hyaleas, Petzeas, Michael Kekaumenos, Eustathios Kamyztes – were part of the new guard that had emerged after the Diogenes conspiracy. They had been obscure figures before the mid-1090s; now they were on the front line of a major fightback in the empire's eastern provinces.[39]

Having caused trouble for the empire for nearly a decade, Çaka himself was finally forced to flee from Smyrna. His fall was dramatic. Arriving in Abydos to take counsel with Kilidj Arslan, he was murdered after a lavish banquet, a sword plunged into his side by the former governor of Nicaea himself. He had become a liability to the Turks of Asia Minor.[40]

Such was the revival in Byzantine fortunes that Kilidj Arslan sought out the emperor to come to terms with him. As Anna Komnene put it, 'these did not fail to meet with success'. Although she does not provide any detail of what was agreed, the fact that 'peace was restored to the maritime provinces' is a telling indication that Byzantium's fortunes in Asia Minor had improved suddenly and decisively.[41]

The most important towns and regions in the eastern provinces were back in imperial hands. And while there was still much to be done if the Turks were to be driven out of the subcontinent altogether, the emperor also had to be pragmatic about how much he could realistically recover in one go. Quite apart from finding enough officers he could trust to reimpose his authority, it was essential that the gains of 1097–8 were made permanent. There was of course the prospect that as the Crusaders marched on from Nicaea, the Turks would regroup and subject the town, and the rest of this region, to renewed pressure. This made the agreement with Kilidj Arslan a welcome development for Alexios, allowing him the scope to rebuild the empire's position in western Asia Minor properly, and to consolidate the improvement in his own position in Byzantium.

The emperor had used the muscle of the Crusader army shrewdly, and benefited from its power both directly – at Nicaea – and indirectly, through the pressure it put on the Turkish presence in western Asia Minor generally. Yet ironically the willingness of Kilidj Arslan to reach a settlement with Alexios and sacrifice a substantial swathe of territory had negative consequences for the Crusaders who now drew the full focus of Turkish attention.

After setting off from Nicaea, the western army divided into two, with Bohemond, Tancred and Robert of Normandy in one group; Robert of Flanders, Raymond of Toulouse, Hugh of Vermandois and the bishop of Le Puy in another. There were practical reasons for splitting the force. Although supplies had so far been ensured by the emperor, the sheer size of the army as it started to move meant that keeping it provisioned was extremely challenging, especially in the baking heat of the central Anatolian plateau in the height of the summer months.

At the start of July, just a few days into the march, Bohemond noticed Turkish scouts shadowing his lead party, as it approached the ruined town of Dorylaion. Although he immediately sent word to the main contingent, he was ambushed by an enormous Turkish force under the command of Kilidj Arslan that was on its way to tackle the western knights. Shock and fear spread through the Crusaders as the enemy bore down on them 'howling like wolves and furiously shooting a cloud of arrows'.[42]

The noise made by the Turks was terrifying. 'They began to gabble and shout, saying in their language some devilish word which I do not understand', wrote one eyewitness. They were likely to have been shouting 'Allahu akbar!' – 'God is great!' Yet it was not just the sounds that frightened the westerners. The attack was so ferocious that priests on the expedition prayed to God through streaming tears, so certain were they of their imminent doom.[43] 'What shall I say next?' recorded another westerner. 'We were all indeed huddled together like sheep in a fold, trembling and frightened, surrounded on all sides by enemies so that we could not turn in any direction. It was clear to us that this happened because of our sins . . . By now we had no hope of surviving.'[44]

Surrounded by mounted archers, Bohemond's men were pushed back towards the nearby river. This turned out to be fortunate: for knights wearing metal armour and fighting with heavy swords, access to drinking water could make the difference between life and death. In addition, the Turkish horses found the marshy land hard going.

Thus falling back to more advantageous terrain, the Crusaders held
their line in spite of heavy casualties and fought a fierce rearguard
action until reinforcements arrived. Bohemond's tactics and his ability
to maintain discipline explains why the Norman leader's star rose
steadily amongst the rank and file of the expedition. He urged his
men to hold their ground, leading by example in the first major open
encounter with the enemy. The Crusaders maintained their faith: 'we
passed a secret message along our line, praising God and saying, "Stand
fast all together, trusting in Christ and in the victory of the Holy
Cross. Today, please God, you will all gain much booty!"'[45] It seems
it was not just faith that sustained the knights.

With the arrival of detachments from the contingents of Godfrey
of Bouillon, Raymond of Toulouse and Hugh of Vermandois, the
balance began to shift in the westerners' favour. The appearance of
Adhemar of Le Puy proved decisive, with the bishop ransacking the
Turkish camp, setting it on fire and then attacking the enemy from
the rear. This spread confusion amongst the attacking force, which
now began to disperse. A battle that had threatened to bring the
Crusade to an ignominious and early end turned into a spectacular
victory. No wonder some commentators regarded it as yet another
sign of God's grace and protection: 'It was a great miracle of God
that during the next and the third days the Turks did not cease to
flee, although no one, unless God, followed them further. Gladdened
by such a victory, we all gave thanks to God. He had willed that our
journey should not be brought entirely to naught, but that it should
be prospered more gloriously than usual for the sake of that Christianity
which was His own.'[46]

Nevertheless, the Turks had made a startling impression on the
Crusaders; their skill on horseback, their impressive use of the bow,
and their military ability earned them western admiration. Some
Crusaders regretted that they were not Christians: '[The Turks] have
a saying that they are of common stock with the Franks, and that
no men, except the Franks and themselves are naturally born to be
knights. This is true and nobody can deny it, that if only they had
stood firm in the faith of Christ and Christendom . . . you could
not find stronger or braver or more skilful soldiers; and yet by God's
grace they were defeated by our men.'[47] Despite the knights'
grudging admiration for their enemy – Kilidj Arslan was referred to

as 'a very noble man, but nevertheless a heathen' – the threat posed by the Turks to the expedition outweighed such niceties.[48] As Alexios had stressed in Constantinople, the Turks were formidable fighters; unless strict discipline was maintained in battle, the Crusaders would be massacred.[49]

Having seen off the attack at Dorylaion, the knights continued their march across central Anatolia. They made rapid progress, meeting little meaningful opposition as the Turks they encountered melted away, rather than daring to engage. As the Crusaders approached Herakleia, on the northern coast of modern Turkey, the enemy fled 'as quickly as an arrow, shot by a strong hand, flies from the bowstring'.[50] The lack of resistance was due to the western knights' spectacular victory at Dorylaion. As one Arabic writer noted, 'when news was received of the shameful calamity to the cause of Islam, the anxiety of the people became acute, and their fear and alarm increased'.[51]

With Asia Minor opening up to the advancing army, Tatikios made sure that strategically important towns were taken along the way. These were identified in advance: the Byzantine commander therefore led the Crusaders not along the most direct route to the Holy Land, but via a series of locations that were to serve as bases from which further conquests could be launched in future. One such place was the town of Plastencia, east of Caeserea (modern Kayersi) which was recovered in the autumn of 1097. In accordance with the agreements between the Crusaders and the emperor, the town was placed in the hands of an imperial governor, in this case Peter Aliphas, who had taken service with Alexios in the mid-1080s. Now occupying an influential liaison role with the Crusaders, Peter took on the responsibility of securing the town 'in fealty to God and to the Holy Sepulchre' – rather than in the name of the emperor, at least according to one commentator.[52]

Similar arrangements were put in place to take control of other locations as the Crusader army marched east. A certain Simeon took command of a tract of territory in south-eastern Asia Minor, vowing to protect it from Turkish attack.[53] Then there was Welf, a native of Burgundy who had expelled the Turks from Adana and taken control of the town by the time a small Crusade detachment arrived to assess the situation on the southern coast. Like Peter Aliphas, he was a westerner in imperial service who had been reclaiming towns for Byzantium as the Crusade made its way across Asia Minor.[54]

Two forays involving Baldwin of Bouillon, the younger brother of Godfrey, and Tancred seem to have had much the same purpose. In the autumn of 1097, Baldwin detached himself from the main body of the expedition and marched into Cilicia, his departure sanctioned by the Crusade leadership. Tancred set off around the same time – but without the same consent. He claimed he had resolved to make his own way to Antioch; in fact, he wanted to see what Baldwin was up to.[55]

The two men soon came to blows after they both made for Tarsos, a wealthy and strategically important town on the south-eastern coast of Asia Minor. Tancred arrived first, and thanks to a series of well-judged threats managed to raise his banner over the ramparts without having to launch an attack on the town. Baldwin reached Tarsos soon after and immediately had Tancred's banner replaced with his own. Antagonism between the two men worsened as Tancred moved on to Adana and then to Mamistra, with Baldwin following close behind. Eventually their forces broke into open battle with Tancred's surprise attack easily beaten back by Baldwin's men.[56]

It is difficult to interpret this episode; it is usually presented as a case of personal profiteering, a chance for both men to enrich themselves by chasing the opportunities that opened up during the Crusade and then fighting over the spoils. In fact, it is to Constantinople again that we should look for an explanation.

Baldwin had caught the emperor's eye in the capital, impressing Alexios by chastising the arrogant knight who had dared to sit on the imperial throne. His reprimand is quoted in full in the *Alexiad*: 'You ought never to have done such a thing, especially after promising to be the emperor's liegeman. Roman emperors don't let their subjects sit with them. That is the custom here and sworn liegemen of His Majesty should observe the customs of the country.'[57]

Alexios was on the lookout for westerners whom he could trust. Even Bohemond, with his blue eyes, smooth face and a reputation that inspired terror in Byzantium, had been carefully considered by the emperor as he looked for commanders to take on responsibilities during the Crusade. Baldwin appeared to fit the mould perfectly. It was no coincidence, therefore, that he was put in command of a force that made for the coast, nor that he advanced on Tarsos and the south-eastern corner of Asia Minor. The capture of the town was a vital precursor for the assault on Antioch, the next focus of the Crusader expedition. It was an important base with a good natural harbour, making it an obvious location from which the Turks might harass the coast of Syria once the westerners arrived, threatening supply lines to Antioch not only from southern Asia Minor, but also from Cyprus. Alexios was already in the process of establishing Cyprus as a primary base from which to provision the Crusaders. Protecting maritime traffic in the eastern Mediterranean was essential if the expedition was to prove successful in Syria. Taking Tarsos and other towns targeted by Baldwin – like Mamistra – was a crucial part of the wider plan to recover Antioch, until recently the most important city in the Byzantine east.

Thus the dispatch of Baldwin to oversee the capture of Tarsos and the towns of its hinterland had nothing to do with profiteering, but was a foray executed under the direction of the emperor. This was the reason why Baldwin's departure from the main army, which was still being led by Tatikios, was agreed to in the first place. It also explains Baldwin's determination to drive off Tancred. The latter was a difficult character, headstrong and ambitious. Baldwin's eventual use of force against him was a necessary step to keep the framework of the expedition intact.

Having secured Tarsos, Adana and other locations in the south-western corner of Asia Minor, Baldwin handed them over to Tatikios and the Byzantines. This was why, less than six months later, Tatikios was himself able to place the towns under Bohemond's control when he left the Crusader camp in search of supplies and reinforcements.[58] Baldwin had shown himself to be willing to defend Alexios' interests aggressively, and it was not long before other towns and local populations who were keen to drive out the Turks appealed to him, as the emperor's representative, for help. After briefly rejoining the main army, Baldwin set off on his second foray, this time into the Caucasus. He was invited to Edessa by its governor T'oros, a Byzantine appointee who had done what he could to defend the town, fighting the Turks 'with the bravery of a lion', according to one local source.[59]

Baldwin was welcomed as a saviour by the region's inhabitants. 'When we were passing through the towns of the Armenians', reported one eyewitness, 'it was a wonder to see them coming out to greet us, carrying crosses and banners, kissing our feet and our clothes so much did they love God and because they had heard that we were going to protect them against the Turks who had oppressed them for so long.'[60] The joy with which he was greeted must have stemmed from the belief that the emperor was actively trying to protect and secure this region against the Turks, as he had been desperately trying to do immediately before the Crusade, according to the most likely reading of an inscription from the Harran gate in the town.[61] It also explains the offer made by the people of Edessa to give Baldwin half the revenues and taxes of the town. This was not intended to line Baldwin's pockets; these were funds earmarked for the emperor and were being handed to his agent in the traditional fashion.[62]

Like Plastencia and Tarsos, Edessa was strategically well placed to dominate a wider region and Baldwin's securing of the town was clearly part of a wider plan. Alexios was building a network of key towns and locations in the east which were held by trusted lieutenants. It was a role that suited Baldwin perfectly. Devout, experienced and capable, the youngest of three brothers whose patrimony had been reduced in the eleventh century, Baldwin had sold almost his entire landholdings before setting off for Jerusalem. He was one of the Crusaders who saw the expedition not only as a pilgrimage to Jerusalem but as offering the prospect of a new life in the east.

Baldwin formally took charge of Edessa on behalf of Constantinople. We can tell this not just from the fact that he started to wear Byzantine clothes and grew his beard in local fashion, but from other more substantial clues. It was striking, for example, that after settling into his position in Edessa, Baldwin took to having two trumpeters ride ahead of him to announce his imminent arrival when touring the region. Baldwin would travel in his chariot, which bore on a golden shield the unmistakable image of the authority with which he acted: the imperial eagle of Constantinople.[63]

Baldwin's appointment as Alexios' representative in Edessa and the surrounding area was formalised by granting him the official title of *doux*, governor. This was why Latin sources began to talk of Baldwin in this period as having the rank of duke – a title that he did not hold at home.[64] His obligations in Edessa also explain why it was that Baldwin was later reluctant to leave the city and rejoin the Crusade: he had responsibilities that he could not ignore.[65] A marriage to the daughter of a local potentate following the death of his English wife

Godevere likewise suggests that he was putting down roots.[66] In short, he was an excellent choice of lieutenant for Alexios in his ambitious and extensive plan to recover the Byzantine east.

While Baldwin was making headway in extending the emperor's authority, the rest of the Crusader army continued east. In October 1097, they finally arrived at the great city of Antioch. The city was not only strongly defended but well located: set back against mountains on two sides, with the river Orontes to the west serving as a further obstacle, Antioch was protected by walls twenty metres high and two metres thick, with numerous towers offering full sight of any hostile activities below.[67]

It was not just the physical location and the defences of Antioch that were a cause for concern; so was its size. The circuit of walls stretched for five kilometres around the city, encompassing an area of some 1,500 acres. As one observer put it, as long as the inhabitants were supplied with enough food, they would be able to defend the city for as long as they liked.[68] In so large a city, enough could be grown within its walls to sustain it almost indefinitely.

Antioch's governor, Yaghi Siyan, was so confident about the city's defences that he did little to oppose the expedition when it arrived. This gave the knights precious time to survey the city properly and regroup following the long march. Moreover, the Crusaders reached Antioch at a favourable time of year, when the scorching heat of the summer had dissipated and food was in plentiful supply. They were delighted to find 'fruitful vineyards and pits full of stored corn, apple trees laden with fruit and all sorts of other good things to eat'.[69]

To start with, there was a curious normality about the scene. Those in the city went about their business seemingly unworried about the presence of a major army outside the walls; and those who had come to attack it set about making plans, oblivious to the perils and strains which lay ahead. As the chaplain of Raymond of Toulouse wrote wistfully, at the beginning the westerners 'ate only the best cuts, rump and shoulders, scorned brisket and thought nothing of grain and wine. In these good times, only the watchmen along the walls reminded us of our enemies concealed inside Antioch.'[70]

The Crusaders established themselves in the surrounding area, taking the city's port at St Simeon to open up supply lines by sea to

Cyprus, where a new Byzantine governor had recently been appointed, after the restoration of Alexios' authority there, to oversee provisioning of the knights.[71] As Tarsos and other coastal towns had been captured already, there was little disruption to maritime traffic, either from Cyprus or elsewhere.

The Crusaders now tried to impose a blockade on Antioch. Although this initially affected the price of goods in the city, its geography and scale made it all but impossible to seal off completely. As a Muslim chronicler noted, 'oil, salt and other necessities became dear and unprocurable in Antioch; but so much was smuggled into the city that they became cheap again'.[72]

The ineffectiveness of the siege was one thing; the other problem was that living conditions soon deteriorated for the attackers. Finding enough food and pasture was a problem for any besieging force tackling a large target. Maintaining a single horse could require between five and ten gallons of fresh water per day, as well as a good supply of hay, and plenty of pastureland. It is difficult to estimate the precise number of horses outside Antioch, but there would have been thousands, with leading aristocrats having brought several mounts with them. The cost and practicalities of keeping so many horses supplied, to say nothing of those who rode them, was substantial.

Ominously, supplies started to run out a few weeks after the army's arrival at Antioch. The land that had been so pregnant when they reached the city was quickly stripped bare. By the end of the year, conditions became atrocious. As Fulcher of Chartres reported: 'Then the starving people devoured the stalks of beans still growing in the fields, many kinds of herbs unseasoned with salt, and even thistles which because of the lack of firewood were not well cooked and therefore irritated the tongues of those eating them. They also ate horses, asses, camels, dogs and even rats. The poorer people ate even the hides of animals and the seeds of grain found in manure.'[73]

By mid-November, those leaving the safety of the camp to seek food – or for other reasons – ran serious risks. One young knight, Abelard of Luxemburg, 'a very high-born young man of royal blood', was found 'playing dice with a certain woman of great birth and beauty in a pleasure garden full of apple trees'. He was ambushed and beheaded on the spot; his companion, seized by Turks, was repeatedly violated and also decapitated. The heads of both were then catapulted into the Crusader camp.[74] The Turks demonstrated their confidence no less forcefully by hanging John the Oxite, the patriarch of Antioch, upside down over the walls, beating his feet with iron bars in sight and within earshot of the western army.[75]

Food shortages were soon followed by disease. According to one chronicler from Edessa, as many as one in five of the Crusaders died outside Antioch from starvation and illness.[76] Infection raged through an increasingly malnourished and enfeebled force which was camped close together. Water carried deadly typhus and cholera bacteria. Tents rotting from the endless rain did nothing to improve morale or to stem the spread of disease.[77]

The situation worsened further when a large army under Duqaq, the emir of neighbouring Damascus, moved to relieve Antioch shortly after Christmas 1097. By a stroke of good fortune, the advancing force was spotted by Bohemond and Robert of Flanders who were on a foraging mission, and decided to engage the enemy. Vastly outnumbered, the western knights held rank and managed to avoid being encircled by Duqaq's men by breaking through enemy lines.[78] The Crusaders' resistance had a surprising effect on Turkish morale. Duqaq had made for Antioch expecting to finish off a weakened and exposed western army. But Bohemond and Robert of Flanders had shown formidable determination and discipline when they came under attack, which startled the governor of Damascus and his men. Rather than continue on to Antioch, to the westerners' great surprise Duqaq decided to return home. The first major Muslim army to attack the Crusaders at Antioch had folded at the first opportunity.

The sense of relief in the western camp did not last long. Barely a month later, at the start of 1098, scouts reported that another large relief army, led by Ridwan, the governor of Aleppo, was approaching fast. The principal leaders of the crusading force met in council and decided that some 700 knights would move against the Aleppan force, while the rest of the expedition was to remain at Antioch to maintain the siege as best they could.

Bohemond, Robert of Flanders and Stephen of Blois left camp on 8 February 1098 under the cover of nightfall.[79] When they encountered the Aleppan army, Bohemond once more took a leading role in battle. As had been the case with Duqaq's force, the Turks again threatened to overwhelm the western knights. Bohemond stood firm, urging those close to him: 'Charge at top speed, like a brave man, and fight valiantly for God and the Holy Sepulchre, for you know in truth that this is no war of the flesh, but of the spirit. So be very brave, and become a champion of Christ. Go in peace and may the Lord be your defence!'[80]

Bohemond's ferocious determination inspired his men and startled the enemy. But the Crusaders' battlefield tactics were also important. Part of the western cavalry hid from view, waiting for the right moment to ambush the enemy. They chose their moment impeccably, successfully dispersing the Turks so they could be picked off in smaller groups. As the Crusaders counter-attacked, Ridwan's army fell apart. Once again, a miraculous victory had been delivered against all the odds.

The stock of the commanders who had overseen the success rose dramatically. Raymond of Toulouse's ill health had prevented him from taking part and he had been left in command of those who remained at Antioch. Tatikios and the Byzantine force too could not take any credit for the successes over the governors of Damascus and Aleppo. Bohemond, on the other hand, had been inspirational. As one eyewitness reported, 'Bohemond, protected on all sides by the sign of the Cross, charged the Turkish forces like a lion which has been starving for three or four days which comes out of its cave thirsting for the blood of cattle and falls upon the flocks careless of their own safety, tearing the sheep as they flee hither and thither.'[81] It marked the beginning of a personality cult that was to prove enormously powerful in the years that followed.

The rout of Ridwan's army was a major boost to morale. Equally, it was a huge shock to the city's inhabitants who were presented with the sight of Turkish heads on posts in view of the city's gates. It was a grim reminder of what would happen to them if they continued to hold out.[82]

Three times now, in their encounters with Kilidj Arslan, Duqaq and now Ridwan, the Crusaders had come within a hair's breadth of catastrophe. While they had survived on each occasion, the odds of them succeeding each time an army set out against them diminished. The governors of Nicaea, Damascus and Aleppo might have failed. But there were other local rulers, to say nothing of the mighty sultan of Baghdad and the vizier of Cairo, who were likely to intervene sooner or later. The question was whether the Crusaders could break Antioch before their good fortune ran out.

10

The Struggle for the Soul of the Crusade

Even after repelling Ridwan's attack, the Crusaders were still highly exposed. And the longer the siege went on, the more vulnerable the western army, depleted by illness and disease, grew. The struggle for Antioch in the first half of 1098 now fuelled dangerous levels of discord within the leadership of the expedition. The careful balance of interests between east and west – Byzantine reconquest and Christian Crusade – was thrown off-kilter by the loss of morale and the competing personal ambitions that emerged outside the walls of Antioch.

In an attempt to break the deadlock, Adhemar of Le Puy urged the knights to fast for three days and march in a solemn procession around the city walls. He decreed that Mass be celebrated and psalms be recited more frequently, and suggested that fortunes might improve if everyone shaved their beards.[1] He also thought that too few Crusaders were wearing a cross and insisted that all should attach the symbol to their garments.[2] For the bishop there was a clear link between the terrible suffering in the camp and the lack of piety shown by the Crusaders.

As morale was plummeting, desertion became commonplace among the rank and file. The Crusade leadership took an uncompromising line, with severe punishments handed out to anyone found trying to flee. When Peter the Hermit, Walter the Carpenter and William of Grantmesnil were discovered slipping away, they were caught by Tancred and taught a humiliating lesson: Walter was made to lie on the floor of Bohemond's tent 'like a piece of rubbish' before being chastised in front of the rest of the force.[3] Those who abandoned the siege were fit for the sewers, wrote one commentator.[4] So fragile was morale in the Crusader camp that even the leaders took oaths, promising each other that they, at least, would not leave until Antioch had been taken.[5]

These commitments were a way of binding together the most senior figures, some of whom were now developing misgivings about the siege. Bohemond, for instance, had threatened to leave early on in the blockade, complaining not only about the loss of life amongst his men, but also protesting that he was not wealthy enough to provide for his force as food prices rocketed.[6] Others were less direct. Stephen of Blois retired to Tarsos, ostensibly to regain his health – a euphemism for not having the stomach to endure the suffering at Antioch.[7] Robert of Normandy too felt he would rather view proceedings from comfortable surroundings, and had withdrawn to a more hospitable location on the south coast of Asia Minor by Christmas 1097.[8] Although it took repeated attempts to encourage him back to the siege, at least he did not leave for home. One contemporary chronicler was surprised that Robert did not give up and return to Normandy, given his weakness of will, his prodigality when it came to money, his love of food, and general indolence and lechery.[9]

The burning question was how to provision the Crusader army. The nearby city of Tarsos had been retaken by forces loyal to Byzantium in 1097; so too had Laodikeia, the last remaining Turkish-held port on the southern coast. Alexios now established Laodikeia as the primary supply base for Antioch, the hub for 'wine, grain and great numbers of cattle' being sent from Cyprus.[10] Operations were overseen by the island's governor, Eumathios Philokales, who also took charge of Laodikeia by the spring of 1098.[11]

Yet although the threat of pirate raiding had all but disappeared, Cyprus was not able to supply resources in great enough quantities to keep thousands of men and horses nourished through the lean winter months. There were two solutions to the dilemma: either to improve supply lines dramatically or increase the number of men at Antioch so the city could be properly cordoned off and the siege brought to an end. As Bruno of Lucca put it when relaying news of the situation in the east to the inhabitants of his hometown, Antioch had been surrounded by the Crusaders, 'but not very well'.[12]

It fell to Tatikios to take the initiative. The Byzantine commander had been responsible for quartermastering the Crusader army and ensuring smooth progress to Antioch. At the end of January 1098, he left the Crusade, promising to send 'many ships laden with corn, barley, wine, meat, flour and all sorts of required provisions'. Yet although he left his possessions in the camp, he did not return.[13]

Tatikios' departure became notorious, and was used later to show that he – and therefore the emperor Alexios – betrayed the Crusaders, abandoning them to their fate at Antioch. He set off, said one chronicler, 'in false faith . . . to carry a message about the promised relief, which he had not done faithfully at all, since he did not return to Antioch again'.[14] In the words of Raymond of Aguilers, who was present during the siege, Tatikios left 'with God's curse; by this dastardly act [of not returning], he brought eternal shame to himself and his men'.[15] 'He is a liar', was the verdict of the author of the *Gesta Francorum*, 'and always will be.'[16]

These judgements were unjustified. On 4 March 1098, a few weeks after Tatikios had left, a fleet put in at St Simeon's port bringing essential foodstuffs, provisions, reinforcements and materials to use against Antioch's formidable defences. The timing of the fleet's appearance was no coincidence. Nor was its identification by Bruno of Lucca, who sailed with it, as English; Alexios had established an English garrison in Laodikeia after its recapture, and it was presumably these men who now brought emergency supplies to Antioch.[17] Tatikios had delivered what he had promised.

The reason why this was not acknowledged by the Crusaders and their chroniclers was that misgivings had already started to grow about the Byzantine role in the expedition. For one thing, with Tatikios absent, it was not clear to whom Antioch should be handed if and when it was taken, in accordance with the oaths given to Alexios in Constantinople. This led to unease amongst the western force, which began not only to question whether the Byzantines had lost faith in the operation, but also why the city was being besieged in the first place, at such heavy cost to the westerners.[18] Antioch did have Christian significance; after all, it was the original see of St Peter. But its capture had little to do with the liberation of the Holy Sepulchre; why not simply advance to Jerusalem and leave Antioch to one side?

It appears that the Crusaders remained at Antioch in spite of the suffering because they were bound by the commitments they had made to the emperor who was providing the leadership of the expedition, albeit from a distance. Thus the oaths that the emperor had

insisted upon were proving to be highly effective: they subjected the
Crusade leaders to Alexios' authority and gave the Byzantine ruler
the power to set the military and strategic objectives of the expedition. The emperor evidently felt comfortable enough to think that it
was not necessary to dispatch Tatikios back to the western camp, or
to send a senior representative in his place to ensure that the obligations remained intact.

One reason for this was a major miscalculation on Alexios' part
concerning Bohemond. In Constantinople, Bohemond had been keen
to position himself as a perfect foil for the emperor, the ideal right-
hand man who would protect the emperor's best interests and mediate
for him with the other main leaders of the expedition. On more than
one occasion, he had done so successfully, intervening on Alexios'
behalf.[19] If the emperor thought that Bohemond would continue to
represent him faithfully, he was wrong.

By the spring of 1098, following the departure of Tatikios and in
the absence of any Byzantine authority, Bohemond saw a golden
opportunity. He began broaching the idea of a new agreement on the
future of Antioch – one that did not involve Alexios. The suggestion
he came up with was provocative: the oaths to the emperor were null
and void, he said, since Alexios had not fulfilled his side of the agreement. The emperor had not accompanied the Crusaders in person;
the small force he had sent with the knights had withdrawn; he had
failed to provide military support in the hour of need; and he had not
kept the knights supplied. In short, he was a traitor.[20]

Bohemond concluded that Antioch should not be handed over to
Alexios. He proposed that whoever was able to breach the walls and
deliver the city should be allowed to claim personal control of it.
Although he was given short thrift by his fellow leaders, who were
wary of the Norman's wider ambitions, Bohemond persisted. At the
end of May 1098, he raised the issue of Antioch again.

This time, however, his audience was more receptive. Conditions
in the Crusader camp had not improved and no progress had been
made against the city's defences. News had also been received that
Kerbogha, the ambitious governor of Mosul, was approaching with
a large army aiming to defeat the westerners once and for all. So
well resourced were Kerbogha's forces that the Latin and Greek
sources assumed that it must have been funded and sent by the Seljuk

sultan Barkyaruq himself.[21] The crisis at Antioch was reaching its climax.

Intelligence reports on Kerbogha's movements and objectives were so troubling that when the leaders met in council, they resolved to keep the news secret from their troops to avoid destroying morale and provoking mass desertion. Given these dire circumstances, Bohemond's return to the question of the future of Antioch seemed misplaced; in the face of complete annihilation, the Norman persistently questioned the legal status of the oaths and made demands about the control of the city and the distribution of the spoils of victory. It seemed that Bohemond knew something the other leaders did not.

In fact, Bohemond had made a secret arrangement with an enemy captain, named Firouz, who was in charge of one of the defence towers along Antioch's walls, to allow the Crusaders into the city. Some eyewitnesses reported that Bohemond had captured Firouz's son and was holding him hostage. Others believed that Firouz had been inspired by God, and had had a vision instructing him to hand Antioch over to the Christians; that he was an Armenian with misgivings about the ill-treatment of the city's inhabitants by the Turks; or that he was a man who could not resist the promise of a handsome reward.[22] Whatever the case, Bohemond had found himself a trump card – and kept it hidden from the other leaders. His negotiations with Firouz would have been helped by the fact that both men spoke Greek, the latter the result of living in Byzantine Antioch, the former thanks to his upbringing in southern Italy – even if, as Anna Komnene sniped, Bohemond did have a terrible accent.[23]

With Kerbogha bearing down on Antioch, Bohemond's proposals about the fate of the city were again discussed. Raymond of Toulouse, the richest and most influential of the Crusade leaders, refused point-blank to give his approval to what he saw as an outright betrayal of the oaths sworn to the emperor in Constantinople.[24] Raymond had been the most reluctant of all to give Alexios the undertakings demanded of him; now he was the most reluctant to break them.

Although most other leading Crusaders had misgivings about Bohemond's proposals, he eventually extracted some support, albeit heavily qualified: it was agreed that if a single leader was able to take Antioch, he could hold it. However, this would be on a strictly conditional and temporary basis; control of the city was ultimately to be ceded to Byzantium. The agreement was carefully recorded in writing.[25] Attention now turned to the preparations for an all-out assault on the city – the final roll of the dice before Kerbogha's army arrived.

On 2 June 1098, four days after the council of leaders, the Crusaders commenced their attack. They began by feigning the departure of a large contingent to put the defending garrison off guard. Returning silently under the cover of nightfall, the knights joined up with another detachment by the Gate of St George, led by Robert of Flanders and Godfrey of Bouillon. A smaller group took up position with Bohemond by the tower that was under the command of Firouz.

After establishing that the coast was clear, the first group of Bohemond's men made their way up a ladder that had been secured to the top of the battlements. Firouz was waiting for them, as agreed. 'Micro Francos echomé!' he exclaimed in despair – 'We have few Franks!' As he saw it, there were nowhere near enough men to stand a chance of taking the city.[26]

Getting up the ladder in the darkness was not easy, and it was not made any easier by the fact that too many eager attackers, including Fulcher, a Knight from Chartres, attempted to climb it at the same time.[27] The weight of so many men caused the ladder to topple over, injuring some and making a terrific noise. Through a stroke of fortune, interpreted as a mark of divine protection, a strong wind muffled the sound, and the ladder was once again raised and the attackers clambered up as fast as they could.[28] Assembling at the top, the Crusaders made their way along the walls in silence, killing those they met until they were in position to signal to Godfrey and Robert of Flanders, who were waiting below, that the time had come to storm one of the city's gates.[29]

Breaching the gate, the Crusaders streamed into Antioch, bludgeoning and hacking their way deeper and deeper into the city as its bewildered inhabitants were roused from their sleep. Bohemond was focused on one thing: to raise his battle standard on the highest point of the walls as quickly as possible. This would show that the city had been captured and was now in Christian hands. But it was also a declaration to the other Crusaders that Antioch had fallen to Bohemond; even in the heat of battle, he was already thinking about its aftermath.[30]

Things quickly went the Crusaders' way as Antioch's other gates were flung open by its non-Muslim inhabitants. Some took the full brunt of the furious onslaught of the soldiers fighting their way through the city street by street, with many of the Christians living in the city killed in the process. In the dark, overwrought with fear and adrenaline, there was no time to separate friend from foe. The storming of Antioch was brutal. For days afterwards, corpses lay in the streets, the rotting bodies producing a putrid smell in the heat of the early summer. 'All the streets of the city on every side were full of corpses,' reported one eyewitness, 'so that no one could endure to be there because of the stench, nor could anyone walk along the narrow paths of the city except over the corpses of the dead.'[31]

The city's commander, Yaghi-Siyhan, fled in panic, escaping into the neighbouring mountains. He was recognised by three locals, all of them Christian, who dragged him off his mule and decapitated him with his own sword. His distinctive head – huge, with great hairy ears and a waist-length beard – was brought back to Antioch as a trophy and presented to the Crusaders.[32]

After eight long, painful months, Antioch finally fell on 3 June 1098 – although the citadel, the strong fort within the city, still held out. Thousands of Crusaders had died during the siege, and countless numbers had been wounded. Others had deserted and headed home. Nevertheless, it had ended in triumph. Those who made it into the city had no time to enjoy their success, however; Kerbogha's army arrived the very next day.

The advancing force was far larger than those assembled by the governors of Damascus and Aleppo. Rather than rush his assault, Kerbogha deployed his resources carefully, setting up camp by the walls and making contact with the defenders of the citadel. Having established that the Crusader army was exhausted, depleted and apprehensive, he ordered a ferocious assault from the citadel's garrison.

The Crusaders managed to resist the initial attack and Kerbogha now decided to suffocate the city by mounting a blockade. The besiegers had become the besieged. Communications from Antioch to the outside world were cut off, although a delegation to the Byzantine emperor with a desperate message calling for help had managed to set off just before Kerbogha's arrival. Later attempts to break out of the city were dealt with by the Turks with ease.

Kerbogha's blockade quickly had an effect. After months of siege, there were no more supplies within the city. 'Our men ate the flesh of horses and asses and sold it to one another', reported one chronicler; 'a hen cost 15 shillings, an egg two and a walnut a penny . . . so terrible was the famine that men boiled and ate the leaves of figs, vines, thistles and all kinds of trees. Others stewed dried skins of horses, camels, asses, oxen and buffaloes which they then ate.'[33] Indigestible plants were gathered and cooked, often poisoning those who ate them. Some resorted to eating shoes and other leather goods; others drank the blood of their horses.[34] For some, like Fulcher of Chartres, there was an obvious explanation for this suffering: many Crusaders had slept with local women both before and after taking the city. God was now punishing such wanton fornication.[35]

More than at any point during the expedition so far, the Crusaders needed a miracle – and they got one. A man of no particular distinction named Peter Bartholomew came forward to tell Raymond of Toulouse and the bishop of Le Puy that visions of St Andrew had been appearing to him for several months in which the saint revealed the location of the lance that had pierced Christ's side. After searching the city under Peter's direction, part of the Holy Lance was eventually recovered under the floor of the Church of St Peter in Antioch.[36] The find provided a major boost at a time when morale was at an all-time low. To the Crusaders, the discovery of such an important relic, particularly one that typified suffering, seemed highly significant – even if later commentators were dismissive of its authenticity. It helped strengthen resolve at a critical moment, when the knights 'did not have the strength to suffer these things and linger; so great and small consulted together, saying it was better to die in battle than to perish from so cruel a famine, growing weaker day by day until overcome by death'.[37]

The expedition leaders now decided to meet the enemy army head-on. The order was given that although supplies were all but exhausted, horses should be given as much feed as possible to boost their stamina. For three days before engaging the Turks, the Crusaders took part in solemn processions, celebrations of the Eucharist, and making confession.[38] Then, on 28 June 1098, the westerners marched out from Antioch and crossed the Bridge Gate over the Orontes, fanning out in front of the city in four brigades. This took Kerbogha by complete surprise. Playing chess when he heard that a sortie was under way, he lost precious time asking for confirmation that the reports were accurate and considering how he should respond. He simply could not believe that anyone would be so brave – or so stupid – as to try to break out of the city.[39]

At this point, the Crusade could have unravelled. Antioch itself was left essentially undefended, save for a small contingent under the command of Raymond of Toulouse, who remained behind, once again suffering from illness. The group that stayed with him, numbering just 200 knights, was all that there was to stop the garrison in the citadel retaking control of the city. Kerbogha, meanwhile, did nothing, failing to attack the Crusaders at their most vulnerable as they crossed the river.[40]

When Kerbogha finally ordered an attack, the western knights once again crucially managed to hold their formation. This caused panic in Kerbogha's army, already unnerved by the reputation the westerners had gained from previous successes. The Crusader forces kept their discipline, sending small units into the heart of the enemy army, which splintered under the pressure of the heavy cavalry charges. Kerbogha's troops started to melt away, their commander fleeing like a deer, according to one eyewitness. His camp and everything in it was captured, including many Turkish women who had been brought along in anticipation of the celebrations that were to accompany Kerbogha's recovery of Antioch and his destruction of the Crusader army. The westerners did these women no evil, wrote Fulcher of Chartres, 'but they did drive lances into their stomachs'.[41]

What had looked like the endgame for the expedition to Jerusalem suddenly became its most glorious hour. So extraordinary was the success against Kerbogha's army that even those who witnessed it struggled to understand how the victory had been achieved. According to Raymond of Aguilers who fought in the battle, Kerbogha's flight was caused by God sending a divine shower on to the Christian army which inspired it with graces, fortitude and hatred of the enemy.[42] Another eyewitness agreed that divine intervention had been involved, with the appearance of countless supernatural knights, all bearing white standards and led out by saints George, Mercurius and Demetrius, alongside the Crusaders.[43] For yet another chronicler, it was the relic of the Holy Lance itself that had brought victory, striking cold fear into Kerbogha's heart the moment he saw it and causing him to flee.[44] Arab contemporaries had a little more insight. Kerbogha was an arrogant man whose personality and behaviour had not endeared him to other emirs, they reported; his refusal to let them kill captured knights had proved particularly unpopular. Moreover, he was let down in the battle by enemies within his own army who had taken a vow to betray him at the first opportunity.[45]

The collapse of Kerbogha's army may well have seemed miraculous to the Crusaders, but there were more mundane reasons for the triumph. The confusion that quickly spread through the Turkish army was the result of incompetent leadership and poor communication. This gave way to panic, as limited Crusader operations, in some cases simply holding positions, gave the impression that the Muslim army was being driven back. In the chaos of combat, with dust being kicked up by the hooves of horses and the noise of clashing metal and battle cries filling the air, the already excitable Turkish army was undermined by its own size, with multiple commanders on the field trying to ascertain what was going on, while trying to take orders from Kerbogha.

The Crusader force, nimble, disciplined and well led, owed their most stunning success so far to their ability to hold their ground. The westerners had now repelled three major Muslim armies and gained permanent control of Antioch. They had nothing left to fear; and they needed no further signs that God was truly with them. It was a matter of course, surely, that the Holy City itself would be returned to Christian hands.

The aftermath of the battle for Antioch saw the Crusade leaders take stock of their position. They decided that the advance south to Jerusalem would not take place until the winter, to allow the expedition to consolidate and recover its strength. Morale was further boosted by the surrender of Antioch's citadel in the wake of Kerbogha's defeat, and by the support the Crusaders received from those living in the surrounding area, which began to supply the new overlords of the city.

There was, however, more to the decision to delay the march on Jerusalem than allowing time to regroup. The Chronicler Raymond of Aguilers, for one, was keen for the Crusaders to push on. He was certain that they would be unopposed if they marched directly on the Holy City, arguing that the populations of Syria and Palestine were so scared and weak after the defeat of Kerbogha that no one would dare even throw a stone at the western knights if they marched now.[46] In fact, the delay was caused by confusion and disagreement over what should happen to Antioch. With the city captured, the practicalities of occupation began to bog down the Crusaders. How would control of this city, and of other towns, forts and locations, be maintained? Under whose auspices and authority should they fall? What was reasonable to expect from the local population in terms of food supply and co-operation – especially when they were Muslims? Who could claim personal overlordship of towns beyond Byzantium's frontiers? Was the purpose of the expedition as a whole the liberation of Jerusalem alone – or were there other goals to consider? The months that followed the defeat of Kerbogha were taken up with a struggle for the soul of the First Crusade.

Central to this crisis was the emerging stand-off between Bohemond, who was clamouring for personal control of Antioch, and Raymond of Toulouse, who insisted that oaths to Alexios should be obeyed and was adamant that the expedition's integrity as an armed pilgrimage – rather than a campaign of conquest – should be respected. The result was a stalemate. Bohemond refused to leave Antioch; Raymond refused to set out for Jerusalem until Bohemond agreed to relinquish his claims.

The Crusade began to disintegrate. The leaders of the expedition had previously shown remarkable solidarity, both in battle and in council. But after the capture of Antioch, competing ambitions threatened the viability of the enterprise. An extraordinary announcement was made soon after the defeat of Kerbogha that all taking part in the expedition were free to take service with whichever lord they wished; it was an open admission of how divided the campaign had become. It meant that all the traditional ties, bonds and loyalties that had had so much value in the west had not only loosened but were removed altogether. This dramatic volte-face worked largely in Raymond's favour; his popularity and honourable reputation did much to recommend him to those not already serving with him.[47] One who joined him was author of the *Gesta Francorum* who had accompanied

Bohemond from southern Italy but had grown frustrated with the delay in heading for Jerusalem.

Other Crusaders also looked to benefit from the unravelling situation. A number of knights and foot soldiers, left impoverished by the long siege at Antioch, made for Edessa, drawn by Baldwin's promises of financial reward in return for service.[48] Baldwin's brother Godfrey, meanwhile, set about capturing local forts and towns, such as Tell-Bashir, extracting levies from the inhabitants which he shared with his men.[49] This increased his popularity and attracted others into his fold. Even low-ranking knights seized the opportunity. Raymond Pilet assembled a force with the promise of easy pickings and headed into the fertile Jabal as-Summaq plateau. After initial success, the expedition ended in disaster, all but annihilated in an ill-advised assault on the town of Maarrat an-Numan in July 1098.[50]

The First Crusade was in freefall. What the expedition needed now was strong and decisive leadership but instead dissent started to swell, at first in private and then in public. Rumours began to spread that the rank-and-file participants might take matters into their own hands and tear down the walls of Antioch to bring the leaders to their senses. It is hard to think of a more dramatic course of action than to destroy the prize that had been won at such great cost. But their anger was understandable: disagreement over Antioch was the cause of the problems.[51]

To overcome the impasse, the Crusaders turned to Emperor Alexios. As we have seen, when Kerbogha approached Antioch, a delegation led by Stephen of Blois had been sent to the emperor begging him to march at the head of the imperial army to relieve the western force. Stephen found Alexios at Philomelion and asked for a private meeting with him. His summary of how things looked could barely have been more bleak: 'I tell you truly that Antioch has been taken but the citadel has not fallen and our men are all closely besieged; I expect that by this time they have been killed by the Turks. Retreat therefore as fast as you can, in case they also catch up with you.'[52] Stephen and others reported that in all probability, Kerbogha had already arrived at the city and slaughtered the besieged knights. Antioch was likely back in Turkish hands, and the Crusade at a bloody finale. This hardly encouraged the emperor to march across to the Crusaders' aid. With an agreement already reached with Kilidj Arslan in western Asia Minor following the success of the Byzantine campaign of 1097–8, he sounded the call for the imperial forces to return to Constantinople.[53]

Unaware of the emperor's decision, rumours circulated for several months after the fall of Antioch that Alexios' arrival in the east was imminent.[54] In the meantime the absence of a senior Byzantine representative created a vacuum. In the case of Nicaea and elsewhere, a Byzantine appointee – men such as Manuel Boutoumites, Peter Aliphas, Welf of Burgundy and Baldwin of Bouillon – had stepped forward to take control of the situation. There was no such figure in Antioch, and without the emperor to look to for instruction and guidance, the Crusaders were at a loss.

To break the deadlock, a second embassy was sent to Alexios, again led by a senior figure in the Crusader army, with the aim of persuading the Byzantine ruler to take control of the expedition. In the late summer of 1098, 'our leaders, Duke Godfrey, Raymond Count of Saint-Gilles, Bohemond, the Count of Normandy and the Count of Flanders and all the others sent the high-born knight Hugh the Great to the emperor at Constantinople asking him to come and take over the city and fulfil the obligations which he had undertaken towards them'.[55] Although one source suggests that Hugh of Vermandois behaved aggressively towards Alexios when he met him in Constantinople, it seems much more likely that he was placatory. But if Hugh did intimate, gently or otherwise, that unless the emperor came to Antioch to assume leadership of the expedition there would be devastating consequences, then it had little effect. Alexios would not head east.[56]

Had the emperor done so, he might well have unblocked the impasse that stymied the progress of the Crusade. He might also have avoided the hostility towards him that was quickly building up. Some weeks after the capture of Antioch, Peter Bartholomew, who had identified the location of the Holy Lance, started having more visions. This time St Andrew was telling him that the Byzantines should not take possession of Antioch, for if they did so, they would desecrate it, as they had supposedly done with Nicaea.[57] Attitudes towards Alexios and Byzantium were becoming poisonous.

In the circumstances it did not help that Adhemar of Le Puy had died of fever on 1 August 1098. The bishop had not only been the Pope's envoy during the expedition, but had gained the respect of the other leaders and the lower-ranking men with his unstinting bravery. His obvious delight at being sent seventy Turkish heads by Tancred increased his popularity.[58] The *Chanson d'Antioche*, a poetic song recording the glory of the First Crusade, also described how Adhemar shared the excitement of a crowd as it watched knights devouring the flesh of dead Turks and washing it down with wine.[59]

In the emperor's absence, the bishop might have been able to soothe tensions in the Crusader camp, as he had done at a low point during the siege when his suggestions on how to appease God's wrath had been acted upon.[60] As the Pope's representative, Le Puy was the bridge between east and west, 'ruler and shepherd' of the Crusader army, and a calming influence. Adhemar, 'beloved by God and mankind, flawless in the estimation of all', died at precisely the wrong moment.[61]

On 11 September 1098 a letter was sent to Pope Urban II in the names of the expedition's senior figures, including Bohemond, Raymond of Toulouse, Godfrey of Bouillon, Robert of Flanders and Robert of Normandy. While the Turks and the pagans had been subdued, the letter reported, it had been impossible to overcome the heretics: Armenians, Jacobites, Syrians – and also the Greeks.[62]

This was a key moment in the Crusade. Giving up on the emperor, the western leaders turned to the Pope for leadership, imploring him to join them in the east. 'In this way, you will complete the expedition of Jesus Christ which we began and you preached. Thus you will open the gates of both Jerusalems, liberate the Sepulchre of the Lord and exalt the Christian name over every other one. If you do come to us to complete with us the expedition you began, the whole world will obey you . . . Amen.'[63]

In its final paragraph, the letter went even further: the emperor was not only rebuked for not having done enough to help the expedition, he was also accused of having actively sought to harm the campaign. 'You should separate [us]', the leaders wrote, 'from the unjust emperor who has never fulfilled the many promises he has made us. In fact, he has hindered and harmed us in every way at his disposal.'[64] The Pope, however, was no more willing than Alexios to join the expedition. He instead sent a high-ranking cleric, Daimbert of Pisa, to replace Adhemar.

In the meantime, little progress was made at Antioch. In the months that followed the capture of the city, Bohemond played a truculent game, trying to provoke Raymond wherever possible in order to get his own way. When the Count of Toulouse moved against Maarrat an-Numan, Bohemond raced to the town to prevent him from taking it and using it to secure the wider region for himself. When the town finally fell after a long and difficult siege, the Norman then brazenly occupied parts of Maarrat, refusing to hand these over to Raymond, in order to gain leverage in Antioch.

Efforts to mediate between the two Crusaders ended in failure. Meeting in the Basilica of St Peter in Antioch, Raymond solemnly repeated the oath to Alexios, stressing that the commitment could not be rescinded on a whim. In response, Bohemond produced a copy of the agreement made between the leaders before the storming of Antioch, noting that this too was binding. The Count of Toulouse again emphasised that 'we swore upon the Cross of the Lord, the crown of thorns and many holy relics that we would not hold without the consent of the emperor any city or castle in his dominion'.[65] He offered to submit to the judgement of his peers, specifically Godfrey of Bouillon, Robert of Flanders and Robert of Normandy – on the condition that Bohemond would travel on with them to Jerusalem. He was prepared to compromise, in other words, as long as the issue was resolved later.[66]

This sounded reasonable enough – but many could see both sides of the argument. The oaths had been clear and categorical; and yet it seemed that Alexios had not kept his side of the agreement. As impatience grew within the Crusader army, Bohemond realised that his best bet was to sit tight. Eventually, his intransigence paid off. At the start of 1099, Raymond of Toulouse finally gave up trying to resist Bohemond's demands and prepared to set off for Jerusalem without him.

Yet the other leaders had learnt from Bohemond, and demanded concessions from the wealthy count of Toulouse in return for continuing on their journey. As substantial payments of 10,000 solidi to Godfrey of Bouillon and Robert of Normandy, 6,000 to Robert of Flanders and 5,000 to Tancred show, they had learnt that their co-operation to make the final move to Jerusalem could have a price. The idealism that had characterised the expedition at its outset had been replaced by something altogether more pragmatic: upfront payments for marching to the Holy Land, unilateral declarations that sworn oaths no longer applied – and if not the jettisoning of spiritual incentives, then at least the demand for material benefits alongside them. The expedition had taken on a decidedly new dimension since the capture of Antioch.[67]

There were further difficulties during the journey to Jerusalem. The capture of Maarrat an-Numan over the winter of 1098–9 was followed by deprivation that was worse than even the terrible scenes at Antioch twelve months earlier. Starved and weakened and with few taboos still to break, the Crusaders were so desperate that they reportedly cut the flesh from the buttocks of dead Muslims and ate them. And so acute was the hunger that many tried to eat the human flesh even before it had been properly cooked.[68]

Local rulers controlling territory on the route to Jerusalem anxiously made truces with the western army as it approached, having heard how the Crusaders had dealt with the armies of Duqaq, Ridwan and Kerbogha, and after receiving gory reports about their cruelty in places like Maarrat where captives' stomachs were sliced open in the belief that they had swallowed gold coins to keep them hidden. The emirs of Shaizar, Homs, Jabala and Tripoli, for example, sent lavish gifts to Raymond of Toulouse to win his goodwill and prevent attacks on their towns.[69]

Progress slowed dramatically when the army reached Arqa, and subjected the town to a siege that dragged on for three months. By this time, Alexios had learnt of the Crusaders' survival at Antioch – and of the change in attitude towards him. He dispatched ambassadors to complain about the flagrant violations of the oaths when he found out about their refusal to restore Antioch and other former Byzantine possessions to him. The envoys now advised the western leaders that the emperor would join the expedition on 24 June 1099 and that the Crusaders should therefore hold position and wait for him. This caused debate within the western army, with a divide quickly emerging between those who welcomed the arrival of Alexios and of reinforcements, and those who were no longer willing to co-operate with the Byzantines. Even the promise of substantial gifts, suggested by the ambassadors, had little impact on those who had now sided against the emperor.[70]

It may be that the prospect of Alexios joining the expedition spurred the decision to move on Jerusalem in order to strengthen their position, for at the start of May 1099, the Crusaders abandoned the siege of Arqa and marched at full speed on Jerusalem. After eighteen months, during which the scope, aims and nature of the expedition had changed out of all recognition, the purpose of the Crusade suddenly returned.

11

The Crusade Unravels

After all they had been through – disease and deprivation at Antioch, countless casualties sustained in combat and along the long march, and conditions so bad that the battle-hardened had turned to cannibalism – it was not surprising that the arrival of the Crusader force at Jerusalem on 7 June 1099 was accompanied by rejoicing and exultation. One chronicler wrote of tears of happiness flowing when the army reached its destination.[1]

Yet there was still much to be done. Jerusalem was heavily fortified, with impressive walls and defences and a garrison that had been preparing for months for the arrival of the western knights. As the Crusaders met in council and pondered how to storm the city, Tancred, suffering from an acute case of dysentery, made for a nearby cave; there he found a pile of equipment for building siege engines, remnants of past attempts to take the city. It was another moment of great good fortune for the Crusaders.[2] Useful materials were gathered locally before news was received that six Genoese boats had put in at Jaffa, carrying supplies and provisions, as well as ropes, hammers, nails, axes and hatchets.[3] Even though bringing the materials back to camp involved a fifty-mile round trip across hostile terrain, this was a godsend that made the difference between success and failure of the entire expedition.[4]

In spite of the many successes and the fearsome reputation which preceded the western knights, Jerusalem's garrison had good reason to think that they could repel the attacks. Like Antioch, the city enjoyed the protection of formidable defences. Moreover, while it was still substantial, the attacking army had decreased dramatically in size over the course of the previous two years, losing men in battle as well as to illness and disease. It has been estimated that by the time it reached Jerusalem, the western army had been reduced to a third of its original strength.[5] The inhabitants of the Holy City could also take heart from the difficult conditions the Crusaders were experiencing in front of the city walls. This time the primary problem was not food. As Fulcher of Chartres reported: 'Our men did not suffer from lack of bread or meat. Yet because the area was dry, unwatered and without streams, our men as well as our beasts suffered for lack of water to drink.'[6]

All the wells outside Jerusalem had been blocked up or poisoned in anticipation of the imminent assault, with the result that a round trip of twelve miles was needed to fetch fresh water from the nearest source. Ox and buffalo hides were stitched together to try to transport it safely and in large volume. Those brave enough to go and find water ran the risk of ambush. And when they returned to camp, the returning water-bearers often met with furious argument, so acute was the thirst, so strong the heat. Some saw the chance to make money from such ventures, feeling they deserved more than the thanks and appreciation of their comrades, and insisted on payment for water. As a result, water was not shared out equally but sold at prices that were nothing short of extortionate. For those able or willing to pay, it was not always good value for money: at times the water was dark and muddy, and on occasion even contained leeches. Filthy water led to disease; eyewitnesses described how drinking unclean water caused severe swelling of the throat and stomach, and often led to an agonising death.[7]

There were few alternatives for those who could not afford to buy from their unscrupulous peers. One was the Pool of Siloam, just outside the walls of Jerusalem; fed by a natural spring and safe to drink, water could be found there at least some of the time. But getting to the pool was another matter: as it was located close to the city's battlements, a well-judged shot from the walls could prove lethal.[8] There was also the risk of ambush; some Crusaders who ventured there were attacked and killed, while others were captured never to be heard of again.[9]

The inhabitants of Jerusalem were also reassured by messages they received from the powerful vizier of Cairo, al-Afdal, telling them that he was coming to their rescue and was a mere fifteen days away. The capture of one of his messengers, who revealed this information under torture, spread alarm among the Crusaders. Their concerns were heightened after the interception of a carrier pigeon brought down by a hawker. Describing the western knights as foolhardy, headstrong and disorderly, the note it was carrying urged the Muslim governors of Acre and Caeserea to attack the Crusaders, stressing that if they did so, they would find easy pickings.[10]

The westerners' response was to accelerate plans to capture the city. On 8 July 1099 they held a solemn procession with knights bearing crosses, walking barefoot round the walls of Jerusalem, imploring God for help and mercy. The inhabitants of the city used the spectacle to indulge in target practice, shooting arrows at the men marching around the city. It seemed to them that they had little to fear from the bedraggled and beleaguered western army.[11]

The Crusaders were not relying on divine inspiration alone for their success, however. Two assault towers were built at speed, and as soon as they were ready, they were set up against the walls, one to the south of the city, the other close to the imposing Quadrangular Tower defending the western side of Jerusalem. The construction and positioning was watched closely by the city's garrison, who reinforced defences and deployed resources accordingly.[12]

In the searing heat of July, the Crusaders now pulled off a tactically brilliant move that brought them a decisive advantage. The siege tower that had been assembled by the Quadrangular Tower was dismantled during the night of 9 July and re-erected to the north of the city where weaker defences had been identified and the ground was flat.[13] The attack on Jerusalem now began in earnest. A defensive ditch was quickly filled in and a tranche of the outer wall dismantled. Stone-throwing devices provided vital cover, as did Crusade archers, raining arrows on to the defenders. A huge battering ram was used to make a breach in the defences that was large enough for the siege tower to be brought up against the main wall. Rather than pull the ram back out of the way, and lose precious time, it was then set on fire. As the tower was hauled into position under furious enemy fire, sappers set about mining the wall from below. Others climbed up to the top of the tower, fighting the defenders manning the wall, and before long gaining a position on the battlements.[14] Jerusalem was suddenly teetering.

While there was rapid progress on the defences to the north of the city, concerted efforts were being made simultaneously on a southern section of the walls. Another siege tower, well built and robust, had been pushed against the battlements. Its value, however, proved to lie less in its operational efficiency than in the fact that it drew enemy fire and distracted attention from the assault elsewhere. The defenders had concluded that they were more vulnerable to attack from the south of the city and concentrated resources there as a result: nine of the fifteen projectile devices in Jerusalem were positioned to protect the southern approach. Other contraptions that flung fireballs of fat, resin, pitch and hair into the Christian army were also concentrated in this part of the city. The defence of the southern section was successful, for the siege tower was set ablaze and substantial casualties were sustained by the westerners. The counter-attack was so well directed that the Crusaders, led by Raymond of Toulouse, contemplated withdrawal. It was only when news was received that the attack was progressing well elsewhere that efforts were renewed. As the siege engine to the south burned and missiles, oil and arrows rained on the western knights, reports came through that the Crusaders had breached the northern wall and were streaming into the city.

Resistance within Jerusalem collapsed immediately. The town's commander, Iftikhar ad-Dawla, looked to his own safety and cut a deal with the western leaders, handing control of the Holy City over in return for safe transit to the citadel, where he planned to hold out until the vizier of Cairo's forces arrived. The agreement that he, his wives and selected others would be able to leave the city unharmed was respected by the Crusaders.[15] The Muslim commander must nevertheless have worried; the governor of Maarrat an-Numan had made a similar agreement with Bohemond in the spring of 1099, only to be butchered as he left the town.[16]

The city of Jerusalem fell to the Crusaders on 15 July 1099. The Latin sources leave little to the imagination in their description of the behaviour of the westerners as they poured into the city: 'Some of the pagans were mercifully beheaded, others pierced by arrows from the towers, and yet others, tortured for a long time, were burned to death in searing flames. Piles of heads, hands and feet lay in the homes and streets, and men and knights were running to and fro over corpses.'[17]

The slaughter was on a scale which shocked even the most sanguine of eyewitnesses: 'Almost the whole city was filled with their dead bodies so the survivors dragged the dead ones out in front of the gates and piled them up in mounds as big as houses outside the city gates. No one has ever heard of such a slaughter of pagans, for they were burned on pyres like pyramids and no one save God knows how many of them there are.'[18]

Another author, not present at the time, concurred about the horror of the attack. 'If you had been there, your feet would have been stained to the ankles in the blood of the slain. What shall I say? None of them were left alive. Neither women nor children were spared.'[19] The accounts of the sack of Jerusalem were dramatic and bleak. But the portentous language and imagery of many of the victors' accounts were also deliberate – with the Book of Revelation providing a specific reference point to underline the significance of the Christian success.[20]

Nevertheless, other sources reveal something of the scenes that accompanied the capture of the city. One horrified Muslim writer claimed that 70,000 were murdered in the al-Aqsa mosque alone, including imams, scholars and righteous men.[21] Jews too were massacred as cries of vengeance for Christ's crucifixion hung thick in the air. The Crusaders seemed not in the mood to celebrate so much as to settle scores.[22]

Some visited the Holy Sepulchre to thank God for having delivered them finally to their destination. But for many, there were other priorities. The appetite for loot seemed inexhaustible. The Crusaders had heard rumours that Muslims had swallowed their most precious belongings to prevent them from being looted. 'How astonishing it would have seemed to you', Fulcher of Chartres reported, 'to see our squires and footmen, after they had discovered the trickery of the Saracens, split open the bellies of those they had just slain in order to extract from their intestines the bezants which the Saracens had gulped down their loathsome throats while alive! For the same reason, a few days later, our men made a great heap of corpses and burned them to ashes in order to find more easily the above-mentioned gold.'[23]

Those who had entered Jerusalem seized whatever property they wished; many Crusaders of previously limited means suddenly occupied houses in the most important city in the Christian world.[24] Eventually, after two days of bloodshed and chaos, the expedition's leaders decided to clear corpses from the streets to prevent the spread of disease. And as the bloodlust subsided, the Crusaders became more restrained in their dealings with the city's inhabitants. One Jewish commentator even preferred the Crusaders to the previous Muslim overlords – at least they were given food and drink by their new masters.[25]

Jerusalem was finally restored to Christian hands. It was the culmination of a journey of almost unimaginable ambition, of unprecedented scale and organisation that had seen tens of thousands of men cross Europe and Asia Minor campaigning against all the odds and in astonishingly hostile conditions. The logistics of keeping a substantial force supplied with food and water while maintaining order and discipline had been highly challenging. In terrain that was more gruelling and hotter than these men had experienced before, the Crusaders had attacked many well-defended forts, towns and cities. There was no mistaking the achievement – three of the biggest cities in the eastern Mediterranean, cornerstones of Christianity, had been conquered in the space of two years: Nicaea, Antioch and Jerusalem.

It was the third and last that was the most important to those who had left western Europe in 1096. The capture of Jerusalem was an extraordinary feat, a testimony to the determination, skill and tenacity of the Crusaders. All had endured hardship, tension and fear; many had not made it. It was a time for celebration.

'With the fall of the city it was rewarding to see the worship of the pilgrims at the Holy Sepulchre, the clapping of hands, the rejoicing and singing of a new song to the Lord', said Raymond of Aguilers, who was among those present at the fall of the city. 'Their souls offered to the victorious and triumphant God prayers of praise which they could not explain in words. A new day, new gladness, new and everlasting happiness, and then fulfilment of our toil and love brought forth new words and song for all. This day, which I affirm will be celebrated in centuries to come, changed our grief and struggles into gladness and rejoicing. I further state that this day ended all paganism, confirmed Christianity and restored our faith. "This is the day which the Lord has made; we shall rejoice and be glad in it", and deservedly because on this day, God shone upon us and blessed us.'[26]

In the aftermath of the capture of Jerusalem, the Crusaders were faced with difficult decisions. How should the city be governed; how should they engage and interact with the local population; what reliance, if any, would they have on Byzantium and the emperor Alexios;

how would the city and its new masters be supplied; what opposition were they going to face in future? Steps had to be taken as it dawned on the westerners that they would have to try to ensure that the capture of the city was not a transient success, but the basis of permanent Christian rule.

There was not much time for debate. Jerusalem and the surrounding region needed to be secured quickly, for even as the city was being looted, news came of a huge army bearing down on them from Cairo. As a first move, a week after taking the city, the Crusade's leaders met and proposed to elect the richest, worthiest and most devout of them as monarch. The establishment of royal government was of course partly a replication of a political system the knights were most familiar with. But there was also a deliberate purpose behind vesting authority in one individual: to avoid the fragmentation and indecision that had plagued the expedition after the capture of Antioch. Raymond of Toulouse was the obvious choice for this role. Yet against the expectations of the Crusaders, Raymond refused; his devout response was that the royal title was suitable only for the Son of God, at least in this most holy of cities. This piety was all very well, but the Crusaders recognised the need for authoritative leadership. If Raymond was not prepared to step up, who else might be suitable to take the role?

Godfrey of Bouillon had also performed well during the Crusade; he had been diligent and reliable throughout, and perhaps most importantly, he had not been divisive. His argument with the emperor in Constantinople about taking the oath showed that he was prepared to stand his ground when necessary, and his apparent intention to remain in the Holy Land after the expedition also counted strongly in his favour. Godfrey did not need to be asked twice. Sensitive, however, to Raymond's objections to the royal title of king, he was shrewd enough to find a way to get round the issue. On 22 July 1099, Godfrey was named as Advocate of the Holy Sepulchre. It was up to him to turn the western conquerors into settlers.

While the capture of Jerusalem reverberated around Europe, its local impact was no less profound. The city had been home to Muslims, Jews and indeed Christians for centuries, producing and exporting olive oil, fragrances, marble and glass around the Mediterranean. It was an important pilgrimage centre for Islam as well; according to one eleventh-century visitor, many thousands of Muslim pilgrims came to Jerusalem as it was a much easier destination for them to reach than Mecca.[27]

The Christian conquest dramatically altered the social, ethnic and economic structure of the city. Muslims fled Jerusalem and other towns and locations in Palestine and left behind everything that they could not carry.[28] As a result, the production of oils, ceramics, fruit preserves and other goods for which this region was famous came to a standstill. Yet in addition to resuming economic production, there was also the need to establish new links to replace the web of largely Muslim networks that dominated trade to and from the Levant. Genoese and Venetian merchants were only too willing to step in and negotiated highly favourable terms for themselves. In return for supplying the new Crusader colonies, the Italian city-states were granted quarters and extensive properties in the main cities on the eastern seaboard of the Mediterranean, notably Antioch, Jerusalem and eventually Tyre, the main port for the Holy City.[29]

The first priority, however, was to secure lasting control of the Holy City. The Crusaders had received envoys from the Fatimids of Cairo as they made their way south in the spring of 1099 proposing an alliance against the Sunni Turks.[30] Although this was not rebuffed outright, the Fatimids had drawn their own conclusions as the Crusader force marched on Jerusalem. A very substantial army under the command of the vizier al-Afdal had already been dispatched and was on its way north by the time the Crusaders reached the Holy City, and it arrived at the beginning of August. On 10 August, the knights rode out from Jerusalem and met the enemy near Ascalon, catching the Fatimid army by surprise. In the panic that ensued, many tried to hide in the trees, only to be shot like birds by arrows or speared with the knights' lances. Yet again, the discipline of the knights brought about an unlikely victory against vastly superior numbers, scattering al-Afdal's force and driving it back within the walls of Ascalon from where the demoralised survivors soon set sail for home.[31]

Despite the success, the first stages of Crusader settlement were precarious, with Muslim forces putting almost constant pressure on the towns that had been captured in 1098-9. To try to alleviate the situation, urgent appeals for help from Europe were issued by the Crusade leadership. In the spring of 1100, Archbishop Daimbert

of Pisa, sent east by the Pope as his representative after the death of
the bishop of Le Puy, wrote to 'all the archbishops, bishops, princes
and all Catholics in the Germanic region', begging them to send
reinforcements to the Holy Land to help the Christians hold on to
the towns and territories they had taken.[32]

The appeals fell on fertile ground, with many in Europe enthralled
by news of the capture of Jerusalem and the exploits of those who
had taken part in the expedition. The fact that the heroes who had
captured the Holy City were now badly exposed inspired a new wave
of armed men to set out for Jerusalem in 1100. Contingents from
Lombardy, Burgundy, Aquitaine and Austria reached Byzantium by
the spring of the following year, together with several knights – such
as Hugh of Vermandois and Stephen of Blois – who had taken part
in the original campaign but had returned home without reaching
Jerusalem.

Determined to emulate the deeds of their peers, the new Crusaders
gathered near Nikomedia in the early summer of 1101. Ignoring the
advice of Emperor Alexios to take the most direct route across Asia
Minor, they instead headed into the heart of Turkish-held territory.
When they reached Mersivan in Paphlagonia, they were attacked by
Kilidj Arslan at the head of a massive Turkish army and all but annihilated. The few survivors, including Raymond of Toulouse, who was
escorting the fresh force to Jerusalem, returned to Constantinople.
The attempt to strengthen the Christian position in the east had been
a fiasco.[33]

The chronic vulnerability of the Crusaders in the Holy Land was
underlined by the death of Godfrey in the summer of 1100, almost a
year to the day since the fall of Jerusalem.[34] Around the same time,
Bohemond was captured on the battlefield near Melitene by a Turkish
emir.[35] This deprived the westerners of some of their senior and most
respected figures, and further weakened the Crusaders' ability to
withstand the assaults of their Muslim neighbours.

The turbulence was made worse by the ambitions of Tancred, who
quickly assumed his uncle Bohemond's mantle in Antioch, and of
Daimbert of Pisa, who had managed to have himself declared patriarch
of Jerusalem after his arrival in the east.[36] Seeing the power vacuum
that emerged after Godfrey's death and Bohemond's capture, the two
men attempted to take control of Jerusalem for themselves. This met

with opposition from an important faction within the Holy City, who sent a delegation to Baldwin in Edessa, asking him to come urgently to take his brother's place.[37]

Historians have traditionally paid little attention to the motivations for the call to Edessa, but the appeal to Baldwin was significant because it was also aimed at repairing relations with Alexios. Although the Crusaders had seen off the Muslims at Ascalon, the pressure on the new settlements was chronic. There were also severe problems with supply. The arrival of fleets from Pisa, Genoa and Venice promised the opening of new routes to the Christian east, but there was still the more significant problem of ensuring that the supply links from Cyprus and the ports of southern Asia Minor, which were in Byzantine hands, were kept open in the aftermath of the conquest of Jerusalem. Baldwin, who had performed his duties as the emperor's representative in Edessa effectively and reliably, was the obvious choice to help rebuild relations with Byzantium.

After appointing his kinsman, Baldwin of Le Bourg, to govern Edessa in his absence, Baldwin set off for Jerusalem. When he arrived, he worked tirelessly to outmanoeuvre the anti-Byzantine animosities that were rapidly rising in the city. Led by Daimbert and Tancred, this group had further antagonised the Byzantines by engineering the flight of John, patriarch of Antioch, to Constantinople in the summer of 1100 and appointing a Latin Church leader in his place.[38] It was telling that when Baldwin reached Jerusalem in November, his arrival was greeted by cheering crowds made up not only of westerners but also of Greek and Syrian Christians.[39] On Christmas Day 1100, Baldwin was crowned in Bethlehem, taking the title of king of Jerusalem; his elder brother had been buried at the entrance to the Holy Sepulchre.[40]

Baldwin was keen to dampen anti-Byzantine sentiment and make peace with the emperor but tensions simmered in the city until the summer of 1101 when the troublesome Daimbert was suspended by a papal legate, who had been sent east following heavy lobbying of the Pope by Baldwin.[41] Soon afterwards, Baldwin captured Jaffa, which provided the Crusaders with essential access to the sea. It was no coincidence that the town was placed in the hands of Odo Arpin of Bourges, a knight who was close to Alexios and was to become an important conduit for the emperor to central France in the early twelfth century: it was another positive step forward in relations with Byzantium.[42]

By the spring of the following year, the need for Byzantine support had become even more urgent. In the summer of 1102, another huge Muslim army, which had been sent north from Cairo to prise the Crusaders out of Jerusalem, inflicted a massive blow on the westerners at Ramla, crushing a force led by Baldwin that was woefully unprepared and badly outnumbered. Although the king was lucky to escape, the weakness of his position was painfully exposed; with increasingly skeletal garrisons holding on to the towns still controlled by the Crusaders and manpower dwindling drastically following setbacks on the battlefield and the lack of reinforcements, the situation looked bleak.[43]

It was imperative to rebuild bridges with Constantinople. One step was the forced deposition of the anti-Byzantine Daimbert as patriarch of Jerusalem and his replacement with Evremar, an elderly French priest, who was a more malleable character.[44] But the key step came with the dispatch of an embassy to the imperial capital with the express aim of cementing an alliance with Byzantium. Baldwin resolved to approach Alexios 'in the most humble way he could, and with mild entreaties . . . appeal to the emperor of Constantinople about the Christians' miseries'.[45] High-ranking officials were sent to the capital, along with two pet lions as gifts, to appeal for help, particularly in the supply of provisions from Cyprus and other parts of the empire. An accord was reached with Alexios, who demanded guarantees that Baldwin's ambassadors would repair the damage done to his relations with the papacy caused by the rumours about his supposed betrayals of the Crusaders. In return, he swore to 'show mercy . . . and to show honour and love to King Baldwin'. The good news was swiftly transmitted back to Jerusalem.[46]

Alexios had his own reasons for reconciling with the Crusaders. Although Bohemond was safely out of the way, held captive by Turks in eastern Anatolia, Tancred was still proving to be a thorn in the emperor's side. Using Antioch as a base, the knight had made significant inroads into newly recovered imperial territory in Cilicia, taking the town of Marash and moving against Laodikeia.[47] This threatened to destabilise the new alliance between Constantinople and Jerusalem, with the result that senior Crusaders took steps against Tancred. Raymond of Toulouse tried to relieve Laodikeia on behalf of the emperor in 1102, but without success.[48] Baldwin of Le Bourg openly declared himself to be an enemy of Tancred and set about raising money to pay Bohemond's ransom in the hope that the latter would return to Antioch to stamp his authority over his feisty nephew.[49]

Initially, this was precisely what happened. Released from captivity in 1103, Bohemond resumed control of Antioch, sidelining Tancred, establishing cordial relations with Baldwin in Edessa and taking part in joint attacks in northern Syria.[50] However, things soon started to go wrong. Bohemond responded petulantly to an embassy sent from Constantinople in late 1103 or early 1104, raising concerns about his willingness to co-operate with the agreement reached between the emperor of Byzantium and the king in Jerusalem.[51] Bohemond's relations with other leading western knights also began to deteriorate after his release, who took a dim view of his attempts to expand his territories. Things were so bad that one eyewitness wrote of the complete collapse of relations between the Crusaders at this time.[52]

Matters took a decisive turn in the early summer of 1104 when Bohemond and Tancred commanded a force from Antioch in support of an attack, led by Baldwin of Le Bourg and a contingent from Edessa, on the town of Harran in south-eastern Asia Minor. When the westerners were comprehensively routed and Baldwin was taken captive, Bohemond and Tancred merely looked on from a safe distance before withdrawing – at least according to the Muslim sources.[53]

The defeat at Harran was a major setback for the Crusaders. The Christians were disheartened by their loss, reported one chronicler in nearby Damascus, their resolve shaken by the Muslim victory. It was a huge boost to the morale of the latter, who took this as a sign that fortunes were finally reversing.[54] That reversal had a wider impact, however, for it seems to have profoundly destabilised the delicate balance of power in the Latin settlements in the Holy Land and their relations with Byzantium. Part of the problem was that following Baldwin's capture and that of other senior officers who had been stationed with him in Edessa, Tancred moved north and took possession of the town. Although the inhabitants of Edessa do not appear to have been unduly discomfited by this, his arrival would not have been welcomed by Alexios – even though he had himself taken advantage of the chaos finally to restore imperial authority in Cilicia and Laodikeia.[55]

A more serious problem, however, came from Bohemond's response to the defeat at Harran. The Norman seems to have realised that with Antioch secure, Edessa under the control of his nephew, Baldwin out of the way in captivity and the Christian hold on Jerusalem looking precarious, an unmissable opportunity had opened up for Bohemond to make himself master of the Crusader states in their entirety. He therefore refused to pay a ransom for Baldwin of Le Bourg when approached by his captors, and instead launched another assault on Laodikeia, though this was unsuccessful.[56] In the autumn of 1104, he gathered his retinue in the Basilica of St Peter in Antioch. 'We have irritated the two richest powers in the world', he said; however, there were not enough men in the east to continue to hold out against Byzantium and Persia. 'We must search for help from the men across the sea. The people of the Gauls must be roused. Their bravery will arouse us, or nothing will.' Bohemond would head for Europe and raise an army of his own.[57] His eye was on Jerusalem and Constantinople – and possibly both.

According to Anna Komnene, Bohemond was so convinced that the emperor would take revenge for his treachery during the Crusade that he travelled home in secret. He even spread reports that he had died and had a coffin designed which purported to be carrying his corpse. As his ship passed through imperial waters, he lay in the sarcophagus alongside a dead chicken whose rotting carcass lent the coffin a powerful and unmistakable smell of death.[58]

As soon as he made land in Italy, Bohemond began gathering support for a new military expedition, lighting the same tinder that Urban had so skilfully ignited in the mid-1090s. On that occasion, the purpose of the terrible descriptions of the dangers in the east, the ravagings of the Turks and the plight of the Eastern Church, had been to help Byzantium. Now, the aim was to destroy it.

12

The Consequences of the First Crusade

The participants in the expedition to Jerusalem were feted when they returned home. News of their deeds was met with wild celebration. Songs about the Crusaders' successes and the capture of Jerusalem were composed in central France, forming the basis of the epic song cycles of the First Crusade, such as the *Chanson d'Antioche* and the *Chanson de Jerusalem*.[1] The exploits of the Crusaders were also commemorated in a rash of new religious endowments and foundations in western Europe made by those who had returned from Jerusalem. Robert of Flanders refounded a monastery close to Bruges, dedicating it to St Andrew in thanks for the saint's help at Antioch in 1098 and his role in finding the Holy Lance.[2] Crusaders brought countless relics with them back from Jerusalem, physical evidence not just of the success of the campaign, but of a new direct link between the churches and monasteries of Europe and the Holy Land.[3]

The returning Crusaders maximised the political capital gained from their exploits. Fulk V of Anjou, Robert of Flanders and Rainold of Château-Gontier were just three of those who adopted the epithet 'Jerosolimitanus' when signing acts and charters after their return from the Holy City.[4] Others sought to benefit vicariously from the kudos of the returning knights. In the first years of the new century, Philip I of France married off four of his children to prominent Crusaders or to the daughters of leading figures who had fought their way to Jerusalem. His heir, the future Louis VI, was married to the daughter of Guy of Rochefort, who took part and evidently did well in the expedition of 1101;[5] another of the king's sons, Philip, Count of Mantes, married the daughter of Guy of Trousseau – whose career in the east was rather undistinguished, to put it mildly.[6]

Not everyone had done well from the expedition. Stephen of Blois and Hugh of Vermandois had both left the western force to convey news to the emperor Alexios before and after the capture of Antioch respectively; neither rejoined the Crusader army, choosing instead to head home. In order to fulfil their vows to reach Jerusalem, both men set off again, taking part in the ill-fated campaign of 1101, yet they both died without reaching their destination. While Hugh was celebrated as an excellent soldier who died a martyr,[7] Stephen of Blois was lampooned in the popular songs about the Crusade, held up as a traitor and a buffoon.[8]

Many Crusaders did not make it home. Although it is difficult to assess the numbers of casualties during the expedition, it is clear that a substantial proportion of those who set out died on the way to Jerusalem, whether victims of disease or killed in battle; including deserters, perhaps as many as three-quarters never made it to the final destination.[9] For those left behind, not knowing the fate of their loved ones proved a heavy burden. The wife of Baldwin of Hainault, for example, was devastated to hear that her husband had disappeared after being sent to the emperor together with Hugh of Vermandois in 1098. While there were reports that he had been killed, there was also news that he had been captured and was alive. Having exhausted all avenues of investigation and refusing to give up hope, Ida set out for the Holy Land herself to look for her husband. This was just one of many stories of loss during that time.[10]

Of those who did return, it was Bohemond who stood out above all. His exploits during the Crusade, in particular his courage in battle, marked him out as the idol of the campaign. Reports of his bravery and resolve when facing the armies of Kilidj Arslan, Duqaq, Ridwan and Kerbogha had made him a legend before he even reached the shores of Italy. There were many exotic stories about his exploits in the aftermath of the fall of Antioch and Jerusalem – his captivity at the hands of the Danishmenids and his secret communications with his fellow Crusaders from prison; his wooing of his captor's daughter to secure his own release;[11] or the tale that the Turks referred to him as the 'little god of the Christians'.[12]

The cult that was built up around Bohemond and his adventures immediately after the Crusade owed much to the wide circulation of the *Gesta Francorum et aliorum Hierosolimitanorum* – 'The deeds of the Franks and the others who reached Jerusalem'. Ostensibly written by a member of the expedition from southern Italy who travelled east in 1096 before joining the contingent of Raymond of Toulouse at Antioch, it became wildly popular in the early twelfth century. Its central character was Bohemond.[13]

By the time that the Norman arrived back in Europe at the end of 1105, he was not just a member of the successful expedition; he was its undisputed hero. He was more prominent than any of the other leaders, his exploits commemorated in more detail and with greater resonance than those of his peers. There was some irony in the fact that Bohemond had not been present at the fall of Jerusalem, refusing to move from Antioch for fear of losing control of the city. Indeed, he had only completed his Crusade vow to reach Jerusalem in the winter of 1099, making sure that he travelled south with Baldwin of Bouillon to prevent Alexios' principal client making a move on Antioch in his absence.[14] But this did nothing to dim his star.

On his arrival in Italy, Bohemond was received by Urban's successor, Pope Paschal II. In a letter to the Pope he referred to himself as 'prince of Antioch', using this high title regularly after his return home.[15] Still unmarried, Bohemond was seen as the best catch in Europe, the epitome of the early medieval knight: handsome, brave, adventurous and selfless.

Eligible heiresses were soon being lined up for him to choose from. One who should not have been included was Constance of France, daughter of King Philip I, who was already engaged to Hugh of Troyes, Count of Champagne. Yet such was Bohemond's cachet that Constance speedily abandoned her fiancé, who was promptly declared to have been an unsuitable match – though what he had done to deserve such a slur was unclear.[16] Having not taken part in the exped-ition himself, Constance's father was more than happy to bask in the reflected glory of the famed Crusader and eagerly gave his blessing to the match.

Bohemond did not need to think twice about marrying the most powerful woman of her generation, whose grandparents included the king of France, a princess of Kiev, and the counts of Holland and of Saxony. In the spring of 1106, a lavish ceremony took place in Chartres cathedral, attended by the great and the good of France, including men who had fought alongside Bohemond in Asia Minor and Syria – and many more who wished they had.[17]

Bohemond was becoming unstoppable. Before the wedding, he had begun recruiting men for his new expedition to the east. He obtained a papal blessing for his campaign, and was given the banner of St Peter to carry into battle as well as a legate to help gather further support.[18] According to one author, the Pope was prompted to give his backing to Bohemond's campaign against Byzantium after hearing what a disaffected legate to the east had to say about Alexios.[19] More plausible, however, is that Paschal II did not sanction an all-out assault on the Byzantine Empire at all, but what seemed to be a major initiative to support the Holy Land – at least to start with. The Pope does not appear to have harboured animosity towards the Greek church, to Byzantium or to Alexios, and the assistance he provided should be seen in this light.[20]

Bohemond's ambitions, conversely, were unambiguous as his call to arms accelerated. Travelling extensively over the course of 1105–6, he promised those willing to follow him that they would take part in victories no less spectacular than those at Nicaea, Antioch and Jerusalem. His first targets: Dyrrakhion and then Constantinople.[21] With his new royal connections to help him, he gathered a substantial force in southern Italy in 1107 and prepared to launch his attack on Byzantium's western flank.

Men flocked to join Bohemond from all four corners of the world, wrote Orderic Vitalis, eager not only to deprive Alexios of his empire but to kill him too.[22] Bohemond was an effective propagandist against Alexios, regaling spellbound church congregations with stories of his exploits, urging his listeners to take the Cross and set out for Jerusalem – but attacking the emperor of Constantinople first.[23] In a letter sent to the Pope, Bohemond crudely underlined a long list of supposed heresies perpetrated by the Orthodox Church to justify action against fellow Christians.[24]

Yet in England Bohemond's appeals fell on stony ground. Having informed King Henry I that he wished to cross the Channel to look for support, he was bluntly told that he was not welcome. The king replied simply that it was wintertime and that the crossing would be too rough for the Norman.[25] It may be that Henry I was unwilling to share his military resources with Bohemond at a time when the king of England had extensive designs of his own, namely in Normandy. But the king might have had other reasons for refusing to let Bohemond into England. At some point in the early twelfth century, he received an embassy from Constantinople led by a certain Ulfricus who brought precious gifts from Alexios, which are likely to have included an arm of St John Chrysostom that was later housed in Abingdon. It is not inconceivable, therefore, that the emperor had been looking for allies to neutralise Bohemond's activities.[26] Certainly, there is other evidence that Alexios continued to cultivate important relationships in western Europe in the aftermath of the Crusade.[27]

Despite the enthusiasm generated by Bohemond's call to arms, his assault on Byzantium was an abject failure. Setting out in October 1107, Bohemond first moved on Epirus in the south-western Balkans, a region Alexios had already had to defend twice before during his reign. Replicating the tactics that had devastated Robert Guiscard's force in 1084–5, the emperor made alliances with Italian city-states, cutting western supply lines back to Italy and imposing an effective land blockade. The noose was then tightened remorselessly. Having set off with grandiose plans to dispose of Alexios, seize Constantinople and then march east to join up with Tancred at Antioch, Bohemond found himself ground into the dust. With his men dying from disease and hunger, he eventually had no other choice than to sue for peace. At a humiliating meeting at Diabolis (or Devol), in modern Albania, he accepted Alexios' terms, which are recorded in full in the *Alexiad*.

Bohemond was forced to recognise that he had made an agreement with the emperor when he passed through Constantinople in 1097, though he also stated that this had been violated as a result of 'certain unexpected events'. He admitted that his attack on Byzantium broke the terms of the agreement, but while he had betrayed Alexios, this was the result of temporary insanity. He stated that he had finally regained his senses.[28]

Bohemond now paid new homage: he once again formally became the liegeman not only of Alexios but also of his son and heir, the young prince John Komnenos. He was to defend their lives with honour and resolution, his promise to do so set solid 'like a statue hammered out of iron'. 'Whatever happens', he promised, 'I will not violate this; nor shall there be any reason or method, manifest or obscure, that shall make me appear to be a transgressor of the articles of this present covenant.'[29]

The treaty agreed at Diabolis went on to delineate which provinces, towns and villages belonged to the Byzantine Empire, and over which it claimed jurisdiction. The military district of Tarsos, and the whole of the district of Cilicia between the rivers Kydnos and Hermon were subject to the emperor; Laodikeia and the surrounding area was identified as Byzantine, as were Aleppo and other towns in northern Syria and in the Caucasus.[30] The purpose of listing these regions was to establish clearly which areas were subject to Alexios' authority – either de facto, or de jure. This went beyond redrawing the boundaries of land that had been subject to imperial authority before the First Crusade, for in many cases, notably in Cilicia, the Byzantine military had also had to resist and repel forces led by Bohemond and Tancred that had taken control of territories recovered from the Turks. Bohemond agreed to restore possessions to the empire, and to wage relentless war on the emperor's enemies and rivals – including his nephew Tancred – until they relinquished towns that rightfully belonged to Byzantium.[31]

The question of Antioch, the jewel of the Byzantine east, was finally resolved, with Bohemond agreeing to cede it to the empire. The Norman was to retain a life interest in the city, holding it as an imperial governor on behalf of Alexios until his death, whereupon it would pass 'to the empire of New Rome, the Queen of Cities, Constantinople'. However, the emperor retained the right to claim it before this point, should Bohemond fall short in any way of his obligations as 'servant and liegeman'.[32] It was also agreed that Antioch was to have an Orthodox patriarch and that the city would follow the Greek rite; this was to be binding in perpetuity.[33] This reversed the appointment of a western cleric following the expulsion of John the Oxite in 1100, when Bohemond had set about cementing his control of the city.[34]

While Tancred continued to cause trouble in the east – he had yet again moved into Cilicia when Byzantine troops were recalled from the region in 1107 – Alexios rewarded Bohemond with the high title of sebastos and a fat annual salary, and appointed him formally as Antioch's governor. This was not a concession; Alexios knew that his best chance of regaining Antioch lay in Bohemond doing so as his agent.[35]

All these terms were accepted by the Norman, who gave a further, sweeping commitment to the emperor: 'I will abide by all the undertakings I have given . . . and in no way whatsoever will I breach my oath, break my promises or evade my responsibilities. In thought and deed, I, and all my men, will do everything in my power to help and honour the empire of the Romans.'[36] The treaty was concluded with Bohemond swearing to honour the terms in the name of Christ, while placing his hand on the Holy Gospels and in the presence of some of the most important relics in Christendom. These included the Cross of Christ, the crown of thorns and, significantly, the spear that pierced Jesus on the Cross – a tacit admission that the lance recovered so conveniently in Antioch in 1098 was a fake.[37]

This was a crushing victory for Alexios. The legitimacy of his claims had been established incontrovertibly. But it was Antioch, 'the jewel of Asia Minor', that provided the crowning glory. For the knights of the First Crusade, the culmination of the expedition came with the capture of Jerusalem in 1099. For Emperor Alexios, it came nine years later with the Treaty of Diabolis. The Crusader army had helped Byzantium to recover Nicaea and the coast of Asia Minor. But the agreement reached with Bohemond marked the point at which the emperor's appeals for help from the west were finally resolved – it vindicated his policies, as well as his reign.

In practice, however, Alexios' success looked less assured. His reputation in the west had been severely damaged in the wake of the expedition to Jerusalem. Doubtless there were many Crusaders who still respected the emperor – and the lavish reception given to Robert of Flanders and Robert of Normandy as they passed through Constantinople on their way home from Jerusalem was designed to leave them with a favourable impression of Byzantium.[38] Alexios had also taken care to ransom knights captured by the Muslims, and to treat survivors of the doomed 1101 expedition with great generosity.[39] However, the two earliest written accounts of the Crusade both painted an overwhelmingly negative picture of the emperor.

The *Gesta Francorum* was particularly poisonous in its portrayal of Alexios. The emperor, wrote its author, rejoiced when he learnt that Peter the Hermit and his force had been utterly smashed at Xerigordos.[40] He was wretched and wicked, ordering his men to kill Crusaders whenever they had the chance.[41] Alexios was 'troubled in mind and fairly seething with rage, and planned how to entrap these Christian knights by cunning and fraud; but by God's grace, neither he nor his men found place or time to harm them'.[42] The emperor was a fool and a knave. At Nicaea, he ensured that Turks were spared and brought to Constantinople so they could be briefed and sent back to fight against the western knights. At every step of the way, Alexios had sought to hinder the expedition to Jerusalem.[43]

The account of Raymond of Aguilers, who travelled as part of the contingent of Raymond of Toulouse, also did not spare the emperor. Alexios, he wrote, bribed agents to deliver rosy reports about Constantinople as the army marched towards the capital on their way east; his words of friendship were without meaning or substance.[44] In fact, the emperor was an out-and-out liar, declared Raymond. He made promises at Nicaea about founding a hospice for needy Franks and giving lavish rewards to the Crusaders. 'The Franks trusted these sincere words and prepared for surrender. But once in possession of Nicaea, Alexios afforded the army such an example of gratitude that as long as he might live, people would ever revile him and call him a traitor.'[45] Central to this was the sense that the emperor had sent the Crusaders into Asia Minor and towards Antioch; according to Raymond, Alexios had knowingly sent the westerners to their doom.[46]

These savage attacks on Alexios need to be understood in the context of the oaths that the emperor had demanded in Constantinople in 1096–7, and serve to explain why the Crusaders kept possession of cities like Antioch that should have reverted to Byzantium. The first historians of the Crusade produced such fiercely negative portrayals of the emperor to justify Bohemond's decision to turn his back on the solemn commitments given to Alexios. This was because the emperor had not fulfilled his promises: Alexios' betrayals – not the Crusaders' – rendered the oaths void. According to the *Gesta Francorum*, the emperor swore to protect the knights and to keep them supplied by land and sea; Alexios also promised to accompany the expedition, bringing soldiers and a fleet with him.[47] His failure to appear at Antioch during or after the siege meant that the oaths sworn by the Crusaders were no longer valid.[48]

The argument was forcefully made, but the accusations were dubious. Alexios had kept the Crusaders adequately supplied on their way to Constantinople and oversaw an effective system of provisioning at Kibotos and during the assault on Nicaea. The westerners crossed Asia Minor without complaint about inadequate supplies, which suggests that provisioning had been carefully planned and well executed. When the army arrived at Antioch in the autumn of 1098, measures had been put in place by the Byzantines to support a lengthy siege; this was why Anselm of Ribemont could write home reporting that stocks of corn, wine, oil and other goods were larger than could be imagined.[49]

That supplies ran short in the winter of 1097–8 was unfortunate; but it was hardly surprising given how hard it was to gather foodstuffs during the winter, and the difficulty of getting provisions through to Antioch across challenging terrain. And in any event, it was not clear how much Alexios was to blame for the hardship that ensued. In a letter Stephen of Blois wrote to his wife from Antioch in March 1098 – at a time when conditions in the Crusader camp were at their worst – he said nothing about the emperor's failings.[50]

On the contrary, provisions clearly continued to reach the Crusaders from Cyprus and Laodikeia, even after Tatikios' departure from the camp. It was Alexios presumably also behind the food and other materials being sent to the westerners by local commanders in Cilicia and by the Greek monks of the Black Mountain monastery in northern Syria, an institution that historically had close connections with Constantinople.[51] And as one Crusade historian freely admits, Alexios' heralds continued to urge the local population to supply the Crusaders with grain by land and sea.[52] After Antioch fell, Byzantine ships carried on bringing supplies to the western armies, attempting to do so, for instance, during the siege of Arqa in 1099.[53]

Alexios certainly thought that he kept his part of the bargain in supporting the knights on the expedition. In a reply to a letter by the abbot of Montecassino, sent in June 1098 – just before he received reports of how dire the situation at Antioch had become – the emperor wrote: 'I implore you earnestly to provide aid to the army of the Franks, your most thoughtful letter states. Let your Venerable Holiness be assured on that score, for my empire has been spread over them and will assist and advise them on all matters; indeed I have already helped them to the best of my ability, not as a friend or a relative, but as a father . . . By God's grace, they continue to prosper in the service in which they have begun, and they will continue to prosper as long as good purpose leads them on.'[54]

There is other evidence that the Crusaders were satisfied with their progress around this time. In his letter to Manasses, archbishop of Rheims, in February 1098, Anselm of Ribemont made light of the problems facing the expedition, concentrating instead on the fact that the passage across Asia Minor up to Antioch had met with no obstacles.

Two hundred towns and fortress had been recovered by the Christians, which Anselm thought to be a considerable achievement. 'Let the Mother Church of the west', he concluded, 'rejoice that she has produced men capable of bringing such a glorious reputation to her and such marvellous aid to the Eastern Church.'[55] In short, there were many in the Crusader army who felt that the expedition progressed successfully in the first part of 1098, and had no grievance or complaint with Alexios. Indeed, the reluctance of the other Crusader leaders to lend support to Bohemond as he agitated for control of Antioch shows that they did not consider the emperor to have breached his obligations.

Quite the opposite, in fact: messages were sent repeatedly from Antioch to Alexios to ask for advice and direction. This was why Stephen of Blois was dispatched just before Antioch was captured; Hugh of Vermandois was sent not long afterwards. Even the hostile *Gesta Francorum* noted that the message Hugh took to Alexios was unequivocal: Godfrey of Bouillon, Raymond of Toulouse, Bohemond, Robert of Normandy, Robert of Flanders and all the other knights wanted the emperor to come and take possession of Antioch. This is clear evidence that the oaths given to the emperor were considered intact even after the city's fall.[56]

It seems it was only after the Crusaders began to argue amongst themselves that attitudes towards Alexios began to harden. By the autumn of 1098, he had become a lightning rod for criticism, a convenient cipher for the squabbles and rival ambitions amongst the Crusade leadership. In September, a letter was sent to the Pope by the most prominent knights taking part in the expedition to report on the terrible difficulties of the previous two years. Jesus Christ had delivered the Crusaders from the Turks who had attacked them from all corners, the letter explained. Nicaea had been taken and, at great cost to the western army, Antioch had also been captured. The knights now begged the Pope to join the Crusade himself, take personal control of the expedition, and finish what he had started.[57]

The letter-writers laid out a clear reason for their appeal to the Pope: Alexios had failed the Crusade. They claimed that the emperor had not just neglected to help God's soldiers, but had actively worked against them: 'he has placed whatever obstacle he could in our way'.[58] Fulcher of Chartres, who reproduced a version of this letter in his chronicle, chose not to include these final comments, feeling them to be unfair and unjustified.[59] There is no doubt that by late 1098 a concerted effort was under way to taint the emperor Alexios as the Crusade unravelled after the capture of Antioch.

The main line of attack on the Byzantine ruler now was his failure to come to the city to take control of the situation as the leading Crusaders squabbled among themselves. Hence it was the emperor, and not the western knights, who had broken the bonds made in Constantinople. But again, there was questionable substance to this claim. It was by no means clear that Alexios needed to come in person – nor indeed that his failure to do so constituted a breach of the agreement. Why could the city not be handed to one of his representatives, as had been the case at Nicaea and at many other towns in Asia Minor?

In addition, eyewitnesses to the oath-taking ceremonies in Constantinople were clear that Alexios did not give specific guarantees about joining the expedition. On the contrary, as Raymond of Aguilers set out, the emperor stated categorically in the imperial capital that he would not be able to take part in the campaign because of the variety of problems he had to contend with close to home.[60]

The Crusaders, in other words, were on shaky ground – and it seems that Raymond of Aguilers for one was aware of it. The chronicler avoided discussing the oaths altogether: 'Shall I write of the most fraudulent and abominable treachery of the emperor's counsel? Let anyone who wants to know about this find out from someone else.'[61]

As we have seen, Bohemond, keen to hold Antioch for himself, had remained impervious to the wishes of the other leaders and the rank and file who wanted to move on Jerusalem. When the Crusaders met in the Basilica of St Peter in Antioch to try to reach a compromise, Raymond of Toulouse calmly dismissed accusations that the commitments given to Alexios were void, repeating the words of the oaths that had been given to the emperor.[62] He reminded everyone of what had been said: 'We swore upon the Cross of the Lord, the crown of thorns and many holy relics that we would not hold without the consent of the emperor any city or castle in his dominion.'[63]

It is tempting to see the arguments about the oaths given to Alexios as turning exclusively on definitions of fealty and on the moral rectitude of those like Raymond, who considered themselves to be bound by their vows, and those like Bohemond, who did not. While clearly there were important legal implications to what had been agreed with

the emperor, there were also practical issues underpinning the arguments between the Crusade leaders themselves. The positioning of the
various leaders relative to each other was of course a factor in
the refusal of the Count of Toulouse to let Bohemond have free
rein to take Antioch for himself; it was not simply that the former
wanted to respect the oaths given to Alexios, but also that he did not
want to countenance one of his peers – and rivals – gaining an undue
upper hand. In that respect, the oaths given to the emperor were a
useful shield to hide behind – offering Raymond the chance to attack
Bohemond while retaining the high ground.

From the Byzantine perspective too, the practical reality of the
situation in Antioch and beyond was complex and subtle, and required
a more nuanced approach than recourse to high-level notions of what
exactly bonds of fealty meant. There can be no doubt that Alexios
knew exactly what he was doing when he insisted on commitments
being given to him in a format and manner that he knew would be
understood by the principal leaders of the Crusade. But his main
priority, at least in 1096 and early 1097, was ensuring that the passage
of the expedition was trouble-free as it passed Constantinople at a
time when the emperor's hold on power was precarious. As it
happened, the promises he extracted became very useful as time went
on, offering Alexios the opportunity to claim that he had been wronged
by individual leaders and by the Crusade as a whole.

But within this mix of accusation and counter-accusation, and what
would seem to be rather arcane arguments about agreements being
void (or otherwise), it became important for Bohemond to be able to
demonstrate simply and clearly just how he came to hold Antioch in
the face of claims from Byzantium and indeed from some Crusaders
too that he had no right to do so. It was this political imperative that
underpinned attitudes towards the emperor which circulated through
Europe at the start of the twelfth century. Thus, while some effort
was made by chroniclers writing in the early twelfth century to demon-
srate that Alexios had not fulfilled his commitments to the expedition's
leaders, a great deal more went into mounting a full-scale character
assassination of the emperor Alexios.

The real damage to the emperor's reputation was not done by the
Gesta Francorum and by the chronicle of Raymond of Aguilers, but by
a string of accounts composed around the time that Bohemond began

to recruit men for the expedition against Byzantium, after his return to Italy at the end of 1104. Histories of the Crusade written by Robert the Monk, Baldric of Dol and Guibert of Nogent in or soon after 1107 all made extensive use of the *Gesta Francorum*, faithfully repeating the negative portrayal of the emperor. The delight Alexios was purported to have felt at the massacre of the People's Crusade in 1096 was dutifully reported by all three.[64] Paraphrasing the *Gesta*, they stated coldly that the emperor did not advance to Antioch because he was a coward.[65]

Yet these authors went further than simply repeating and para-phrasing the *Gesta*, for they all elaborated on Alexios' supposed shortcomings and faults. Guibert of Nogent was especially creative. The emperor's mother, he wrote, was a sorceress with a firm command of the dark arts. Alexios, furthermore, was so iniquitous that he issued a proclamation by which families with more than one daughter had to give one girl up to be a prostitute; money raised from the sale of her services helped fund the imperial treasuries. He ordered families with more than one son to offer one up for castration. With so many young men deprived of their virility, little wonder Alexios had needed help from the west, wrote Guibert.[66]

Such outlandish charges were gleefully circulated and added to by historians writing in the twelfth century and later. One such history stated that Alexios was only able to defeat Robert Guiscard in 1085 because he told the Norman's wife that he would marry her if she poisoned her husband, which she duly did.[67] This was embroidered by others, like Roger of Hoveden, who stated that Alexios did indeed marry Sickelgaita, only to burn her alive after having her crowned as his empress.[68]

The hostility towards Alexios intensified rapidly in the early twelfth century. He was a man, said William of Malmesbury, who was 'better known for treachery and his cunning than for honest dealing'.[69] William of Tyre, writing several decades later, summed up how the emperor was seen in the Latin East. Alexios could not be trusted, wrote the archbishop; he was 'like a scorpion; for while you have nothing to fear from its face, you do well to avoid injury from its tail'.[70]

This view was perpetuated over the centuries. In the eighteenth century, Edward Gibbon, for example, followed the medieval caricature closely. 'I should compare the emperor Alexius', he wrote, 'to the jackal, who is said to follow the steps of and devour the leavings of the lion.' Even the empress Eirene, he claimed, thought little of her husband, sharing the opinions of others. After the emperor died, therefore, she insisted that an epitaph be inscribed on Alexios' tomb saying: 'You die, as you lived – an HYPOCRITE.'[71]

The reputation of the emperor Alexios has never recovered and his vilification has had a wider impact in shaping interpretations of the First Crusade. The emperor has been barely visible in accounts of the expedition to Jerusalem, particularly of its origins, because he was airbrushed from history in the wake of the disputes at Antioch. Deliberately set to one side by Latin historians at the time, Alexios has remained on the periphery ever since – merely an incidental player in the campaign.

If anything, Alexios' success at Diabolis in 1108 only served to reinforce this image, as western historians strove to undermine his claims as to what were now seen as legitimate Crusader possessions – above all Antioch. As it happened, Bohemond never returned to the city to take up his new 'appointment', which meant that imperial authority over Antioch remained notional. Envoys sent by the emperor to Tancred to enforce the terms reached at Diabolis were given short thrift; the Norman refused to accept the emperor's demands, assuring his ambassadors that he would never release his grip on Antioch even if his adversaries came at him with hands of fire.[72]

When Bohemond died in 1111 possession of Antioch should have passed to Byzantium, as set out in the treaty. But his death came at an inopportune moment for the emperor, for as long as Bohemond was alive there was hope that he would exert influence over Tancred. Now Alexios had little opportunity to make political capital out of the terms reached with Bohemond – or indeed use the resulting settlement as a corrective to the inflammatory statements made in the early Crusade chronicles.

Instead of becoming known as a traitor, Bohemond was commemorated in a quite different fashion. His popularity in the west was little affected by the last, disastrous attack on Epirus, the settlement he reached with the emperor little known outside Byzantium. In the words of Albert of Aachen, who wrote a decade after his death, he was: 'Bohemond, magnificent prince of Antioch, appointed by God'.[73] Inscriptions on the cupola of the cathedral of Canosa in southern Italy where he was buried likewise preserve a rather more positive memory of Bohemond than justified by the treaty of Diabolis:

The magnanimous prince of Syria lies under this roof;
No better man than he will be born again in the universe.
Greece was conquered four times, while the greater part of the world
Knew for a long time the genius and strength of Bohemond.
He conquered columns of thousands with a battle line of tens because
    of his virtue, as the city of Antioch knows so well.

How noble Bohemond was, say inscriptions above the bronze doors at the southern end of the church. He conquered Byzantium and protected Syria from its enemies. He could not be called a god; but he was certainly more than a normal man. Pray for the mighty Bohemond as you enter the church, it goes on, that this great soldier is happy in heaven.[74]

To say that Bohemond defeated Byzantium four times was stretching things. All three of the assaults on Epirus that the Norman took part in – in 1081–3, 1084–5 and 1107–8 – had ended in failure, while the Crusade hardly represented a victory for Bohemond over the empire – especially in the wake of his ignominious surrender at Diabolis. But the inscriptions at Canosa are by no means the only evidence of elasticity with the truth from this period. One poem produced by a monk from the Loire region in France presented Bohemond's last invasion of the empire as a great success. The hero of Antioch not only took on the emperor Alexios, who fought like a cornered boar, but scattered the imperial armies sent against him. The campaign concluded not in a crushing Byzantine victory, but quite the opposite: a peace treaty extended by Bohemond and readily agreed to by the emperor who was only too pleased to recognise the Norman's superiority. It was Alexios, according to this poem, who swore an oath to Bohemond, and not the other way round.[75] It appears that memory and reality were two different things when it came to Bohemond – and indeed to the emperor Alexios.[76]

In fact, it was not just these two leading characters whose roles and reputations were recast in the years that followed the First Crusade. Perhaps more surprisingly, so was the position of the Pope. The contribution made by Urban II was central and decisive when it came to laying the foundations for the campaign to Jerusalem. His galvanisation of the knighthood of Europe was instrumental and proved enormously effective in inspiring tens of thousands of men to take the Cross and make for the Holy Land. His role was clearly recognised by the Crusader leadership when they wrote to him from Antioch in 1098 following the fall of the city.[77]

Urban is, however, conspicuously absent from the first accounts of the Crusade. Neither the *Gesta Francorum* nor the *Historia Francorum* of Raymond of Aguilers seems to suggest that the First Crusade was conceived, inspired and put into motion by Pope Urban II. Raymond of Aguilers, who travelled alongside the Count of Toulouse, does not even mention the papacy at the start of his account of the expedition to Jerusalem. The moment that supposedly defined the expedition and changed the medieval world forever – the rousing speech at Clermont – is not referred to, directly or indirectly. Nor does the influential *Gesta Francorum* mention Clermont. Its author reports that the Pope travelled north of the Alps and encouraged men to take up arms and head east – but he is not cast as the originator of the Crusade. He simply fanned 'the great stirring of heart throughout all the Frankish lands'. According to this author, at least, he was tapping into the zeitgeist rather than shaping events.[78]

It was only in the accounts written a decade after Clermont that the role of the papacy was clearly articulated and accentuated. Robert the Monk, Baldric of Dol and Guibert of Nogent, writing several years after the capture of Jerusalem, reshaped the origins of the Crusade, casting Urban as the main protagonist, placing him firmly at the heart of the expedition. Intentionally or otherwise, he now filled the void left by the expurgation of Emperor Alexios; the central figure behind the mobilisation of western knights was cast into the shadows in the decade that followed the Crusade, and has remained there ever since.

It is not that Urban did not deserve credit for the liberation of Jerusalem, or even that his efforts to draw thousands of men to the defence of the Eastern Church did not have a monumental impact. He almost certainly did not learn of the fall of the Holy City, even though he died at the end of July 1099 just a few weeks after it had been captured: news cannot have reached him that quickly. Nor did he live to see the effect of his effort to unite the church. While reconciliation talks with the Greek church had taken place at the Council of Bari in 1098, matters did not progress quite as well as he might have hoped. But in western Europe, at least, his backing of the Crusade

proved to be a masterstroke, and had laid the basis for the transform-
ation of the papacy's role in the western world.

Urban had been elected pope in 1088 in Terracina, because he and
the other senior bishops had been expelled from Rome. In the early 1090s
his position remained precarious as he was outmanoeuvred by Clement,
the rival pope, who was backed by the powerful emperor of Germany,
Henry IV. But the success of the First Crusade decisively concluded the
competition in Urban's favour: Clement III swiftly became irrelevant.
Such was the collapse in the fortunes of the antipope that his successor
had to be chosen in secret and under the cover of nightfall following
Clement's death in the autumn of 1100 to protect his safety.

By then, Henry IV was openly talking about submitting to Urban's
successor, Paschal II.[79] The German emperor had missed out on the
First Crusade because of his enmity with the Pope; following the fall
of Jerusalem, he soon declared that he also intended to set off for the
east in a succession of solemn Masses in the winter of 1102.[80] He also
sought to mend the rift in the Western Church by writing to his
godfather Hugh, the powerful abbot of Cluny, at the start of the
following year to try to reopen discussions with Rome, as well as to
profit from the status of knights returning from Jerusalem.[81]

This did not stop the new Pope demonstrating the extent of the
authority that the Crusade had given him: by 1102, Henry was already
being accused of heresy, and there were calls for those who had come
back from Jerusalem to attack him as a result.[82] The Pope's power was
such that by the start of the following year, the German emperor
was admitting to one of the pontiff's most senior supporters that he was
to blame for the split in the church and wished for reconciliation.[83]

It was not until the Concordat of Worms in 1122 and the First
Lateran Council at the start of the following year that the investiture
crisis – the name given to the dispute between the papacy and the
German emperors – was finally brought to a close. While it was
up to the second generation of chroniclers of the expedition to
Jerusalem to restore Pope Urban II to his central position in the
narrative, there could be little doubt that the First Crusade had been
a triumph for the popes of Rome.

In fact, for the man who had triggered Urban's call to arms, Alexios
I Komnenos, the expedition was also an astonishing success. The
Crusade had brought an almost epic reversal in the empire's fortunes.

In the spring of 1095, Byzantium was in a perilous condition, forced to confront the total failure of its policy in Asia Minor, and bereft of a foothold from which to carve out the recovery of the subcontinent. To the north of the capital, things were little better, with Serbs and Cuman nomads stretching already depleted military resources to the limit. Constantinople all but collapsed under the pressure, with a full-scale mutiny threatening to bring about the emperor's deposition and murder.

Twelve years later, things could not have looked more different. Nicaea had been restored to imperial authority, while the west coast of Asia Minor and the vital river valleys of the interior were back under Byzantine control. Troublesome figures from the Turkish world had been dealt with once and for all, and a good relationship built with Kilidj Arslan, secured by a peace that had held since the summer of 1098.[84] Cilicia and the important ports on the south coast of Anatolia had been recovered. Even the Serbs had been pacified, thanks to a well-judged intervention by Raymond of Toulouse on his way to Constantinople in 1097. And to crown it all Antioch was back in Christian hands, with Byzantine claims over the city established emphatically.

While Tancred's intransigence after the signing of the treaty of Diabolis in 1108 was galling, it turned out to be a temporary inconvenience. As the experiences of the Crusaders in Jerusalem had shown, the threat posed by the Muslims was not going to diminish. Alexios and Byzantium were key allies, and the knights who had established themselves in the east knew that they needed their support. This was why the chronicler Fulcher of Chartres, chaplain to Baldwin of Bouillon in Edessa and Jerusalem, was careful not to inflame passions. His account of the Crusade is conciliatory throughout towards the emperor; as we have seen, he even chose to excise the inflammatory final paragraph of the letter sent to the Pope in 1098 from Antioch, which accused Alexios of failing to help the Crusaders and of actively seeking to harm them during the expedition. Unlike his peers in the west, Fulcher realised there was little to be gained from antagonising those whose support might be vital in the future.[85] Others too were cautious in their appraisals of Alexios and of Byzantium, and deliberately pulled back from the vitriolic assessments of some of their peers.[86]

Alexios continued to keep a close eye on the situation in the east. After the death of Raymond of Toulouse in 1105, he sent an embassy to ensure the loyalty and support of his successor in Tripoli, the base where Raymond had established himself at the start of the twelfth century.[87] Three years later he took an oath from Bertrand of Toulouse, who journeyed to Constantinople where he received the same treatment the Crusade's leaders had been given a decade before: an impressive reception, lavish gifts and careful attention by the emperor in person.[88]

The benefits that the Crusade brought to Byzantium could be measured in many different ways. A new empire emerged in the twelfth century, strident, self-confident and militaristic, very much in Alexios' own image. The economy, in tatters at the time of the Komnenoi coup in 1081, was again in bloom, stimulated by the re-coinage of the currency, increased trade with Venice and the other Italian city-states, and of course by the Crusade itself. Expenditure on the army finally stabilised; while Alexios had been in the field almost every year in the first half of his reign, he rarely led the army in person after the passage of the Crusade through imperial territory. By 1107, the empire's tax system had been completely overhauled, reset on a basis of documented land ownership that gave the state much clearer assessment of – and income from – private property in Byzantium. Stability and prosperity had been restored to the empire.

There is a remarkable poem, written as a guide to John II, the emperor's heir, around the time of Alexios' death in 1118. It reviews Alexios' reign, noting the difficult and turbulent times he faced after taking the throne. But later, all, including 'the massed movement of horsemen from the west', yielded before the great ruler, cowering and withdrawing. As long as John II used the same techniques, he too would be able to benefit from his father's expertise and skill. Money and gifts should be given 'readily and with a gentle manner', urged Alexios. The new emperor should stuff gold and presents into the 'opened jaws' of westerners and do so unstintingly. To prepare for this, John was urged to accumulate 'many things' in strong rooms, 'so that you may fulfil the greed of the nations who are on the move all around us just as long ago'. In short, the new emperor should therefore treat Constantinople as 'a fountain of gold' from which rewards and inducements should be actively and generously distributed. As long as he did so, his reign would be stable. This was a startlingly confident view of the world, based firmly on Alexios' policies and their success.[89]

The poem reflects how robustly the emperor emerged from the

Crusade. This can also be seen in how Alexios conducted himself in the later years of his reign. After Henry IV of Germany's younger son and successor, Henry V, marched on Rome in 1111, taking Pope Paschal II into captivity, Alexios sent embassies to Montecassino to offer his sympathies for the pontiff and the way he had been treated. The emperor was willing to come to Rome in person. To ensure that the city and the papacy were safe in the future, he proposed that either he, or his son John, take the imperial crown of Rome.[90] So greatly had the fortunes of Byzantium been transformed as the result of the Crusade that Alexios' ambitions now extended to taking power in Rome itself.

Persistent misgivings about Byzantium and its emperors cemented themselves in western European consciousness, but it was only when the Second Crusade fell into chaos as it crossed Asia Minor in 1146–7 that these negative portrayals of Alexios began to have an effect. After the German and French armies ran into trouble, the familiar need arose to find a scapegoat for the failure of men who were supposed to be doing God's work. Blame was laid on the emperor in Constantinople, Manuel I Komnenos, the grandson of Alexios, who became the subject of vicious personal attacks across Europe. The same accusations that had been thrown at his grandfather were now levelled at him: treachery, double-dealing, sympathy with Islam, and betrayal of the defenders of Christianity. There were now calls for a full-blown Crusade against Byzantium itself. The empire's reputation in the west never recovered.[91]

It was also the precise moment when Anna Komnene decided that the time had come to rehabilitate her father's reputation and to record his achievements. But she faced the difficult problem of how to provide a balanced account of Alexios' reign. On the one hand, he had saved Byzantium from the jaws of defeat; on the other, he had sown seeds that were to bring a slew of new problems. The resulting text, the *Alexiad*, is florid, contradictory and pregnant with hidden meanings. It has disorientated, confused and misled people ever since.

When we try to unscramble the erratic sequence of events provided by Anna's account we see a clear picture. In the mid-1090s, the Byzantine Empire was teetering on the brink of catastrophe. Alexios' policies in the east had spectacularly failed, while renewed pressure and setbacks to the north of Constantinople threatened what remained of imperial control elsewhere. With imperial finances in tatters, Alexios lacked the resources to engineer a serious fightback in the east, leading to the failure of confidence in his leadership and a full-scale revolt by the entire Byzantine aristocracy.

As Anna Komnene put it, it was one thing to deal with troublesome knights from the west; but 'the rebellious spirit of his own subjects caused no less trouble – in fact he suspected them even more and hastened to protect himself as best he could, dealing with their plots with skill. But who could possibly describe the ferment of troubles which descended on him? It compelled him to become all things to all men, to accommodate himself as far as he could to the circumstances.'[92]

The emperor, wrote his daughter, was like a helmsman guiding his vessel through endless battering waves. Scarcely had one wave broken than the next rolled towards him: 'There was a never-ending succession of woes, an ocean of trouble, as it were – so that he was allowed no chance to breathe nor even rest his eyes'.[93] Alexios had responded to this onslaught with extraordinary boldness.

The story of the First Crusade has been told many times before. The exploits of men like Bohemond, Godfrey of Bouillon and Raymond of Toulouse have passed from one generation to another for centuries. The names and deeds of Baldwin of Calderun and Achard of Montmerle, who failed to return, were preserved for posterity, to be remembered for their heroism and selflessness in trying to liberate the Holy City of Jerusalem.

Less well known are the names of those who caused the First Crusade. Yet Abu'l-Kasim, Çaka, Bursuk, Togortak and Nikephoros Diogenes should feature in any discussion of the expedition that reshaped medieval Europe. They brought Byzantium to the verge of collapse and forced Alexios to look to the west. The attacks, intransigence and revolts of these men led, ultimately, to the restoration of Christian control of Jerusalem more than 450 years after it had fallen to the Muslims.

But it is one man, above all others, who stands out. Alexios I Komnenos put in motion the chain of events that introduced the Crusades to the world. The call from the east was to reshape the medieval world, massively expanding the geographic, economic, social, political and cultural horizons of Europe. After more than 900 years in the gloom, Alexios should once again take centre stage in the history of the First Crusade.

Abbreviations

Albert of Aachen	*Historia Iherosolimitana*, ed. and tr. S. Edgington (Oxford, 2007).
Anna Komnene	*Alexiad*, revised tr. P. Frankopan (London, 2009).
Baldric of Dol	*Historia Jerosolimitana*, in *RHC, Occ.* vol. 4, pp. I–III.
Barber and Bate, *Letters*	*Letters from the East: Crusaders, Pilgrims and Settlers in the 12th–13th Centuries* (Farnham, 2010).
Bernold of Constance	*Die Chroniken Bertholds von Reichenau und Bernolds von Konstanz*, ed. I. Robinson (Hanover, 2003).
Ekkehard of Aura	*Frutolfs und Ekkehards Chroniken und die Anonymen Kaiserchroniken*, ed. F-J. Schmale and I. Schmale-Ott (Darmstadt, 1972).
Fulcher of Chartres	*A History of the Expedition to Jerusalem 1095–1127*, tr. F. Ryan (Knoxville, 1969).
Geoffrey Malaterra	*De rebus gestis Rogerii Calabriae et Siciliae Comitis et Roberti Guiscardi Ducis fratris eius*, ed. E. Pontieri, in *RIS*, 2nd edition (Bologna, 1927–8).
Gesta Francorum	*Gesta Francorum et aliorum Hierosolimitanorum*, ed. and tr. R. Hill (London, 1962).
Gregory VII, *Register*	*The Register of Pope Gregory VII 1073–1095*, tr. H. E. J. Cowdrey (Oxford, 2002).
Gregory Pakourianos	P. Gautier, 'Le typikon du sébaste Grégoire Pakourianos', *Revue des Etudes Byzantines* 42 (1984), pp. 6–145.
Guibert of Nogent	*Gesta Dei per Francos*, ed. R. Huygens (Turnhout, 1986).

Hagenmeyer, *Epistulae*   *Epistulae et chartae ad historiam primi belli sacri spectantes: die Kreuzzugsbriefe aus den Jahren 1088–1100* (Innsbruck, 1901).

Ibn al-Athir   *The Chronicle of Ibn al-Athir for the Crusading Period from al-Kamil fi'l-Ta'rikh*, Part one, tr. D. S. Richards (London, 2002).

John the Oxite   P. Gautier, 'Diatribes de Jean l'Oxite contre Alexis Ier Comnène', *Revue des Etudes Byzantines* 28 (1970), pp. 5–55.

John Skylitzes   *Ioannis Scylitzae Synopsis historiarum*, ed. I. Thurn (New York, 1973).

John Zonaras   *Epitome Historiarum*, ed. M. Pinder and T. Büttner-Wobst, 3 vols. (Bonn, 1841–97).

Katakalon Kekaumenos   *Sovety i rasskazy Kekavmena*, ed. and tr. G. Litavrin (Moscow, 1972).

Manuel Straboromanos   P. Gautier, 'Le dossier d'un haut fonctionnaire d'Alexis Ier Comnène, Manuel Straboromanos', *Revue des Etudes Byzantines* 23 (1965), pp. 168–204.

Matthew of Edessa   *Armenia and the Crusades*, tr. A. Dostourian (Lanham, 1993).

MGH, SS   *Monumenta Germaniae Historica, Scriptores*, 32 vols. (Hanover, 1826–).

Michael Attaleiates   *Michaelis Attaliotae Historia*, ed. I. Bekker (Bonn, 1853).

Michael the Syrian   *Chronique de Michel le Syrien*, ed. and tr. J-B. Chabot, 4 vols. (Paris, 1899–1910).

Miklosich and Müller   *Acta et diplomata graeca medii aevi sacra et profana*, 6 vols. (Vienna, 1860–90).

Nikephoros Bryennios   *Nicephori Bryennii historiarum Libri Quattuor*, ed. and tr. P. Gautier (Brussels, 1975).

Orderic Vitalis   *The Ecclesiastical History of Orderic Vitalis*, ed. and tr. M. Chibnall, 6 vols. (Oxford, 1967–80).

Patrologia Latina   *Patrologia Latina*, ed. J-P. Migne, 221 vols. (Paris, 1844–64).

Ralph of Caen   *The Gesta Tancredi of Ralph of Caen*, tr. B. Bachrach and D. Bachrach (Aldershot, 2005).

Raymond of Aguilers   *Historia Francorum qui ceperunt Iherusalem*, tr. J. Hill and L. Hill (Philadelphia, 1968).

RHC, Occ.   *Recueil des Historiens des Croisades, Historiens Occidentaux*, 5 vols. (Paris, 1841–95).

RHC, Or.	*Recueil des Historiens des Croisades, Historiens Orientaux*, 4 vols. (Paris, 1869–98).
RIS	*Rerum Italicarum Scriptores.*
Robert the Monk	*Robert the Monk's History of the First Crusade, Historia Iherosolimitana*, tr. C. Sweetenham (Aldershot, 2006).
Theophylact of Ohrid	P. Gautier, 'Discours de Théophylacte de Bulgarie', *Revue des Etudes Byzantines* 20 (1962), pp. 93–130.
William of Apulia	*La geste de Robert Guiscard*, ed. and tr. M. Mathieu (Palermo, 1961).
William of Tyre	*Chronicon*, ed. R. Huygens, 2 vols. (Turnhout, 1986).

Notes

Introduction

1. Fulcher of Chartres, I.2.i, pp. 62–3. • **2.** Robert the Monk, I.1, p. 79. • **3.** Ibid., pp. 79–80. • **4.** Fulcher of Chartres, I.3.iv, p. 66. • **5.** Baldric of Dol, IV.1, p. 15. • **6.** Robert the Monk, I.1, pp. 79–80. • **7.** All the main accounts of Urban's speech were written at the start of the twelfth century, after the Crusade. For some comments on the significance, see below, Chapter Twelve, pp. 200–1. • **8.** Guibert of Nogent, I.1, p. 87; also Fulcher of Chartres, I.3.v–viii, pp. 66–7; Robert the Monk, I.2, p. 81; R. Somerville, *The Councils of Urban II: Decreta Claromontensia* (Amsterdam, 1972), p. 74. • **9.** Robert the Monk, I.2, pp. 81–2; Fulcher of Chartres, I.4.iv, p. 68; Guibert of Nogent, II.5, p. 117. • **10.** V. Tourneur, 'Un denier de Godefroid de Bouillon frappé en 1096', *Revue belge de numismatique* 83 (1931), pp. 27–30; cf. N. Bauer, 'Der Fund von Spanko bei St Petersburg', *Zeitschrift für Numismatik* 36 (1926), pp. 75–94. • **11.** See, for example, J. Riley-Smith, *The First Crusade and the Idea of Crusading* (London, 1986), pp. 31ff. • **12.** For the decree about Jerusalem that was passed at Clermont, see Somerville, *Councils of Urban II*, pp. 74, 124, and also R. Somerville, *Papacy, Councils and Canon Law* (London, 1990), pp. 56–65 and 325–37. Also Riley-Smith, *First Crusade*, pp. 13–30. • **13.** The letter states that the Crusade force numbered 300,000 as it gathered at Nicaea in 1097, and just over 20,000 at the battle of Ascalon in September 1099, although this figure did not include the garrison at Jerusalem or other towns held at this time by Western knights. Barber and Bate, *Letters*, pp. 34–5. For the size of the Crusader army, see J. France, *Victory in the East: A Military History of the First Crusade* (Cambridge, 1993), pp. 122–42. • **14.** Raymond of Aguilers, I, p. 18; Albert of Aachen, V.40, pp. 392–4. • **15.** Albert of Aachen, III.28, p. 182. • **16.** Ralph of Caen, 119, p. 135. • **17.** See, for example, J. Riley-Smith, *The First Crusaders 1095–1131* (Cambridge, 1997); M. Bull, *Knightly Piety and the Lay Response to the First Crusade: The Limousin and Gascony* (Oxford, 1993); France, *Victory in the East*; T. Asbridge, *The First Crusade: A New History* (London, 2004). For surveys of the Crusades in general, C. Tyerman, *God's*

War: A New History of the Crusades (London, 2006), J. Phillips, *Holy Warriors: A Modern History of the Crusades* (London, 2010). • **18**. J. Nesbitt, 'The rate of march of crusading armies in Europe: a study and computation', *Traditio* 19 (1963), pp. 167–82; A. Murray, 'The army of Godfrey of Bouillon 1096–9: Structure and dynamics of a contingent on the First Crusade', *Revue Belge de Philologie et d'Histoire* 70 (1992), pp. 301–29; B. Bachrach, 'Crusader logistics: From victory at Nicaea to resupply at Dorylaion', in J. Pryor (ed.), *Logistics of Warfare in the Age of the Crusades* (Aldershot, 2006), pp. 43–62. • **19**. For example, S. Edgington, 'Albert of Aachen reappraised', in A. Murray (ed.), *From Clermont to Jerusalem: The Crusades and Crusader Societies* (Turnhout, 1998), pp. 55–67; J. France, 'The use of the anonymous *Gesta Francorum* in the early twelfth century sources for the First Crusade', in ibid., pp. 29–42; J. Rubenstein, 'What is the *Gesta Francorum* and who was Peter Tudebode?', *Revue Mabillon* 16 (2005), pp. 179–204. • **20**. A. Vauchez, 'Les composantes eschatologiques de l'idée de croisade', in A. Vauchez (ed.), *Le Concile de Clermont de 1095 et l'appel à la Croisade* (Rome, 1997), pp. 233–43; H. Möhring, *Der Weltkaiser der Endzeit: Entstehung Wandel und Wirkung einer tausendjahrigen Weissagung* (Stuttgart, 2000), and B. E. Whalen, *Dominion of God: Christendom and Apocalypse in the Middle Ages* (Cambridge, Mass., 2009). • **21**. J. Bliese, 'The motives of the First Crusaders: A social psychological analysis', *Journal of Psychohistory* 17 (1990), pp. 393–411; G. Anderson, R. Ekelund, R. Herbert and R. Tollinson, 'An economic interpretation of the medieval crusades', *Journal of European Economic History* 21 (1992), pp. 339–63. • **22**. C. Ottoni, F-X. Ricaut, N. Vanderheyden, N. Brucato, M. Waelkens and R. Decorte, 'Mitochondrial analysis of a Byzantine population reveals the differential impact of multiple historical events in South Anatolia', *European Journal of Human Genetics* 19 (2011), pp. 571–6. • **23**. A. Johansen and D. Sornett, 'Finite time singularity in the dynamics of the world population and economic indices', *Physica A* 294.3–4 (2001), pp. 465–502, citing J. DeLong's University of California, Berkeley 'Estimating World GDP' project. • **24**. Bernold of Constance, p. 520. • **25**. Anna Komnene, XIII.6, p. 373. • **26**. Ia. Liubarskii, 'Ob istochnikakh "Aleksiady" Anny Komninoi', *Vizantiiskii Vremennik* 25 (1965), pp. 99–120; for Anna's sources, actual and possible, see J. Howard-Johnston, 'Anna Komnene and the *Alexiad*', in M. Mullett and D. Smythe (eds.) *Alexios I Komnenos – Papers* (Belfast, 1996), pp. 260–302. • **27**. R. Bedrosian (tr.) *Aristakes Lastivertc'i's History* (New York, 1985), p. 64.

I Europe in Crisis

1. Gregory VII, *Register*, I.1, p. 1. • **2**. Ibid., I.25, p. 30. • **3**. See here U-R. Blumenthal, *The Investiture Controversy: Church and Monarchy from the Ninth to* *the Twelfth Century* (Philadelphia, 1988); G. Tellenbach, *The Western Church from the Tenth to the Early Twelfth Century* (Cambridge, 1993); H. Cowdrey, *Pope Gregory VII, 1073–1085* (Oxford, 1998). • **4**. Gregory VII, *Register*, III.6, p. 181; III.10a, pp. 192–3. • **5**. Hugh of Flavigny, II, p. 458; Lampert, *Annales*, pp. 258, 264–5; Berthold, p. 284; Bonizo of Sutri, *Liber*, 8, p. 609. • **6**. Gregory VII, *Register*, VII.14, pp. 342–4. • **7**. Benzo of Alba, *Ad Henricum*, VI, Preface, p. 502. • **8**. C. Erdmann (ed.), *Die Briefe Heinrichs IV* (Leipzig, 1937), 18, p. 28. • **9**. P. Kehr, 'Due documenti pontifici illustranti la storia di Roma negli ultimi anni del secolo XI', *Archivio della Società Romana di storia patria* 23 (1900), pp. 277–83. • **10**. Bernold of Constance, p. 508. • **11**. Urban introduced the prospect of remission from sin for knights who went to fight in Spain, which was to have an important bearing on spiritual rewards available for would-be Crusaders. The Pope's offer in Spain, however, had little impact on the knighthood of Europe as a whole. See J. von Pflugk-Hartung, *Acta pontificum Romanorum inedita*, 3 vols. (Leipzig, 1880–8), 2, pp. 142–3; Urban II, *Epistolae et Privilegia*, in *Patrologia Latina* 151, cols. 288, 302–3, 332–3. Also A. Becker, *Papst Urban II*, 2 vols. (Stuttgart, 1964–88), 1, pp. 246ff. • **12**. F. Liebermann, 'Lanfranc and the antipope', *English Historical Review* 16 (1901), pp. 330–2. • **13**. P. Kehr, 'Papsturkunden in Rom: Erster Bericht', *Nachrichten von der Gesellschaft der Wissenschaften zu Göttingen, Phil-hist. Kl.* (1900), pp. 148–9. • **14**. Only the reply to Clement III's messages survives. A. Pavlov, 'Otryvki grecheskago teksta kanonicheskikh otvetov russkago mitropolita Ioanna II', *Zapiski Imperatorskoi Akademii Nauk*, 22.5 (1873), pp. 169–86. • **15**. Imperial heirs were often crowned co-emperor at or soon after birth – hence spaces for two names in the formula. *De Cerimoniis aulae Byzantinae libri duo*, ed. J. Reiske, 2 vols. (Bonn, 1829–30), 48, vol. 2, pp. 686–92; 46, vol. 2, p. 679. • **16**. C. Will, *Acta et scripta quae de controversiis Ecclesiae Graecae et Latinae* (Leipzig, 1861), pp. 150–4. • **17**. J. Mansi (ed.), *Sacrorum Concilium Amplissima Collectio*, 31 vols. (Florence, 1759–98), 20, cols. 507–8; Gregory VII, *Register*, VI.5b, p. 281. Alexios' excommunication is mentioned by Bernold of Constance, pp. 479–80. • **18**. William of Apulia, IV, p. 230; cf. Anna Komnene, I.13, p. 40. • **19**. The most reliable material here comes from the canons agreed at the council, six letters sent by the Pope to Flanders, Tuscany and Spain, and also contemporary accounts of sermons preached by Urban in France after Clermont, such as in Angers in February 1096. Somerville, *Councils of Urban II*, pp. 74, 124; Hagenmeyer, *Epistulae*, pp. 136, 137–8; W. Wiederhold, 'Papsturkunden in Florenz', *Nachrichten von der Gesellschaft der Wissenschaften zu Göttingen, Phil-hist. Kl.* (1901), pp. 313–14; P. Kehr, *Papsturkunden in Spanien. I Katalonien* (Berlin, 1926), pp. 287–8; L. Halphen and R. Poupardin, *Chronique des comtes d'Anjou et des seigneurs d'Amboise* (Paris, 1913), pp. 237–8. • **20**. Geoffrey Malaterra, IV.13, p. 92; W. Holtzmann, 'Die Unionsverhandlungen zwischen

Kaiser Alexios I und Papst Urban II im Jahre 1089', *Byzantinische Zeitschrift*, 28 (1928), pp. 60–2. • **21**. Anna Komnene, V.9, p. 151. • **22**. Holtzmann, 'Unionsverhandlungen zwischen Kaiser Alexios I und Papst Urban II', pp. 60–2. • **23**. Ibid. • **24**. Ibid., pp. 62–4. • **25**. Theophylact of Ohrid, *Peri egkalountai Latinon*, in P. Gautier (ed. and tr.), *Theophylacti Achridensis Opera* (Thessaloniki, 1980), p. 249. • **26**. Ibid., pp. 251–61. • **27**. Ibid., pp. 271–9. • **28**. H. Seyffert (ed.), *Benzo von Alba. Sieben Bücher an Kaiser Heinrich IV* (Hanover, 1996), I.14–17, pp. 140–54. • **29**. Geoffrey Malaterra, IV.13, pp. 92–3. • **30**. R. Somerville, *Pope Urban II, the Collectio Britannica, and the Council of Melfi (1089)* (Oxford, 1996), pp. 175–80. • **31**. His comments appear in a letter sent to the patriarch of Constantinople, Nicholas III. Holtzmann, 'Unions-verhandlungen zwischen Kaiser Alexios I und Papst Urban II', pp. 64–7. • **32**. Thus Becker, *Papst Urban II*, 2, pp. 80ff. • **33**. Ibid., p. 60. • **34**. Ibid., pp. 59–60. • **35**. Pavlov, 'Otryvki grecheskago teksta', pp. 169–86. • **36**. Anna Komnene, IV.1, p. 109. • **37**. E.g. *Regii neapolitani archivi: monumenta edita ac illustrata*, 6 vols. (Naples, 1845–61) 5, no. 457, pp. 146–7; no. 458, pp. 148–52; no. 462, pp. 157–9; no. 467, pp. 174–8; *Codice Diplomatico Barese*, 6 vols. (Bari, 1897–1902), 3, no. 24, pp. 39–40; no. 35, p. 41; no. 36, p. 42; no. 27, p. 43; no. 28, pp. 44–5; no. 29, pp. 45–6; no. 30, pp. 46–7; D. Morea (ed.), *Il chartularium del monastero* (Montecassino, 1892), p. 136. • **38**. Bernold of Constance, pp. 470–80. • **39**. G. Spata, *Le pergamene greche esistenti nel grande archivio di Palermo* (Palermo, 1861), pp. 163–6, 173–5, 179–82; S. Cusa, *I diplomi greci ed arabi di Sicilia pubblicati nel testo originale*, 2 vols. (Palermo, 1868–82), 2, p. 391. • **40**. Bernold of Constance, p. 483; Anna Komnene, VIII.5, p. 224. • **41**. F. Sisic (ed.), *Letopis Popa Dukljanina* (Belgrade, 1928), pp. 413–16; P. Frankopan, 'Co-operation between Constantinople and Rome before the First Crusade: A study of the convergence of interests in Croatia in the late 11th Century', *Crusades* 3 (2004), pp. 1–13. • **42**. Fulcher of Chartres, I.5.xi, p. 71. • **43**. Bernold of Constance, pp. 458, 462. • **44**. Herrand of Halberstadt, *Epistola de causa Heinrici regis*, *MGH Libelli*, 2, p. 288. • **45**. *MGH Constitutiones et acta publica imperatorum et regum*, 2 vols. (Hanover, 1893), 1, p. 564; Bernold of Constance, p. 520. • **46**. Bernold of Constance, p. 520. • **47**. Geoffrey Malaterra, IV.23, p. 101; Bernold of Constance, p. 463. • **48**. For the proceedings at Piacenza, see R. Somerville, *Pope Urban II's Council of Piacenza* (Oxford, 2011).

2 *The Recovery of Constantinople*

1. C. Mango and R. Parker, 'A Twelfth-Century Description of St Sophia', *Dumbarton Oaks Papers* 14 (1960), pp. 235–40. • **2**. E. Legrand, 'Constantin le Rhodien: Description des œuvres d'art et de l'église des Saints Apôtres, suivie d'un commentaire par Th. Reinach', *Revue des Etudes Grecques* 9 (1896), pp. 32–65. • **3**. The rules and regulations of trade in Constantinople are set out in a text known as the Book of the Eparch. J. Koder, *Das Eparchenbuch Leons des Weisen* (Vienna, 1991). • **4**. K. Ciggaar, 'Une description de Constantinople dans le Tarragonensis 55', *Revue des Etudes Byzantines* 53 (1995), pp. 117–40. • **5**. Fulcher of Chartres, I.9.i, p. 79. • **6**. *The Saga of the People of Laxardal (Laxdaela Saga)*, tr. K. Kunz in *The Sagas of Icelanders* (London, 1997), 72, p. 410. • **7**. Michael Psellos, ed. and tr. E. Theanauld, *Michel Psellos. Chronographie*, 2 vols. (Paris, 1926), VII.25, 2, p. 97, • **8**. *Laxdaela Saga*, 77, p. 419. • **9**. Snorri Sturulson, *Haralds Saga*, tr. L. Hollander, in *Heimskringla: History of the Kings of Norway* (Austin, TX, 1964), 3–6, pp. 579–82. • **10**. R. Savage (ed.), *La Chronique de Sainte-Barbe-en-Auge* (Caen, 1906), pp. 23, 57–8. • **11**. K. Ciggaar, 'L'émigration anglaise à Byzance après 1066', *Revue des Etudes Byzantines* 32 (1974), pp. 338–41. • **12**. Ciggaar, 'Description de Constantinople', p. 119; *Gesta Francorum Iherusalem expugnantium*, in *RHC, Occ.*, 3, p. 494; J. Zepos and P. Zepos (eds.), *Jus Graeco-Romanorum*, 8 vols. (Athens, 1931–62) I, p. 317; Miklosich and Müller, 6, p. 44; P. Lemerle, N. Svoronos, A. Guillou, D. Papachryssanthou (eds.), *Archives de l'Athos: Actes de Lavra* (Paris, 1970), no. 48, 1, pp. 258–9. • **13**. *Actes de Lavra*, no. 35, 1, pp. 233–5. • **14**. M. English Frazer, 'Church doors and the Gates of Paradise: Byzantine bronze doors in Italy', *Dumbarton Oaks Papers* 27 (1973), pp. 147–8. • **15**. P. Lemerle, 'Le testament d'Eustathios Boïlas (Avril 1059)', *Cinq études sur le XIe siècle byzantin* (Paris, 1977), pp. 24–5. • **16**. For the battle of Manzikert and its place in Turkish identity, see C. Hillenbrand, *Turkish Myth and Muslim Symbol: The Battle of Manzikert* (Edinburgh, 2007). • **17**. *Tabula S. Basilii*, in *RHC, Occ.*, 5, pp. 295–8; J. Darrouzès, 'Le mouvement des fondations monastiques au XIe siècle', *Travaux et Mémoires* 6 (1976), p. 173. • **18**. C. Morrisson, 'La dévaluation de la monnaie byzantine au XIe siècle', *Travaux et Mémoires* 6 (1976), pp. 3–29. • **19**. Michael Attaleiates complains bitterly about rising taxes, p. 284; for the chronic inflation in the price of wheat, ibid., pp. 201–4. • **20**. T. Smiciklas (ed.), *Codex diplomaticus regni Croatiae, Dalmatiae et Slavoniae* (Zagreb, 1905), I, pp. 139–41; Gregory VII, *Register*, 5.12, p. 258; P. Stephenson, *Byzantium's Balkan Frontier, 900–1204* (Cambridge, 2000), p. 144. • **21**. Anna Komnene, II.3, pp. 54–5. • **22**. Michael Attaleiates, p. 215; Nikephoros Bryennios, III.16, p. 241. • **23**. Michael Attaleiates, p. 306. • **24**. Anna Komnene, III.11, pp. 103–4. • **25**. Anna Komnene, VI.11, p. 176. • **26**. Anna Komnene, XV.10, p. 463. • **27**. Anna Komnene, I.1, p. 9. • **28**. Anna Komnene, III.2, pp. 82–3. • **29**. Nikpehoros Bryennios, IV.29, p. 299. • **30**. W. Wroth, *Catalogue of Imperial Byzantine Coins in the British Museum*, 2 vols. (London, 1908), 2, p. 539; G. Zacos and A. Veglery, *Byzantine Lead Seals* (Basel, 1972), nos. 99 (a & b), 100; J. Nesbitt, N. Oikonomides et al. (eds.), *Catalogue of Byzantine Seals at Dumbarton Oaks*,

7 vols. (Washington, DC, 1991–), 6, no. 86.1. • **31**. Anna Komnene, II.9, p. 70. • **32**. Alexios' appointment is not mentioned in the *Alexiad* – unsurprisingly given his decision to turn against the capital, rather than take on the Normans. However, see here Romuald of Salerno, *Chronicon, RIS, NS*, 7, 1, p. 192. Also, Dandolo, *Chronica per extensum descripta, RIS, NS*, 12, p. 216, and Michael the Syrian, p. 176. • **33**. Anna Komnene, II.10, pp. 72–3; John Zonaras, XVIII.20, 3, pp. 727–8. • **34**. Anna Komnene, III.5, pp. 89–90. • **35**. John Zonaras, XVIII.20, 3, p. 729. • **36**. Anna Komnene, II.12, p. 78. • **37**. Anna Komnene, III.1, p. 79. • **38**. *De Cerimoniis*, I.38, 1, pp. 191–6. • **39**. Anna Komnene, II.4, p. 58; IV.4, p. 114; III.9, pp. 100–1. • **40**. Anna Komnene, III.4, p. 87, John Zonaras, XVIII.21, 3, p. 732. • **41**. Geoffrey Malaterra, III.41, p. 82. For the Normans and Byzantium, see W. McQueen, 'Relations between the Normans and Byzantium 1071–1112', *Byzantion* 56 (1986), pp. 427–76; H. Taviani-Carozzi, *La Terreur du monde – Robert Guiscard et la conquête normande en Italie* (Paris, 1997); G. Loud, *The Age of Robert Guiscard: Southern Italy and the Norman Conquest* (Singapore, 2000). • **42**. Gregory Pakourianos, p. 43. The scale of the victory was enormous, with Pakourianos lavishly rewarded by the emperor because of his success. The general was mistaken about how his success would be remembered; it was quickly forgotten, and remained so for nearly a thousand years. P. Frankopan, 'A victory of Gregory Pakourianos against the Pechenegs', *Byzantinoslavica* 57 (1996), pp. 278–81. • **43**. Theophylact of Ohrid, p. 111. • **44**. Anna Komnene, VIII.5, pp. 225–6. • **45**. Anna Komnene, VIII.6, pp. 227–8; John Zonaras, XVIII.22, 3, p. 741. • **46**. For example, leading figures from previous regimes were brought on campaign against the Normans in 1081 – many of whom were killed in battle at Dyrrakhion in 1081. Anna Komnene, IV.6, p. 122. • **47**. Anna Komnene, IV.4, pp. 114–15. • **48**. Michael Psellos, II.1–2, 1, p. 25; II.7, 1, p. 29. • **49**. John the Oxite, p. 31. • **50**. Nikephoros Bryennios, II.7, pp. 154–5. • **51**. Anna Komnene, XV.11, p. 464. • **52**. Anna Komnene, XIV.7, p. 423. • **53**. Nikephoros Bryennios, II.7, pp. 154–5; John the Oxite, pp. 37–9; A. Lavriotes (ed.), 'Historikon zetema ekklesiastikon epi tes basileias Alexiou Komnenou', *Ekklesiastike Aletheia* 20 (1900), p. 412. • **54**. Anna Komnene, III.5, p. 89. For her foundation, Miklosich and Müller, 6, pp. 27–8, 33. • **55**. Anna Komnene, III.5, pp. 90–1; V.2, pp. 130–2; V. Grumel, 'L'affaire de Léon de Chalcédoine, le Chrysobulle d'Alexis Ier sur les objets sacrés', *Revue des Etudes Byzantines* 2 (1944), pp. 126–33; Anna Komnene, III.8, p. 96. • **56**. J. Darrouzès, *Georges et Dèmètrios Tornikès – Lettres et Discours* (Paris, 1970), pp. 234–5. • **57**. Manuel Straboromanos, pp. 182–3. • **58**. John Zonaras, XVIII.29, 3, pp. 765–6. • **59**. Anna Komnene, XIV.4, pp. 411–13. • **60**. R. Romano (ed.), *Nicola Callicle, Carmi* (Naples, 1980), pp. 101–2; P. Magdalino and R. Nelson, 'The Emperor in Byzantine art of the 12th Century', *Byzantinische Forschungen* 8 (1982), pp. 123–6. • **61**. Anna Komnene, III.3, p. 93. For his lisp,

I.8, p. 26. The two known images of Alexios appear in manuscripts held in the Vatican Library in Rome, Vaticanus Gr. 666, f. 2r.; 666, f. 2v.

3 Stability in the East

1. I. Mélikoff (ed.), *La geste de Melik Danismend*, 2 vols. (Paris, 1960). • 2. When Alexios was sent to reassert the emperor's authority over Balliol in the mid-1070s, the inhabitants of Amaseia booed and jeered him when he took the Norman prisoner. Anna Komnene, I.2, pp. 11–13. • 3. Matthew of Edessa, II.72, p. 144. • 4. J-C. Cheynet and D. Theodoridis, *Sceaux byzantins de la collection D. Theodoridis* (Paris, 2010), pp. 26–8. • 5. Nikephoros Palaiologos still held this position in 1081. Nikephoros Bryennios, III.15, p. 239. • 6. J-C. Cheynet and J-F. Vannier, *Etudes Prosopographiques* (Paris, 1986), pp. 57–74; Cheynet and Theodoridis, *Sceaux byzantins*, pp. 54– 6; C. MacEvitt, *The Crusades and the Christian World of the East: Rough Tolerance* (Philadelphia, 2008), pp. 41–2. • 7. For example, Michael Angold, *The Byzantine Empire 1025–1204* (London, 1984), pp. 112–13; France, *Victory in the East*, pp. 155–6; J. Flori, *La Première Croisade: l'Occident chrétien contre l'Islam aux origines des idéologies occidentales* (Paris, 2001), p. 64; P. Magdalino, 'The Medieval Empire (780–1204)' in C. Mango (ed.), *The Oxford History of Byzantium*, p. 185; J. Harris, *Byzantium and the Crusades* (London, 2003), pp. 47, 55. Phillips, *Holy Warriors*, p. 15. • 8. Anna Komnene, III.9, p. 100. • 9. Ibid. • 10. Anna Komnene, II.6, p. 65. • 11. Anna Komnene, II.3, pp. 54–5. • 12. J. Darrouzès, *Notitiae episcopatuum ecclesiae constantinopolitanae* (Paris, 1981), pp. 123–4, 134–5. • 13. J-C. Cheynet, 'La résistance aux Turcs en Asie Mineure entre Mantzikert et la Première Croisade', in *Eupsykhia: Mélanges offerts à Hélène Ahrweiler*, 2 vols. (Paris, 1998), 1, pp. 131–47. • 14. For Alexios' fears about his own troops in 1081, Anna Komnene, II.9, p. 71; for the circumstances behind the belated coronation of Alexios' wife, Eirene, III.2, pp. 81–4. • 15. Anna Komnene, III.5, pp. 89–91. • 16. Anna Komnene, III.11, p. 104. • 17. For example, Nikephoros Bryennios, III.16, p. 241; IV.2, p. 259. • 18. Nikephoros Bryennios, IV.4, p. 265; IV.10–13, pp. 275–9. • 19. J. Darrouzès (ed.), *Georges et Dèmètrios Tornikès – Lettres et Discours* (Paris, 1970), pp. 234–5. • 20. Orderic Vitalis, X.12, 5, p. 274. • 21. For the capture of Tatikios' father, Anna Komnene, IV.4, p. 115. • 22. Anna Komnene, III.11, p. 105. • 23. Anna Komnene, V.5.ii, p. 140. • 24. Anna Komnene, IV.4, p. 115; IV.6, p. 123; V.6.iv, p. 159; William of Apulia, IV, pp. 222, 226. • 25. Anna Komnene, VI.12, p. 177. • 26. Matthew of Edessa, II.78, pp. 147–8. • 27. Bar Hebraeus, ed. and tr. E. Budge, *The Chronography of Gregory Abul Faraj*, 2 vols. (Oxford, 1932), 2, p. 227. • 28. *De Administrando Imperio*, ed. and tr. G. Moravcsik and R. Jenkins, (Washington DC, 1967).

• **29**. Nikephoros Bryennios, IV.31, p. 301. • **30**. P. Frankopan, 'The Fall of Nicaea and the towns of western Asia Minor to the Turks in the later 11th Century: The curious case of Nikephoros Melissenos', *Byzantion* 76 (2006), pp. 153–84, and below, p. 82. • **31**. For the empress's commissioning of Nikephoros' history, Nikephoros Bryennios, pp. 71–3; Anna Komnene, Prologue, p. 5. • **32**. After 1081, he is referred to as the 'emir' (i.e. governor) of Nicaea. Anna Komnene, VI.9, pp. 169–70. Anna also states that his quarters in Nicaea were those of the emperor, though in Turkish they were called those of the sultan, III.11, p. 104. Michael Attaleiates, writing at the very end of the 1070s, does not refer to him with a title, calling him a Turkish leader, p. 266. Nikephoros Bryennios avoids using a title when writing about Sulayman for the period before 1081, e.g. III.16, p. 241. • **33**. The two exceptions are the *Alexiad*, and the *Epitome Historion* of John Zonaras. A third author writing in the twelfth century, Michael Glykas, covers Alexios' reign, though this is copied verbatim from Zonaras' work. • **34**. See P. Magdalino, 'Aspects of twelfth-century Byzantine *Kaiserkritik*', *Speculum* 58 (1983), pp. 326–46. • **35**. Albert of Aachen, II.28, p. 108. • **36**. Ekkehard of Aura, p. 200. • **37**. See J-C. Cheynet, 'The duchy of Antioch during the second period of Byzantine rule', in K. Ciggaar and D. Metcalf (eds.), *East and West in the Medieval Eastern Mediterranean: Antioch from the Byzantine Reconquest until the End of the Crusader Principality* (Leiden, 2006), pp. 1–16. • **38**. Michael Attaleiates, p. 301. • **39**. Lead seals belonging to Philaretos that attest to him as *protosebastos* and commander of the armies of the eastern provinces, must date to after 1081, as the title of *protosebastos* was first introduced by Alexios. This in turn shows that the emperor looked to Philaretos in the east, and rewarded him with greater status. J-C. Cheynet, C. Morrisson and W. Seibt, *Les Sceaux byzantins de la collection Henri Seyrig* (Paris, 1991), no. 192; Cheynet and Theodoridis, *Sceaux byzantins*, pp. 54–6. Other dignities from this period show how he was courted, for example, J-C. Cheynet, 'Sceaux byzantins des Musées d'Antioche et de Tarse', *Travaux et Mémoires* 12 (1994), no. 56. • **40**. Anna Komnene, VI.9, pp. 169–70. • **41**. Matthew of Edessa, II.60, p. 137. • **42**. *Anonymi Auctoris Chronicon ad Annum Christi 1234 Pertinens*, tr. A. Abouna and J-M. Fiey, *Chronicle of the Unknown Edessan* (Paris, 1974), p. 39. • **43**. J-C. Cheynet, 'Les Arméniens de L'Empire en Orient de Constantin Xe à Alexis Comnène (1059–1081)', *L'Arménie et Byzance* (Paris, 1996), p. 76. • **44**. Michael the Syrian, 3, p. 178. • **45**. Matthew of Edessa, II.78, p. 147; also Anna Komnene, VI.9, p. 170. • **46**. Ibn al-Ahtir, AH 477/Dec. 1084–Dec. 1085, p. 218; Sibt ibn al-Jawzi, *Mir'at al-Zaman fi Ta'rikh al-A'yan*, ed. A. Sevim (Ankara, 1968), p. 229. • **47**. Ibn al-Athir, quoting the poet al-Abirwardi, AH 477/Dec. 1084–Dec. 1085, p. 218. • **48**. Ibid., pp. 218–19. • **49**. Ibn al-Athir, AH 479/Dec. 1086–Dec. 1087, p. 223. • **50**. Ibn al-Athir, AH 477/Dec. 1084–Dec. 1085, p. 224;

Sibt ibn al-Jawzi, p. 229. • **51.** Anna Komnene, VI.10, p. 171. • **52.** *The History of the Seljuk Turks from the Jami'ak-Tawarikh*, tr. K. Luther (Richmond, 2001), pp. 62, 60–1. • **53.** Anna Komnene, VI.12, pp. 177–8. The letter was written following the Byzantine defeat of Robert Guiscard's attack on Epirus, and before the major Pecheneg invasion of 1087. • **54.** Anna Komnene, VI. 9, pp. 170–1. Anna splits the report of the sultan's proposal in two. • **55.** Anna Komnene, VI.12, p. 178. • **56.** Anna Komnene, VIII.3, p. 220. • **57.** Anna Komnene, VI.9, p. 171. • **58.** Bar Hebraeus, 2, p. 229. • **59.** Ibn al-Athir, AH 485/ Dec. 1091–Dec. 1092, p. 259. • **60.** Anna Komnene, VI.12, p. 177. • **61.** Matthew of Edessa, II.86, p. 153. • **62.** Ibid. • **63.** The reply to the sultan's queries survives. P. Gautier, 'Lettre au sultan Malik-Shah rédigée par Michel Psellos', *Revue des Etudes Byzantines* 35 (1977), pp. 73–97. • **64.** Matthew of Edessa, II.86, p. 153. • **65.** Little is known about the *kouropalates* T'oros, or Gabriel, governors of Edessa and Melitene respectively in this period, or about whether they accepted (or were induced to accept) the authority of Malik-Shah. However, given Matthew of Edessa's scathing comments about Philaretos Braakhamios, and his decision to join the sultan and turn to Islam, we might expect the same vilification in his chronicle had these two men defected to the Turks. Matthew of Edessa, II.85, pp. 152–3. Gabriel seems to have hedged his bets, however, issuing a seal attesting to him with both Byzantine and Arabic titles. J-C. Cheynet, *Sceaux de la collection Zacos se rapportant aux provinces orientales de l'Empire byzantine* (Paris, 2001), no. 41. • **66.** Anna Komnene, VI.10, p. 172. • **67.** Anna Komnene, VI.13, pp. 180–2. • **68.** Ibid., p. 181; VI.14, pp. 183–4. Humbertopoulos' transfer to the west dates the recovery of the town. • **69.** Anna Komnene, VI.13, pp. 180–2. • **70.** Theophylact of Ohrid, pp. 113–14. Theophylact's comments were delivered in a speech to the emperor made just over a year later. • **71.** Ibid., p. 111.

4 *The Collapse of Asia Minor*

1. Miklosich and Müller, 6, pp. 57–8, 40–4. • **2.** Anna Komnene, VII.6, p. 199. • **3.** Ibid. • **4.** Anna Komnene, VII.7, p. 202; VIII.3, p. 220. • **5.** Anna Komnene, VI.10, p. 174. • **6.** Michael the Syrian, 3, pp. 172ff; Mélikoff, *Danismend*, 2, p. 88. • **7.** Anna Komnene, VII.8, p. 202. • **8.** Anna Komnene, VIII.3, p. 220. • **9.** R. Macrides, 'Poetic justice in the Patriarchate: murder and cannibalism in the provinces', in L. Burgmann, M. Fögen, A. Schmink (eds.), *Cupido Legum* (Frankfurt, 1985), pp. 144–5. There is no detailed internal evidence to help date the poem more precisely than on stylistic grounds to the eleventh/ twelfth centuries. However, the references to chronic food shortage, severe winter and the desperate measures of the population certainly resonate with the early 1090s. • **10**. Anna Komnene, VII.8, pp. 202–3. • **11**. Anna Komnene, VIII.3, p. 220. • **12**. John the Oxite, p. 35. Also P. Frankopan, 'Where Advice meets Criticism in 11th Century Byzantium: Theophylact of Ohrid, John the Oxite and their (re)presentations to the Emperor', *Al-Masaq* 20 (2008), pp. 71–88. • **13**. John the Oxite, p. 35. • **14**. Ibid., pp. 29–35. • **15**. J. Shepard, 'How St James the Persian's head was brought to Cormery: A relic collector around the time of the First Crusade', in L. Hoffmann (ed.), *Zwischen Polis, Provinz und Peripherie. Beiträge zur byzantinsichen Geschichte und Kultur* (Wiesbaden, 2005), p. 298. • **16**. For example, Robert the Monk, I.1, pp. 79–80. • **17**. C. Haskins, 'A Canterbury monk at Constantinople c.1090', *English Historical Review* 25 (1910), pp. 293–5; Ciggaar, 'Description de Constantinople', pp. 118–20. • **18**. Hagenmeyer, *Epistulae*, pp. 133–6. • **19**. See, most recently, P. Schreiner, 'Der Brief des Alexios I Komnenos an den Grafen Robert von Flandern und das Problem gefälschter byzantinischer Kaiserschreiben in den westlichen Quellen', in G. de Gregorio and O. Kresten (eds.), *Documenti medievali Greci e Latini. Studi Comparativi* (Spoleto, 1998), pp. 111–40; C. Gastgeber, 'Das Schreiben Alexios' I. Komnenos an Robert I. von Flandern. Sprachliche Untersuchung', in ibid., pp. 141–85; C. Sweetenham, 'Two letters calling Christians on Crusade', in *Robert the Monk's History of the First Crusade* (Aldershot, 2005), pp. 215–18. • **20**. See, for example, M. de Waha, 'La lettre d'Alexis Comnène à Robert Ier le Frison', *Byzantion* 47 (1977), pp. 113–25; J. Shepard, 'Aspects of Byzantine attitudes and policy towards the West in the 10th and 11th centuries', *Byzantinische Forschungen* 13 (1988), pp. 106–12. • **21**. Hagenmeyer, *Epistulae*, p. 132. • **22**. Ibid. • **23**. Hagenmeyer, *Epistulae*, p. 141; John the Oxite, pp. 37–47. • **24**. Anna Komnene, X.5, pp. 273–4. • **25**. Shepard, 'How St James the Persian's head was brought to Cormery', p. 299. • **26**. Miklosich and Müller, 6, pp. 19–21, 34–8, 42–4, 57–8, 81. • **27**. Ibid., pp. 84–90. • **28**. Ibid., p. 81. • **29**. For the Turk's footwear, Anna Komnene, IX.1, p. 237. • **30**. Miklosich and Müller, 6, pp. 82–3. • **31**. Anna Komnene, VIII.3, p. 220. • **32**. Matthew of Edessa, II.90, pp. 157–8. • **33**. Anna Komnene, VI.12, p. 179. • **34**. *Jami'al-Tawarikh*, p. 62. • **35**. Al-Fath ibn 'Ali al-Bundari, *Zubdat al-nusra wa-nukhbat al-'ursa*, ed. M. Houtsma (Leiden, 1889), p. 63. • **36**. Ibn al-Atir, AH 485/1092–1093, pp. 258–9. • **37**. Gautier, 'Synode des Blachernes', pp. 218–19. • **38**. *Jus Graeco-Romanum*, 1, pp. 35–61. • **39**. P. Gautier, 'Jean l'Oxite, patriarche d'Antioche: notice biographique', *Revue des Etudes Byzantines* 22 (1964), pp. 136–8. • **40**. The towns were taken by the Turks fourteen years after Alexios became emperor. Michael the Syrian, VI.6, vol. 3, pp. 178ff. • **41**. *Gesta Francorum*, IV, p. 25. • **42**. Ibid., p. 26. • **43**. William of Tyre, III.1, 1, p. 197. • **44**. Anna Komnene, XI.2, p. 300. • **45**. John the Oxite, p. 35. • **46**. Anna Komnene, VIII.7, p. 229. • **47**. Anna Komnene, VI.10, pp. 172–3. • **48**. Ibid., p. 172; Ibn al-Athir, AH 487/ Dec.

1093–Dec. 1094, p. 271. • **49**. Anna Komnene, VI.11, p. 176. • **50**. Ibid.
• **51**. Anna Komnene, VI,11, p. 177. • **52**. See, for example, J. Haldon, 'Theory
and practice in tenth-century military administration. Chapters 11, 44 and 45
of the Book of Ceremonies', *Travaux et Mémoires* 13 (2000), pp. 201–352.
• **53**. Anna Komnene, VI.10, p. 175. • **54**. Ibid. • **55**. Anna Komnene, VI.12.
ii–iii, p. 178. • **56**. Anna Komnene, VI.12, p. 180. • **57**. Ibid. • **58**. For the size
of Kilidj Arslan's army in 1097, see, for example, Fulcher of Chartres, I.11.
vi, p. 85. • **59**. Fulcher of Chartres, I.9.iv–v, p. 80. • **60**. *Gesta Francorum*, II,
p. 14. • **61**. For example, H. Ahrweiler, 'L'administration militaire de la Crète
byzantine', *Byzantion* 31 (1961), pp. 217–28; P. Gautier, 'Défection et soumission
de la Crète sous Alexis Ier Comnène', *Revue des Etudes Byzantines* 35 (1977),
pp. 215–27; A. Savvides, 'Can we refer to a concerted action among
Rapsomates, Caryces and the emir Tzachas between AD 1091 and 1093?',
Byzantion 70 (2000), pp. 122–34. • **62**. Anna Komnene states that her uncle
had been governor of Dyrrakhion for eleven years before he was recalled to
lead an expedition against western Asia Minor, VII.8, p. 206. Given that
Dyrrakhion fell to the Normans in 1082 and was only recovered the following
year, the soonest Doukas can have been given command of the efforts against
Çaka was 1094. See P. Frankopan, 'The imperial governors of Dyrrakhion
during the reign of the emperor Alexios I Komnenos', *Byzantine and Modern
Greek Studies* 26 (2002), pp. 89–90. • **63**. Miklosich and Müller, 6, pp. 82–3.
• **64**. Anna Komnene, VII.8, pp. 202–6; IX.1, pp. 238–40; IX.3, pp. 242–4; XI.5,
pp. 309–12. • **65**. Anna Komnene, XI.5, p. 309. • **66**. Richard of Cluny, *Chronicon*,
in L. Muratori (ed.), *Antiquitates Italicae*, 4, col. 1250.

5 On the Brink of Disaster

1. John the Oxite, pp. 29, 35. • **2**. John Zonaras, XVIII.29, 3, pp. 766–7. Zonaras
himself fell foul of the Komnenoi, being exiled in the mid-twelfth century
after being the highest-ranked judge in the empire. • **3**. For the grants to
Melissenos, Anna Komnene, III.4, p. 87; John Zonaras, XVIII.21, 3, p. 732;
also N. Oikonomides (ed.), *Archives de l'Athos: Actes de Docheiariou* (Paris,
1984), p. 76. For Adrian, *Actes de Lavra*, 1, pp. 247–51. • **4**. L. Petit, 'Typikon
du monastère de la Kosmosoteira près d'Aenos', *Izvestiya Russkogo
Arkheologicheskogo Instituta v Konstantinopole* 13 (1908), pp. 19–75. • **5**. Frankopan,
'Imperial governors of Dyrrakhion', pp. 65–103. • **6**. Anna Komnene, VI.9,
p. 171. • **7**. Michael Taronites and Nikephoros Melissenos, two more of the
emperor's brothers-in-law, were also awarded high titles and honours, as
were many members of the Doukas family. Anna Komnene, III.4, p. 87.
These awards are well attested in other sources, not least the lead seals issued

by these individuals, e.g. Zacos and Veglery, *Byzantine Lead Seals*, nos. 2698 and 2720 (d). For the Doukas family, see D. Polemis, *The Doukai* (London, 1968). For the full prosopography of the Komnenoi, see K. Barzos, *He Genealogia ton Komnenon*, 2 vols. (Thessaloniki, 1984). • **8**. See, for example, A. Kazhdan, *L'aristocracia bizantina dal principio dell' XI alla fine del XII secolo* (Palermo, 1997), pp. 141–6; J.-C. Cheynet, *Pouvoir et contestations à Byzance 963–1210* (Paris, 1990), pp. 359ff; P. Magdalino, 'Innovations in Government', in M. Mullett and D. Smythe (eds.), *Alexios I Komnenos – Papers* (Belfast, 1996), pp. 146–66. • **9**. P. Frankopan, 'Kinship and the distribution of power in Komnenian Byzantium', *English Historical Review* 495 (2007), pp. 10–13. • **10**. Anna Komnene, IV.4, p. 114. For his small stature, II.4, p. 58. • **11**. Ibid., p. 115; VI.13, pp. 181–2. • **12**. Anna Komnene, V.5, pp. 140–1. • **13**. *Actes de Lavra*, I, nos. 44–5, 48–9 (1083; 1084; 1086; 1089). • **14**. For Aliphas, Anna Komnene IV.6, pp. 122–3. • **15**. Theophylact of Ohrid, p. 114; Anna Komnene, VI.13, p. 182. • **16**. Manuel Straboromanos, pp. 183–5. • **17**. *Diegesis merike ton epistolon Alexiou basileios kai Nicholaou Patriarchou genomene kata diaphorous kairous*, in P. Meyer (ed.), *Die Haupturkunden für die Geschichte der Athos-Klöster* (Leipzig, 1894), p. 172. • **18**. John Zonaras, XVIII.22, 3, p. 738. • **19**. Anna Komnene, III.10, p. 102. • **20**. Anna Komnene, V.2, pp. 131–2. J. Stephanou, 'Le procès de Léon de Chalcédoine', *Orientalia Christiana Periodica* 9 (1943), pp. 5–64; V. Grumel, 'L'affaire de Léon de Chalcédoine, le Chrysobulle d'Alexis Ier sur les objets sacrés', *Revue des Etudes Byzantines* 2 (1944), pp. 126–33. • **21**. John the Oxite, p. 33. • **22**. John Zonaras, VIII.22, 3, p. 732. • **23**. John the Oxite, esp. p. 33; also pp. 29, 31, 35. • **24**. *Actes de Lavra*, I, no. 50; *Actes de Docheiariou*, no. 2; D. Papachryssanthou (ed.), *Actes de Xénophon* (Paris, 1986), no. 2; J. Lefort, N. Oikonomides and D. Papachryssanthou (eds.), *Actes d'Iviron*, 2 vols. (Paris, 1985–90), 2, pp. 28–9. • **25**. Anna Komnene, IX.2, pp. 240–1. The cause of the revolt can be deduced from the appointment of an official with specific tax responsibilities after authority was eventually restored. Anna Komnene, IX.2, p. 242. See P. Frankopan, 'Challenges to imperial authority in Byzantium: Revolts on Crete and Cyprus at the end of the 11th Century', *Byzantion* 74 (2004), pp. 382–402. • **26**. Anna Komnene, VII.8, p. 206; VIII.7, p. 229. • **27**. Anna Komnene, IV.2, p. 111. • **28**. For example, Dandolo, *Chronica brevis*, p. 363; L. Lanfranchi (ed.), *Famiglia Zusto* (Venice, 1955), 6, 9, nos. 1–2. • **29**. Although the two oldest copies of the original grant state that concessions were awarded in May 1092, modern scholars have dismissed this on the grounds that a date in the mid-1080s seems to them more appropriate – although the palaeographic, textual and contextual grounds for this are highly questionable. Great store too is set by the positioning of the report of the grant in the *Alexiad*, even though this is clearly misplaced. For a full discussion here, see T. Madden, 'The chrysobull of Alexius I Comnenus to the Venetians: The date and the debate', *Journal of Medieval History* 28 (2002), pp. 23–41, and P. Frankopan, 'Byzantine trade privileges to Venice in the eleventh century: The chrysobull of 1092', *Journal of Medieval History* 30 (2004), pp. 135–60. • **30**. M. Pozza and G. Ravegnani, *I Trattati con Bisanzio 992–1198* (Venice, 1993), pp. 38–45. • **31**. Ibid., pp. 39–40. • **32**. Ibid., p. 43. • **33**. Ibid, pp. 40–3. • **34**. Dandolo, *Chronica per extensum descripta*, p. 217. Dandolo does not say why the patriarch was in Constantinople in 1092, only that he died there from fever. • **35**. Anna Komnene, VI.7, pp. 166–7; VI.3, p. 156. • **36**. Anna Komnene, VII.3, p. 194. • **37**. Pozza and Ravegnani, *Trattati con Bisanzio*, pp. 42–3. • **38**. Katakalon Kekaumenos, 81, p. 278. • **39**. Anna Komnene, III.10, p. 103. • **40**. For the birth of Alexios' heir, John II, as well as the emperor's other children, A. Kazhdan, 'Die Liste der Kinder des Alexios I in einer Moskauer Handschrift (UBV 53/147)', in R. Stiehl and H. Stier (eds.), *Beiträge zur alten Geschichte und deren Nachleben*, 2 vols. (Berlin, 1969–70), 2, pp. 233–7. John's coronation, and its date, can be deduced from A. Spinelli (ed.), *Regii neapolitani archivi monumenta edita ac illustrata*, 6 vols. (Naples, 1845–61), 5, nos. 457–8, 462, 464–7. • **41**. Anna Komnene, VIII.7–8, pp. 229–32. • **42**. Anna Komnene, VI.8, p. 168. • **43**. Geoffrey Malaterra, III.13, p. 64; Michael the Syrian, 3, p. 176; Bar Hebraeus, 1, p. 227. • **44**. Anna Komnene, IX.6, p. 248. • **45**. Ibid., p. 250. • **46**. Anna Komnene, IX.5, p. 247. • **47**. Anna Komnene, IX.7, p. 252. • **48**. Anna Komnene, IX.8, pp. 253–4. • **49**. Ibid., p. 253, and III.2, p. 81. • **50**. Anna Komnene, IX.6, p. 254. • **51**. Adrian and Nikephoros reminisced about this when the former was sent to investigate the rumours that Diogenes was plotting against the emperor. Anna Komnene, IX.7, pp. 252–3. • **52**. Adrian had become a monk and went by the name of John when he died. B. de Montfaucon, *Paleographia Graeca* (Paris, 1708), p. 47. For his role in the conspiracy, and the consequences for his family, Frankopan, 'Kinship and the distribution of power', pp. 1–34. • **53**. For example, Anna Komnene, VIII.3, p. 219; VIII.8, p. 232. For Melissenos, see Frankopan, 'The Fall of Nicaea', pp. 153–84. • **54**. Melissenos appears only once again before his death, on campaign against the Cumans: Anna Komnene, X.2, p. 264. Alexios often preferred not to leave his rivals in Constantinople but to take them on expedition with him – so he could keep a close eye on them. Almost all the leading figures in Byzantium accompanied the emperor against the Normans in 1081; and of course they were with him during his mission against the Serbs in 1094. • **55**. Anna Komnene, III.4, p. 87. • **56**. Anna Komnene, XI.10, p. 325; XIII.1, p. 357. • **57**. Anna Komnene, IX.8, p. 254. • **58**. Ibid. • **59**. Anna Komnene, IX.6, p. 250. • **60**. Anna Komnene, IX.8, p. 254. • **61**. Anna Komnene, IX.9, pp. 255–6. • **62**. Ibid., p. 256. • **63**. Ibid., pp. 256–7. • **64**. Ibid., p. 257. The author is coy about whether her father ordered the blinding of Nikephoros Diogenes. • **65**. Anna Komnene, IX.1, p. 237. • **66**. Anna Komnene, XV.11,

p. 465. • **67**. Anna Komnene, IX.2, p. 242; E. Sargologos, *La Vie de saint Cyrille le Philéote, moine byzantin (Part 1110)* (Brussels, 1964), pp. 35.i–viii, 146–53. • **68**. For their careers, see B. Skoulatos, *Les personnages byzantins de l'Alexiade: analyse prosopographique et synthèse* (Louvain, 1980), pp. 160–1, 85–7. • **69**. Anna Komnene, X.9, pp. 286–8; John Zonaras, XVIII.22, 3, p. 739. • **70**. *Gesta Francorum*, IV, pp. 25–6. • **71**. Anna Komnene, XI.10, p. 323. • **72**. Anna Komnene, XI.3, p. 305. • **73**. Anna Komnene, XI.3, pp. 304–5; XI.5, pp. 309–12. • **74**. Anna Komnene, VII.8, p. 203; IX.1, p. 238; IX.3, p. 242. • **75**. Anna Komnene, X.2, p. 264. For Melissenos' death, Peter Lambecius, *Commentariorum de Augustissima Biblioteca Caesarea Vindobonensi*, 8 vols. (Vienna, 1665–79), 5, col. 537. Also see D. Papachryssanthou, 'La date de la mort du sébastokrator Isaac Comnène', *Revue des Etudes Byzantines* 21 (1963), p. 252. • **76**. Anna Komnene, X.2–4, pp. 262–73; *The Russian Primary Chronicle*, tr. S. Cross, and O. Sherbowitz-Wetzor (Cambridge, Mass., 1953), p. 180. • **77**. Anna Komnene, XI.2, p. 300.

6 The Call from the East

1. J-C. Cheynet, 'Les Sceaux byzantins de Londres', *Studies in Byzantine Sigillography* 8 (2003) pp. 85–100; also J-C. Cheynet, 'Le rôle des Occidentaux dans l'armée byzantine avant la Première Croisade', in E. Konstantinou (ed.), *Byzanz und das Abendland im 10. und 11. Jahrhundert* (Cologne 1997), pp. 111–28. • **2**. For example, V. Laurent, *Le Corpus des sceaux de l'empire byzantin II: L'administration centrale* (Paris 1981), no. 469 (Bulgarian); G. Zacos, *Byzantine Lead Seals II*, compiled and ed. J. Nesbitt (Bern, 1984), no. 706 (interpreter to the English); ibid. (Anglo-Saxon); Laurent, *Le Corpus des sceaux de l'empire byzantine*, no. 991 (interpreter of the fleet). • **3**. F. Schmitt (ed.), *S. Anselmi Cantuariensis archiepiscopi opera omnia*, 6 vols. (Edinburgh, 1938–61), 3, pp. 252–5. • **4**. See, for example, J. Shepard, 'The uses of the Franks in 11th Century Byzantium', *Anglo-Norman Studies* 15 (1992), pp. 275–305. • **5**. John Skylitzes, p. 486; Michael Attaleiates, pp. 122–5, Matthew of Edessa, II.19, p. 101. • **6**. *Patrologia Latina*, 150, col. 737. • **7**. Ekkehard of Aura, pp. 133–4. • **8**. Gilbert of Mons, *Chronique Hanoniense*, tr. L. Napran (Woodbridge, 2005), 23, p. 25. • **9**. Hagenmeyer, *Epistulae*, pp. 134–5. For some comments on this letter, above, pp. 60–1. • **10**. Shepard, 'How St James the Persian's head was brought to Cormery', p. 299. • **11**. *Narratio Floriacensis de captis Antiochia et Hierosolyma et obsesso Dyrrachio*, RHC, Occ., 5, p. 356, Gilbert of Mons, 23, p. 25. Also Becker, *Urban II*, 2, p. 180, and above all J. Shepard, 'Cross-purposes: Alexius Comnenus and the First Crusade', in J. Phillips (ed.), *The First Crusade: Origins and Impact* (Manchester, 1997), pp. 107–29 • **12**. Ekkehard of Aura, pp. 134–6. • **13**. Guibert of Nogent, I.5, pp. 102–3. • **14**. Baldric of Dol, I, p. 14.

• **15**. Fulcher of Chartres, I.3.ii–iii, pp. 65–6. • **16**. William of Apulia, IV, p. 212. • **17**. Sibt al-Jawzi, p. 244; Bar Hebraeus, 1, pp. 230–1. • **18**. Raymond of Aguilers, XIII, pp. 108–9; William of Tyre, I.7, 1, pp. 116–17; Albert of Aachen, VI.31, p. 442. • **19**. S. Goitein, *A Mediterranean Society: The Jewish communities of the Arab world as portrayed in the documents of the Cairo Geniza*, 6 vols. (Princeton, 1967–93), pp. 308–14. Also see here S. Goitein, 'Jerusalem in the First Arabic period', in *Jewish Settlements in Palestine in the Beginning of the Islamic and the Crusade Period, in the Light of the Geniza* (Jerusalem, 1980); M. Gil, 'Political History of Jerusalem', in J. Prawer (ed.), *Book of Jerusalem, The First Islamic Period, 638–1099* (Jerusalem, 1991). • **20**. See, for example, S. Gat, 'The Seljuks in Jerusalem', in Y. Lev (ed.), *Town and Material Culture in the Medieval Middle East* (Leiden, 2002), pp. 4–40. • **21**. C. Cahen, 'La chronique abrégée d'al-Azimi', *Journal Asiatique* 230 (1938), p. 369. • **22**. Ibn al-Athir, AH 491/Dec. 1097–Dec. 1098, pp. 13–14. • **23**. See C. Morris, *The Sepulchre of Christ in the Medieval West* (Oxford, 2005), esp. pp. 134–9; however also note J. France, 'The Destruction of Jerusalem and the First Crusade', *Journal of Ecclesiastical History* 47 (1996), pp. 1–17. • **24**. Guibert of Nogent, II.10, pp. 125–6. • **25**. Below, pp. 118–19 • **26**. J. Vaissète, C. Devic and A. Molinier (eds.), *Histoire générale de Languedoc*, 3rd edition, 16 vols. (Toulouse, 1872–1904), 5, cols. 737–8. • **27**. J. Venier (ed.), *Chartres de l'abbaye de Jumièges*, 2 vols. (Paris, 1916), 1, pp. 121–3. • **28**. R. Bautier, M. Gilles and M. Bautier (eds.), *Chronicon S. Petri Vivi Senonensis* (Paris, 1979), p. 140. • **29**. Gregory Pakourianos, p. 131. • **30**. *Letopis Popa Dukljanina*, 27, p. 413. • **31**. Hagenmeyer, *Epistulae*, p. 136. • **32**. Robert the Monk, I.1, p. 79. • **33**. See, for example, T. Head and R. Landes (eds.), *Peace of God: Social violence and religious response in France around the year 1000* (Cambridge, 1992). • **34**. Ivo of Chartres, *Panormia*, VIII.147, in *Patrologia Latina*, 161, col. 1343 AC. • **35**. See Vauchez, 'Composantes eschatologiques', pp. 233–43; J. Rubenstein, 'How or How Much, to Re-evaluate Peter the Hermit', in S. Ridyard (ed.), *The Medieval Crusade* (Woodbridge, 2004), pp. 53–69; J. Flori, *L'Islam et la fin des temps. L'interprétation prophétique des invasions musulmanes dans la chrétienté médiévale* (Paris, 2007), pp. 111–47; and more generally, Möhring, *Weltkaiser der Endzeit* and Whalen, *Dominion of God*. • **36**. Lupus, *Annales*, MGH, SS, 5, p. 62. • **37**. Gilbert of Mons, 23, p. 25. • **38**. Theodore Skutariotes, *Synopsis Khronike*, in K. Sathas, *Biblioteca Graeca Medii Aevi*, 7 vols. (Paris, 1872–94), 7, pp. 184–5. • **39**. For these and other fake relics, Guibert of Nogent, *De pigneribus sanctorum*, ed. R. Huygens (Turnhout, 1993), I, pp. 98, 88. • **40**. *Gesta Episcoporum Tullensium*, in MGH, SS, 8, p. 647. • **41**. Anna Komnene, III.10, p. 103. • **42**. F-J. Schmale and I. Schmale-Ott (eds.), *Frutolfs und Ekkehards Chroniken* (Darmstadt, 1972), p. 96; Ekkehard of Aura, *Chronicon Universale*, in MGH, SS 6, p. 205. For the gifts recorded by Anna, *Alexiad*, III.10, p. 103. • **43**. G. Constable (ed. and tr.), *The Letters of*

Peter the Venerable, 2 vols. (Cambridge, Mass., 1967), 2, p. 209. • **44**. Hagenmeyer, *Epistulae*, pp. 135–6. • **45**. Guibert of Nogent, I.5, p. 103. • **46**. Below, p. 106. • **47**. *Miracula S Augustini episcopi Cantuariensis*, in *Acta Sanctorum*, May, 6, p. 410. • **48**. Anna Komnene III.10, p. 102. • **49**. Hagenmeyer, *Epistulae*, p. 141. • **50**. Shepard, 'How St James the Persian's head was brought to Cormery', p. 299. • **51**. Hagenmeyer, *Epistulae*, p. 136. • **52**. Ibid., p. 142. • **53**. Alexios had developed a great sense of trust for Robert, according to Guibert of Nogent, I.5, pp. 100–1. • **54**. Hagenmeyer, *Epistulae*, p. 133. • **55**. Guibert of Nogent, I.5, p. 101. • **56**. Bernold of Constance, p. 483. • **57**. Anna Komnene, VIII.5, p. 224. • **58**. Ekkehard of Aura, p. 136. • **59**. Otto of Freising, *Chronicon*, in *MGH, SS* 20, VII, p. 248. • **60**. Gregory VII, *Register*, I.18, p. 20. The original letter sent by the emperor does not survive. • **61**. Gregory VII, *Register*, I.46, p. 51. • **62**. Gregory VII, *Register*, I.49, pp. 54–5. • **63**. Gregory VII, *Register*, II.31, pp. 122–3. • **64**. Gregory VII, *Register*, II.37, pp. 127–8. • **65**. Gregory VII, *Register*, II.3, p. 95. • **66**. Gregory VII, *Register*, I.46, p. 51. • **67**. Michael Psellos, *Michaelis Pselli scripta minora magnam partem adhuc inedita*, ed. E. Kurtz, 2 vols. (Milan, 1936–41), I, pp. 329–34. • **68**. Gregory VII, *Register*, II.3, p. 95. See here H. Cowdrey, 'Pope Gregory VII's "Crusading" plans of 1074', in B. Kedar, H. Mayer and R. Smail (eds.), *Outremer: Studies in the history of the Crusading kingdom of Jeruslalem* (Jerusalem, 1982), pp. 27–40, and Becker, *Papst Urban II*, 2, pp. 294–300. • **69**. Bernold of Constance, p. 520. • **70**. Ibid. • **71**. Fulcher of Chartres, I.1.iii, p. 62.

7 The Response of the West

1. See Riley-Smith, *First Crusade*, pp. 13–30; Tyerman, *God's War*, pp. 58–89. • **2**. For Urban's itinerary, Becker, *Papst Urban II*, vol. 2, pp. 435–58. • **3**. Gregory VII, *Register*, 1.46, p. 50; Devic and Vaissete, *Histoire générale de Languedoc*, 3, p. 465 • **4**. Devic and Vaissete, *Histoire générale de Languedoc*, 5, pp. 747–8. • **5**. Gregory VII, *Register*, 1.46, p. 50; 8.16, pp. 381–2. • **6**. *Patrologia Latina*, 151, col. 562. • **7**. *Annales Besuenses, MGH, SS*, 2, p. 250; *Annales S. Benigni Divionensis, MGH, SS*, 5, p 43. • **8**. *Patrologia Latina*, 150, col. 1388; 151, col. 422. • **9**. Robert the Monk, I.1 pp. 80–1. • **10**. Robert the Monk, I.2, pp. 81–2; Fulcher of Chartres, I.4.iv, p. 68; Guibert of Nogent, II.5, p. 117. Although the main narrative accounts of the speech at Clermont were written several years later, the message of the sufferings in the east is captured in the contemporary sources, for example, Hagenmeyer, *Epistulae*, pp. 136, 137–8; Wiederhold, 'Papsturkunden in Florenz', pp. 313–14; Kehr, *Papsturkunden in Spanien*, pp. 287–8; Halphen and Poupardin, *Chronique des comtes d'Anjou*, pp. 237–8. • **11**. Baldric of Dol, IV, pp. 15–16. • **12**. Hagenmeyer, *Epistulae*, pp. 136–7

• **13**. Baldric of Dol, IV, p. 16. • **14**. Baldric of Dol, *Vita Beati Roberti de Arbisello*, *Patrologia Latina* 162, cols. 1050–1. • **15**. Hugh of Flavigny, *Chronicon, MGH, SS*, 8, pp. 474–5. • **16**. Bull, *Knightly Piety*, pp. 250–81. • **17**. For Urban's instructions, Baldric of Dol, I, p. 15. • **18**. S. d'Elbenne and L-J. Dennis (eds.), *Cartulaire du chapitre royal de Saint-Pierre de la Cour du Mans* (Paris, 1903–7), no. 11, p. 15. • **19**. J. Richard, 'Le Cartulaire de Marcigny-sur-Loire 1045–1144. Essai de reconstitution d'un manuscript disparu', *Analecta burgundica* (1957), 119, p. 87. • **20**. B. de Broussillon, *Cartulaire de Saint-Aubin d'Angers* (1903), 1, no. 354, p. 407. • **21**. Hagenmeyer, *Epistulae*, p. 136. • **22**. Ibid., pp. 137–8. • **23**. *Chronica Monasterii Casinensis*, IV.11, p. 475. For the spiritual rewards on offer, Riley-Smith, *First Crusade*, pp. 13–30. • **24**. Kehr, *Papsturkunden in Spanien*, p. 287. • **25**. H. Cowdrey, 'Martyrdom and the First Crusade', in Edbury, *Crusade and Settlement*, pp. 45–56; J. Flori, 'L'example de la Première Croisade', *Cahiers de civilisation médiévale* 34 (1991), pp. 121–39; C. Morris, 'Martyrs of the field of battle before and during the First Crusade', *Studies in Church History* 30 (1993), pp. 93–104. • **26**. Guérard, *Cartulaire de l'abbaye de Saint-Victor de Marseilles*, 1, pp. 167–8. • **27**. C. Métais, *Cartulaire de l'abbaye de la Sainte Trinité de Vendôme*, 4 vols. (Paris, 1893–1900), 2, p. 39; V. Thuillier (ed.), *Ouvrages posthumes de D. Jean Mabillon et D. Thierri Ruinart*, 3 vols. (Paris, 1724), 3, pp. 387–90; P. Jaffé (ed.), *Regesta Pontificum Romanorum*, 2 vols. (Leipzig, 1885–8), 1, nos. 5656, 5649; 5647. • **28**. *Gesta Francorum*, I, p. 2; Hagenmeyer, *Epistulae*, p. 137. • **29**. H. Klein, 'Eastern Objects and Western Desires: Relics and Reliquaries between Byzantium and the West', *Dumbarton Oaks Papers* 58 (2004), pp. 283–314. • **30**. Halphen and Poupardin, *Chronique des comtes d'Anjou*, pp. 237–8. • **31**. A. Gieysztor, 'The Genesis of the Crusades: The Encyclical of Sergius IV', *Medievalia et Humanistica* 5 (1949), pp. 2–23 and 6 (1950), pp. 3–34. However, also see H. Schaller, 'Zur Kreuzzugsenzyklika Papst Sergius IV', in H. Mordek (ed.), *Papsttum, Kirche und Recht im Mittelalter. Festschrift für Horst Fuhrmann* (Tübingen, 1991), pp. 135–54. • **32**. *Recueil des chartes de Cluny*, 5, no. 3703. • **33**. Ibid., nos. 3737, 3755. • **34**. Ibid., no. 3712. • **35**. R. Juënin, *Nouvelle histoire de l'abbaie royale et collégiale de Saint Filibert*, 2 vols. (Dijon, 1733), 2, p. 135. • **36**. Robert the Monk, I.2, p. 82; Fulcher of Chartres, I.4.iv, p. 68; Guibert of Nogent, II.5, p. 117; *Gesta Francorum*, I, p. 7. • **37**. C. Chevalier, 'Cartulaire de l'abbaye de St. Chaffre du Monastier', in *Collection de cartulaires dauphinois* (Paris, 1869–1912), 8, pp. 139–41. For these, and many other examples, Riley-Smith, *First Crusade*, pp. 31ff. • **38**. E. Poncelet (ed.), *Cartulaire de l'Eglise St Lambert de Liège*, 5 vols. (Brussels, 1869), 1, p. 47. • **39**. Orderic Vitalis, IX.3, 5, pp. 26, 32; Hugh of Flavigny, II, pp. 474–5. • **40**. Guibert of Nogent, II, 17, pp. 133–4. • **41**. For Philip's excommunication, Somerville, *Councils of Urban II*, pp. 87, 97, 98. For no one having a kind word about Bertrada, *Chronica de gestis consulum Andegavorum*, in Halphen and Poupardin, *Chronique des* *comtes d'Anjou*, p. 67; for Philip abandoning his wife, Bertha of Holland, because of her stoutness, William of Malmesbury, 3.257, p. 474. • **42**. Guibert of Nogent, II.17, pp. 133–4; Mansi, *Sacrorum Concilium Amplissima Collectio* 20, col. 937; J. Verdon (ed.), *Chronique de Saint-Maixent* (Paris, 1979), p. 154; Somerville, *Councils of Urban II*, p. 90. • **43**. *Gesta Francorum*, I, p. 7. • **44**. Robert the Monk, II.3, pp. 91–2. • **45**. *Codice Diplomatico Barese*, 5, p. 41. • **46**. Anna Komnene, XIII.11, pp. 383–4. • **47**. Anna Komnene, V.6, p. 144. • **48**. According to one Arabic author, Roger refused to have anything to do with the Crusade and 'raised his leg to let out a loud fart' when he heard the initial plans – which Ibn al-Athir states involved northern Africa, rather than Jerusalem. This colourful story gives an idea of Roger's unwillingness to antagonise Muslim traders who played a vital role in making Sicily enormously wealthy. AH 491/Dec. 1097–Dec. 1098, p. 13. • **49**. Jaffe, *Regesta pontificum Romanorum*, no. 5608; Hagenmeyer, *Epistulae*, p. 136. • **50**. Guérard, *Cartulaire de Saint-Victor*, p. 802. • **51**. Anna Komnene, X.7, pp. 279–80. • **52**. Albert of Aachen, I.23, p. 96; Guibert of Nogent, VII.31, p. 328. • **53**. Barber and Bate, *Letters*, p. 22. • **54**. *Patrologia Latina*, 157, col. 162B. • **55**. Robert the Monk, I.2, pp. 81–2. • **56**. *Recueil des chartes de l'abbaye de Cluny*, 5, p. 51. • **57**. Wiederhold, 'Papsturkunden', pp. 313–14. • **58**. Hagenmeyer, *Epistulae*, p. 137. • **59**. Devic and Vaissete, *Histoire générale de Languedoc*, 5, pp. 757–8. • **60**. Bernold of Constance, p. 520. • **61**. For example, Fulcher of Chartres, I.4, p. 68; Baldric of Dol, I, pp. 15–16. • **62**. Robert the Monk, II.2, p. 82. • **63**. For example, at Marmoutier and Tours in the spring of 1096. Halphen and Poupardin, *Chronique des comtes d'Anjou*, pp. 237–8; O. Guillot, *Le Comte d'Anjou et son entourage au XIe siècle* (Paris, 1972), p. 242. • **64**. See, for example, W. Purkiss, *Crusading Spirituality in the Holy Land and Iberia, c.1095–c.1187* (Woodbridge, 2008), esp. pp. 120–38. • **65**. Anna Komnene XI.1, p. 297. Also *Gesta Francorum*, II, p. 16; Albert of Aachen, I.15, pp. 283–4. • **66**. For the date of the foundation of the monastery, see J. Gay, 'L'abbaye de Cluny et Byzance au début du XII siècle', *Echos d'Orient* 30 (1931), pp. 84–90, but also J. Shepard, 'The "muddy road" of Odo of Arpin from Bourges to La Charité sur Loire', in P. Edbury and J. Phillips (eds.), *The Experience of Crusading: Defining the Crusader Kingdom* (Cambridge, 2003), p. 23. • **67**. Anna Komnene, X.5, p. 276. • **68**. Albert of Aachen, II.7, p. 70. • **69**. Albert of Aachen, II.17, p. 86. • **70**. Albert of Aachen, II.7, pp. 70–2. • **71**. Robert the Monk, II.11, p. 95. • **72**. Raymond of Aguilers, I, pp. 16–17. • **73**. Raymond of Aguilers, I, p. 17. • **74**. Raymond of Aguilers, I, p. 17. • **75**. For estimates of numbers taking part, France, *Victory in the East*, pp. 122–42; B. Bachrach, 'The siege of Antioch: A study in military demography', *War in History* 6 (1999), pp. 127–46; J. Riley-Smith, 'Casualties and the number of knights on the First Crusade', *Crusades* 1 (2002), pp. 13–28. • **76**. Fulcher of Chartres, I.6.ix, p. 73. • **77**. Fulcher of

Chartres, I.13.iv, p. 88. • **78**. Anna Komnene, X.5, p. 274. • **79**. Anna Komnene, X.5.vi, p. 275.

8 *To the Imperial City*

1. Robert the Monk, I.5, p. 83. • **2**. Albert of Aachen, I.2, pp. 2–4; Guibert of Nogent, II, p. 121. • **3**. William of Tyre, I.3, 1, p. 108; Albert of Aachen, I.2–3, p. 4; Anna Komnene, X.5, p. 275. For Peter the Hermit, see J. Flori, *Pierre l'Eremite et la Première Croisade* (Paris, 1999). • **4**. Albert of Aachen, I.3, pp. 4–6; Guibert of Nogent, II.8, p. 142. • **5**. For example, J. Flori, 'Faut-il réhabiliter Pierre l'Eremite', *Cahiers de civilisation médiévale* 38 (1995), pp. 35–54. • **6**. Albert of Aachen, I.26–8, pp. 50–2. See B. Kedar, 'Crusade Historians and the Massacres of 1096', *Jewish History* 12 (1998), pp. 11–31; R. Chazan, *God, Humanity and History: The Hebrew First Crusade Narratives* (Berkeley, 2000) and also id., '"Let Not a Remnant or a Residue Escape": Millenarian Enthusiasm in the First Crusade', *Speculum* 84 (2009), pp. 289–313. Also here see M. Gabriele, 'Against the Enemies of Christ: The Role of Count Emicho in the Anti-Jewish Violence of the First Crusade', in M. Frassetto (ed.), *Christian Attitudes towards the Jews in the Middle Ages: A Casebook* (Abingdon, 2007), pp. 61–82. • **7**. Albert of Aachen, I.26–7, pp. 50–2. Also *Chronicle of Solomon bar Simson*, tr. S. Eidelberg, *The Jews and the Crusaders* (Madison, 1977), pp. 28ff. • **8**. *Solomon bar Simson*, pp. 24–5. • **9**. For example, Siegebert of Gembloux, in *MGH, SS*, 6, p. 367; Richard of Poitiers, *Cruce signato*, in M. Bouquet et al. (eds.), *Recueil des Historiens des Gaules et de la France*, 24 vols. (Paris, 1737–1904), 12, p. 411. • **10**. Hugh of Flavigny, *Chronicon Virdunensi*, in *Recueil des Historiens des Gaules et de la France*, 13, p. 623. For many other examples here, N. Golb, *The Jews in Medieval Normandy* (Cambridge, 1998), pp. 119–27. • **11**. Guibert of Nogent, II.9, p. 123. • **12**. Anna Komnene, X.5, p. 274. • **13**. Albert of Aachen, I.29, p. 54. • **14**. Albert of Aachen, I.6, pp. 10–12, and Orderic Vitalis, IX.4, 5, p. 30. • **15**. Albert of Aachen, I.9, p. 18. • **16**. Anna Komnene, X.5, pp. 275–6; John Zonaras, XVIII.23, 3, p. 742. • **17**. *Gesta Francorum*, I, p. 3. • **18**. Anna Komnene, X.6, p. 277. • **19**. *Gesta Francorum*, I, p. 3; Robert the Monk, I.7, p. 85. • **20**. *Gesta Francorum*, I, pp. 3–4. • **21**. Albert of Aachen, I.21, p. 42. • **22**. *Gesta Francorum*, I, p. 4. • **23**. Robert the Monk, I.9, p. 86. • **24**. *Gesta Francorum*, I, pp. 4–5; Robert the Monk, I.12, p. 87. • **25**. *Gesta Francorum*, I, p. 4; Anna Komnene, X.6, p. 278. • **26**. Anna Komnene, X.6, p. 279. • **27**. Guibert of Nogent, II.10, p. 124. • **28**. *Gesta Francorum*, I, p. 5. For the importance of the first accounts of the Crusade, and of the *Gesta Francorum* in particular in early twelfth-century Europe, see J. France, 'The Anonymous *Gesta Francorum* and the *Historia Francorum qui ceperunt*

Iherusalem of Raymond of Aguilers and the *Historia de Hierosolymitano itinere* of Peter Tudebode: An analysis of the textual relationship between primary sources for the First Crusade', in J. France and W. Zajac (eds.), *The Crusades and their Sources. Essays presented to Bernard Hamilton* (Aldershot, 1998), pp. 39–69, and also Rubenstein, 'What is the *Gesta Francorum*?', pp. 179–204. • **29**. Anna Komnene, X.7, p. 279. • **30**. Ibid., p. 280. • **31**. Ibid. • **32**. Anna Komnene, X.8, p. 281. • **33**. Fulcher of Chartres, I.6, p. 72; Anna Komnene, X.7, pp. 279–80. • **34**. Albert of Aachen, II.7, pp. 70–2. • **35**. Hagenmeyer, *Epistulae*, p. 143; C. de Coussemaker, 'Documents relatifs à la Flandre maritime. Extraits du cartulaire de l'abbaye de Watten', *Annales du comité flamand de France*, 10 vols. (Paris, 1860), 5, p. 359. • **36**. Fulcher of Chartres, I.8.i–ix, pp. 76–8. • **37**. *Gesta Francorum*, II, p. 11; Albert of Aachen, II.18, p. 88; *Historia Belli Sacri, RHC, Occ.*, 3, p. 177. • **38**. Anna Komnene, X.8, pp. 281–4. • **39**. Raymond of Aguilers, II, p. 21. • **40**. *Gesta Francorum*, II, p. 10. • **41**. *Gesta Francorum*, I, p. 8. • **42**. Nesbitt, 'Rate of march', pp. 167–82. • **43**. *Gesta Francorum*, II, p. 10. • **44**. Raymond of Aguilers, I, p. 18; J. Shepard, '"Father" or "Scorpion"? Style and substance in Alexios' diplomacy', in M. Mullett and D. Smythe (eds.), *Alexios I Komnenos – Papers* (Belfast, 1996), pp. 80–2. • **45**. Anna Komnene, X.9, p. 285. • **46**. Ibid. • **47**. Anna Komnene, X.7, p. 280; X.11, p. 292; *Gesta Francorum*, I, pp. 5–6; II, p. 11. • **48**. Raymond of Aguilers, II, p. 22. • **49**. Barber and Bate, *Letters*, p. 16. • **50**. Ibid., pp. 15–16. • **51**. Fulcher of Chartres, I.9.iii, p. 80. • **52**. Ralph of Caen, 18, p. 42. • **53**. *De Cerimoniis*, II.15, 2, p. 597. • **54**. P. Chiesa (ed.), *Liudprandi Cremonensis. Antapodosis; Homelia paschalis; Historia Ottonis; Relatio de Legatione Constantinopolitana* (Turnhout, 1997), *Relatio*, I.1, pp. 238–9. • **55**. Ibid., *Antapodosis*, VI.5, pp. 197–8. • **56**. Anna Komnene, X.10, pp. 291– 2. For Alexios' methods, Shepard, '"Father" or "Scorpion"?', pp. 60–132. • **57**. Anna Komnene, XIII.10, pp. 383–4. • **58**. Anna Komnene, X.11, p. 292. • **59**. Ibid., pp. 292–3. • **60**. Ibid., p. 293. • **61**. Ibid., pp. 293–4. • **62**. Barber and Bate, *Letters*, pp. 15–16. • **63**. Albert of Aachen, II.17, p. 86. • **64**. Anna Komnene, XIV.4, p. 411. • **65**. Anna Komnene, X.9, pp. 285–6. • **66**. Robert the Monk, II.9, p. 94; Albert of Aachen, II.12–14, pp. 78–82; Anna Komnene, X.9, pp. 286–8. • **67**. Albert of Aachen, I.12, p. 78. • **68**. Albert of Aachen, II.12, p. 78. • **69**. Albert of Aachen, II.16, p. 84. • **70**. Ibid. • **71**. Ibid., pp. 84–6. • **72**. Fulcher of Chartres, I.9.iii, p. 80. • **73**. *Gesta Francorum*, II, p. 12. • **74**. Fulcher of Chartres, I.8.ix, p. 78. • **75**. Anna Komnene, X.9, p. 285. • **76**. Michael the Syrian, XV.6, 3, p. 179. • **77**. Anna Komnene, X.9, pp. 285–6. • **78**. Albert of Aachen, II.10, p. 74. • **79**. Anna Komnene, X.9, p. 285. • **80**. Ekkehard of Aura, pp. 166–7. • **81**. Albert of Aachen, II.16, pp. 84–6. Also see here, E. Patlagean, 'Christianisation et parentés rituelles: le domaine de Byzance', *Annales ESC* 33 (1978), pp. 625–36; R. Macrides, 'Kinship by arrangement: The case of adoption', *Dumbarton Oaks Papers* 44

(1990), pp. 109–18. • **82**. S. Reynolds, *Fiefs and Vassals: The Medieval Evidence Reinterpreted* (Oxford, 1994). • **83**. Anna Komnene, XIII.12, p. 386. For the oaths, see J. Pryor, 'The oath of the leaders of the Crusade to the emperor Alexius Comnenus: Fealty, homage', *Parergon* New Series 2 (1984), pp. 111–41. • **84**. *Gesta Francorum*, II, pp. 11–12. • **85**. Fulcher of Chartres, I.9.iii, p. 80. • **86**. *Gesta Francorum*, II, p. 12. • **87**. Anna Komnene, X.11, pp. 294–5. • **88**. J. Shepard, 'When Greek meets Greek: Alexius Comnenus and Bohemund in 1097–8', *Byzantine and Modern Greek Studies* 12 (1988), pp. 185–277. • **89**. Anna Komnene, X.9, p. 289. • **90**. Raymond of Aguilers, II, p. 23. • **91**. Ibid., p. 24. Also *Gesta Francorum*, II, p. 13. • **92**. *Gesta Francorum*, II, p. 12. • **93**. Raymond of Aguilers, II, p. 24. • **94**. Anna Komnene, X.9, p. 289. • **95**. Ibn a-Qalanisi, AH 490/Dec. 1096–Dec. 1097, p. 43 • **96**. Ibn al-Athir, AH 491/Dec. 1096–Dec. 1097, p. 14. • **97**. *Gesta Francorum*, II, p. 11. • **98**. Anna Komnene, XI.2, p. 300.

9 *First Encounters with the Enemy*

1. Barber and Bate, *Letters*, p. 16. • **2**. For example, *Gesta Francorum*, II, p. 14; Albert of Aachen, II.29, p. 110. • **3**. Albert of Aachen, I.15, p. 30. • **4**. Albert of Aachen, II.28, p. 110. • **5**. Raymond of Aguilers, III, p. 26; Constable, *Letters of Peter the Venerable*, 2, p. 209; P. Magdalino, *The Empire of Manuel I Komnenos, 1143–80* (Cambridge, 1993), p. 44. Also see J. Shepard, 'Cross-purposes: Alexius Comnenus and the First Crusade', in Phillips (ed.), *The First Crusade*, p. 120, and n. 65. • **6**. Anna Komnene, XI.2, p. 300. • **7**. *Gesta Francorum*, II, p. 15. • **8**. Raymond of Aguilers, III, p. 25. For Nicaea's fortifications, A. Schneider and W. Karnapp, *Die Stadtmauer von Iznik-Nicea* (Berlin, 1938); C. Foss and D. Winfield, *Byzantine Fortifications* (Pretoria, 1986), pp. 79–121; R. Rogers, *Latin Siege Warfare in the 12th Century* (Oxford, 1992), pp. 17–25. • **9**. *Gesta Francorum*, II, p. 15. • **10**. Albert of Aachen, II.29, p. 110–12; II.22, p. 96. • **11**. Albert of Aachen, II.33, pp. 116–18. • **12**. Matthew of Edessa, II.108, p. 163; Anna Komnene, VI.12, p. 179. • **13**. Albert of Aachen, II.34, pp. 118–20; Fulcher of Chartres, I.10.vii, p. 82. • **14**. Anna Komnene, XI.1, p. 298. • **15**. Ibid., p. 299. • **16**. Ibid. • **17**. Ibid., pp. 297–8. • **18**. Albert of Aachen II.25–6, pp. 102–4. • **19**. Anna Komnene XI.2, p. 300. • **20**. Ibid., p. 301. • **21**. Anna Komnene, XI.2.vi, p. 327. • **22**. Ibn al-Qalanisi, AH 490/Dec. 1096–Dec. 1097, p. 41. • **23**. C. Foss, 'Byzantine responses to Turkish Attacks: Some sites of Asia Minor', in I. Sevcenko and I. Hutter, *Aetos: Studies in Honour of Cyril Mango* (Stuttgart, 1998), pp. 155–8. • **24**. Barber and Bate, *Letters*, p. 19. • **25**. Anna Komnene, XI.2, pp. 303–4. • **26**. Anna Komnene, XI.3, p. 304: Fulcher of Chartres, I.10.x, p. 83. • **27**. Barber and Bate, *Letters*, p. 19. Later writers also focus on the fate of Nicaea as a turning point in attitudes to Alexios, e.g.

Orderic Vitalis, IX.8, 5, p. 56. • **28**. Anna Komnene, XI.3, p. 304. • **29**. Ralph of Caen, 10, pp. 31–2. • **30**. Anna Komnene, XI.3, pp. 304–5; Ralph of Caen, 18, p. 42. • **31**. Guibert of Nogent, IV.10, p. 81. • **32**. Anna Komnene, XI.3, p. 304. • **33**. Raymond of Aguilers, II, p. 23. • **34**. Anna Komnene, X.2, p. 264. • **35**. Fulcher of Chartres, I.11.i, p. 83. • **36**. Anna Komnene, XI.5, pp. 309–12. • **37**. Fulcher of Chartres, I.13.i, p. 87; Shephard, '"Father" or "Scorpion"', p. 88. • **38**. Anna Komnene, XI.2, p. 301; XI.5, pp. 309–10. • **39**. Anna Komnene, XI.5, pp. 309–12. • **40**. This episode is misplaced by Anna Komnene – Çaka's death evidently took place after the Byzantine recovery of Smyrna, and not beforehand. Anna Komnene, IX.3, pp. 243–4. • **41**. Ibid., p. 244. • **42**. Fulcher of Chartres, I.11.vi, p. 85. • **43**. *Gesta Francorum*, III, p. 18; Ralph of Caen, 40, p. 65; Fulcher of Chartres, I.11.ix, pp. 85–6. • **44**. Fulcher of Chartres, I.11.viii, p. 85. • **45**. *Gesta Francorum*, III, pp. 19–20. • **46**. Fulcher of Chartres, I.12.iv–v, p. 87. • **47**. *Gesta Francorum*, III, p. 21. • **48**. Albert of Aachen, II.22, p. 94. Albert also refers to Kilidj Arslan as 'magnificent', I.16, p. 32; the same praise is given to another Turk further east, Danishmend, whom Albert also says is 'worthy of praise', IX.33, p. 680. • **49**. Anna Komnene, X.10, pp. 291–2. • **50**. *Gesta Francorum*, IV, p. 24. • **51**. Ibn al-Qalanisi, AH 490/Dec. 1096–Dec. 1097, p. 42. • **52**. *Gesta Francorum*, IV, p. 26. • **53**. Ibid., p. 25. • **54**. Albert of Aachen, III.10, pp. 152–4. • **55**. Albert of Aachen, III.3, p. 140; Ralph of Caen, 23, p. 47. • **56**. Albert of Aachen, III.3–18, pp. 140–66. • **57**. Anna Komnene, X.10, p. 291. • **58**. Raymond of Aguilers, IV, p. 37. • **59**. Matthew of Edessa, II.104–8, pp. 161–4; II.117–18, pp. 168–70; Fulcher of Chartres, I.14.i–xv, pp. 88–92; Albert of Aachen, II.19–24, pp. 169–77. • **60**. Fulcher, I.14.xi, p. 91. • **61**. W. Saunders, 'The Greek inscription on the Harran gate at Edessa: Some further evidence', *Byzantinische Forschungen* 21 (1995), pp. 301–4. • **62**. Albert of Aachen, III.19, p. 168. • **63**. Guibert of Nogent, VII.39, pp. 338–9. • **64**. For example, Albert of Aachen, IV.9, p. 262; VII.31, p. 528; Guibert of Nogent, VII.39, p. 338; Orderic Vitalis, IX.11, 5, pp. 118–20. • **65**. Thus Guibert of Nogent, VII.37, p. 335. • **66**. Albert of Aachen, III.31, p. 361. • **67**. Rogers, *Latin Siege Warfare*, pp. 25–39. • **68**. Fulcher of Chartres, I.15.ii, p. 92. • **69**. *Gesta Francorum*, V, p. 28. • **70**. Raymond of Aguilers, VI, p. 49. • **71**. Anna Komnene, XI.7, p. 317. For the appointment of Eumathios Philokales on Cyprus, IX.2, p. 242. • **72**. Ibn al-Qalanisi, AH 490/Dec. 1096–Dec. 1097, p. 242. • **73**. Fulcher of Chartres, I.16.ii, p. 96. • **74**. Albert of Aachen, III.46, pp. 208–10. • **75**. Albert of Aachen, V.1, p. 338. • **76**. Matthew of Edessa, II.114, pp. 167–8. • **77**. Fulcher of Chartres, I.16.iii, p. 96. • **78**. *Gesta Francorum*, V, pp. 30–1. • **79**. Raymond of Aguilers, VI, p. 39. • **80**. *Gesta Francorum*, V, pp. 36–7. • **81**. Ibid., p. 37. • **82**. Ibid.

10 *The Struggle for the Soul of the Crusade*

1. Raymond of Aguilers, IV, p. 36. • **2.** Guibert of Nogent, V.6, p. 206. • **3.** *Gesta Francorum*, VI, p. 33. • **4.** Guibert of Nogent, V.14, p. 217. • **5.** Albert of Aachen, IV.39, pp. 308–10; *Gesta Francorum*, IX, p. 59. • **6.** Raymond of Aguilers, IV, p. 35; *Gesta Francorum*, V, p. 30. • **7.** *Gesta Francorum*, IX, p. 63; Ralph of Caen, 58, p. 84; Albert of Aachen, IV.13, pp. 266–8. • **8.** Ralph of Caen, 58, p. 84. • **9.** Guibert of Nogent, II.16, pp. 132–3. • **10.** Kemal ad-Din, 'La Chronique d'Alep', *RHC, Or.*, p. 578; *Anonymi Florinensis brevis narratio Belli sacri, RHC, Occ.*, 5, p. 371; Ralph of Caen, 58, p. 84. • **11.** Caffaro, *De liberatione civitatum orientis*, in *RHC, Occ.*, 5, p. 66. For supply from Cyprus, also see Baldric of Dol, p. 65; Raymond of Aguilers, VII, p. 54; Ralph of Caen, 58, p. 84. • **12.** Hagenmeyer, *Epistulae*, p. 166. • **13.** *Gesta Francorum*, VI, pp. 34–5; Raymond of Aguilers, IV, p. 37. • **14.** Albert of Aachen, IV.40, pp. 310–12. • **15.** Raymond of Aguilers, IV, p. 37. J. France, 'The departure of Tatikios from the Crusader army', *Bulletin of the Institute of Historical Research* 44 (1971), pp. 137–47. • **16.** *Gesta Francorum*, VI, pp. 34–5. • **17.** Hagenmeyer, *Epistulae*, pp. 165–6; Ralph of Caen, 58, p. 84. • **18.** This found echoes in later accounts of the Crusade with other episodes. Orderic Vitalis, for example, claims that the first seeds of hatred of Alexios were sown at Nicaea, where his capture of the city paled in comparison to the costs incurred, provisions used and blood shed by the Crusaders. IX.8, 5, p. 56. • **19.** Shepard, 'When Greek meets Greek', pp. 188–277. • **20.** *Gesta Francorum*, VIII, pp. 44–5; Albert of Aachen, IV.15, p. 270; Ralph of Caen, 64–5, pp. 89–90; William of Tyre, IV.24, pp. 267–8; cf. Anna Komnene, XI.4, pp. 307–8. • **21.** *Gesta Francorum*, V, p. 45; Fulcher of Chartres, I.19.i, p. 101; Anna Komnene, XI.6, p. 312. Also Barber and Bate, *Letters*, p. 28; Matthew of Edessa, II.119, p. 170. • **22.** *Gesta Francorum*, VI, p. 44; Fulcher of Chartres, I.17, p. 98; Matthew of Edessa, II.120, p. 170; Ibn al-Qalanisi, AH 491/Dec. 1097–Dec. 1098, p. 45. Firouz is identified as a Turk, Raymond of Aguilers, VI, p. 47; Albert of Aachen, III.61, p. 234. Ibn al-Athir talks of the role played by Firouz (Rudbah) and the offer made to him, AH 491/Dec. 1097–Dec. 1098, pp. 14–15; Kemal ad-Din, p. 580. • **23.** Anna Komnene, V.6, p. 144. • **24.** Raymond of Aguilers, IV, p. 37. • **25.** *Gesta Francorum*, VIII, p. 45; Albert of Aachen, IV.14–15, pp. 270–2; Ralph of Caen, 65, p. 654. • **26.** *Gesta Francorum*, VIII, p. 46. • **27.** Raymond of Aguilers, VI, p. 47. • **28.** Albert of Aachen, IV.20, p. 278. • **29.** Raymond of Aguilers, VI, p. 47; Albert of Aachen, IV.21, p. 280. • **30.** *Gesta Francorum*, VII, p. 47. • **31.** *Gesta Francorum*, VIII, p. 48. • **32.** Albert of Aachen, IV.26, p. 286. • **33.** *Gesta Francorum*, IX, p. 62. • **34.** Albert of Aachen, IV.34, pp. 298–300; Raymond of Aguilers, VIII, p. 59; Ibn al-Athir, AH 491/Dec. 1097–Dec. 1098, p. 16. • **35.** Fulcher of Chartres, I.19.iii, p. 101. • **36.** For the

discovery of the Holy Lance and its consequences on the Crusade, see T. Asbridge, 'The Holy Lance of Antioch: Power, devotion and memory on the First Crusade', *Reading Medieval Studies* 33 (2007), pp. 3–36. • **37**. Albert of Aachen, IV.46, p. 320. • **38**. Fulcher of Chartres, I.22.ii, p. 104; *Gesta Francorum*, IX, pp. 67–8. • **39**. Fulcher of Chartres, I.22.v, p. 105. • **40**. Raymond of Aguilers, VIII, p. 61. • **41**. Fulcher of Chartres, I.23.iv–v, p. 106. • **42**. Raymond of Aguilers, VIII, pp. 63–4. • **43**. *Gesta Francorum*, IX, pp. 69–70. • **44**. Albert of Aachen, IV.53, pp. 330–2. • **45**. Ibn al-Athir, AH 491/Dec. 1097–Dec. 1098, pp. 16–17. • **46**. Raymond of Aguilers, IX, p. 65. • **47**. Robert the Monk, II.2, p. 90. • **48**. Albert of Aachen, V.15, p. 396. • **49**. Albert of Aachen, IV.9, pp. 260–2; Raymond of Aguilers, X, pp. 73–4. • **50**. Albert of Aachen, V.15, p. 357; *Gesta Francorum*, X, pp. 73–4. • **51**. Raymond of Aguilers, X, p. 75. • **52**. *Gesta Francorum*, IX, p. 63. • **53**. Anna Komnene, XI.6, p. 313. • **54**. Raymond of Aguilers, IV, p. 37. • **55**. *Gesta Francorum*, X, p. 72; Fulcher of Chartres, I.23.viii, p. 107. • **56**. Albert of Aachen, V.3, pp. 340–2. • **57**. Raymond of Aguilers, IX, pp. 67–8. • **58**. Ralph of Caen, 51, p. 77. • **59**. S. Duparc-Quioc (ed.), *La Chanson d'Antioche*, 2 vols. (Paris, 1976), I, laisse 175. • **60**. Raymond of Aguilers, IV, p. 34. • **61**. Raymond of Aguilers, IX, p. 84. • **62**. Barber and Bate, *Letters*, pp. 32–3. • **63**. Ibid., p. 33; also Fulcher of Chartres, I.24.xiii–xiv, pp. 111–12. • **64**. Ibid. Fulcher does not include this final paragraph, below, p. 203 • **65**. Raymond of Aguilers, X, pp. 74–5; *Gesta Francorum*, X, pp. 75–6, 80–1. • **66**. *Gesta Francorum*, X, pp. 75–6. • **67**. Raymond of Aguilers, X, p. 80. • **68**. *Gesta Francorum*, X, p. 80; Fulcher of Chartres, I.25.ii, p. 112. • **69**. *Gesta Francorum*, X, pp. 82, 86; Raymond of Aguilers, XI, pp. 87, 91. • **70**. Raymond of Aguilers, XIII, p. 105.

11 *The Crusade Unravels*

1. Albert of Aachen, V.45, p. 402. • **2**. Ralph of Caen, 120, pp. 136–7; Baldric of Dol, IV.12, p. 100; Albert of Aachen, VI.2, p. 406. • **3**. Raymond of Aguilers, XIV, p. 119. • **4**. *Gesta Francorum*, X, pp. 88–9; Albert of Aachen, VI.5, p. 410; Raymond of Aguilers, XIV, pp. 119–20. • **5**. France, *Victory in the East*, pp. 122–42. • **6**. Fulcher of Chartres, I.27.iv, p. 119. • **7**. Albert of Aachen, VI.6, pp. 410–12. Also *Gesta Francorum*, X, p. 89; Raymond of Aguilers, XIV, p. 118. • **8**. Fulcher of Chartres, I.26.i, p. 116. • **9**. *Gesta Francorum*, X, p. 89. • **10**. Raymond of Aguilers, XIII, p. 114. • **11**. Albert of Aachen, VI.8, pp. 412–14. • **12**. *Gesta Francorum*, X, p. 90; Raymond of Aguilers, XIV, p. 124. • **13**. Raymond of Aguilers, XIV, pp. 124–5; Ralph of Caen, 125, pp. 140–2; *Gesta Francorum*, X, p. 90. • **14**. Albert of Aachen, VI.10, p. 416; Ralph of Caen, 124, pp. 139–40. • **15**. *Gesta Francorum*, X, pp. 91–2; Ibn al-Athir, AH 492/Dec. 1098–Dec. 1099,

p. 21. • **16**. *Gesta Francorum*, X, pp. 79–80. • **17**. Raymond of Aguilers, XIV, p. 127. • **18**. *Gesta Francorum*, X, p. 92. • **19**. Fulcher of Chartres, I.27.xiii, p. 122. • **20**. B. Kedar, 'The Jerusalem Massacre of July 1099 in the Western Historiography of the First Crusade', *Crusades* 3 (2004), pp. 15–75. • **21**. Ibn al-Athir, AH 492/Dec. 1098–Dec. 1099, p. 21. • **22**. S. Goitein, 'Contemporary letters on the capture of Jerusalem', *Journal of Jewish Studies* 3 (1952), pp. 162–77. • **23**. Fulcher of Chartres, I.28.i, p. 122. • **24**. Fulcher of Chartres, I.29.i, p. 123. • **25**. S. Goitein, 'Tyre–Tripoli–'Arqa: Geniza documents from the beginning of the Crusade period', *Jewish Quarterly Review* 66 (1975), pp. 69–88. • **26**. Raymond of Aguilers, XIV, p. 128, citing Isaiah 65:17, Psalms 118:24. • **27**. *Naser-e Khusraw's Book of Travels (Safarnama)*, tr. W. Thackston (New York, 1986), p. 21. Many pilgrim guides were written in this period for Muslim visitors to Jerusalem, a good example being that of Ibn al-Murajja, written in the first part of the eleventh century. E. Amikam, *Medieval Jerusalem and Islamic Worship* (Leiden, 1995), pp. 68–78. • **28**. M. Gil, *A History of Palestine, 634–1099* (Cambridge, 1997), p. 191, n. 67. • **29**. M-L. Favreau-Lilie, *Die Italiener im Heiligen Land vom ersten Kreuzzug bis zum Tode Heinrichs von Champagne (1098–1197)* (Amsterdam, 1988). • **30**. Barber and Bate, *Letters*, p. 24; William of Tyre, IV.24, I, pp. 267–8. Also note *Gesta Francorum*,VI, pp. 37–8; Raymond of Aguilers, V, pp. 40–1. • **31**. Fulcher of Chartres, I.31.i–xii, pp. 125–8; P. Tudebode, pp. 146–7; Albert of Aachen, VI.45–50, pp. 464–70. • **32**. Barber and Bate, *Letters*,, pp. 37–8. • **33**. For the expedition of 1101, Riley-Smith, *First Crusade*, pp. 120–34. • **34**. Albert of Aachen, VII.20, p. 512; Fulcher of Chartres, I.36.i, p. 136; Matthew of Edessa, II.132, p. 176. • **35**. Bohemond's capture, Fulcher of Chartres, I.35.iii, p. 135; Albert of Aachen, VII.29, p. 526; Matthew of Edessa, II.134, p. 177. • **36**. See. A. Murray, 'Daimbert of Pisa, the *Domus Godefridi* and the Accession of Baldwin I of Jerusalem', in *From Clermont to Jerusalem*, pp. 81–102. • **37**. Albert of Aachen, X.30, p. 528. • **38**. William of Tyre, VI.23, I, p. 340. For John's flight, ibid.; Orderic Vitalis, X.24, 5, p. 356. • **39**. Fulcher of Chartres, II.3.xiii, p. 143. • **40**. Albert of Aachen, VII.43, p. 550. For Godfrey's burial, VII.21, p. 516. • **41**. Albert of Aachen, VII.46–51, pp. 554–60. • **42**. Albert of Aachen, VII.57, p. 566; for his service to the emperor, IX.6, p. 644. Also see here Shepard, 'The "muddy road" of Odo Arpin', pp. 11–28. • **43**. Albert of Aachen, IX.1–6, pp. 638–44; Fulcher of Chartres, II.15.i–vi, pp. 163–4; Anna Komnene, XI.7, p. 316. • **44**. The patriarch was dismissed on charges of embezzlement. Albert of Aachen, VII.62–63, p. 574. It is significant that these were made by envoys sent by Roger of Sicily, erstwhile supporter of the papacy, and of its reconciliation with Constantinople in the 1090s. This suggests that the axis of Rome–Sicily–Constantinople was working together once again. • **45**. Albert of Aachen, VIII.45, p. 634. • **46**. Albert of Aachen, VIII.45–48, pp. 634–6. • **47**. Anna Komnene, XI.7, p. 318; Ralph of Caen, 143–4, pp. 158–60. For the chronology here see R-J. Lilie, *Byzantium and the Crusader States 1096–1204*, tr. J. Morris and J. Ridings (Oxford. 1993), pp. 259–76 and Ia. Liubarskii, 'Zamechaniya k khronologii XI knigi 'Aleksiada' Anny Komninoi', *Vizantiiskii Vremennik* 24 (1964), pp. 47–56. • **48**. Anna Komnene, XI.7, p. 318; Ralph of Caen, 145, p. 160. • **49**. Ralph of Caen, 147, pp. 163–4. • **50**. Kemal ad-Din, p. 591. • **51**. Anna Komnene, XI.9, pp. 320–1. • **52**. Fulcher of Chartres, II.27.vii–viii, pp. 178–9. • **53**. Ibn al-Athir, AH 497/Dec. 1103–Dec. 1104, pp. 79–80; Ibn al-Qalanisi, p. 60. Also here Fulcher of Chartres, II.27.i–viii, pp. 177–9; Matthew of Edessa, III.18, pp. 192–3; Albert of Aachen, IX.39; Ralph of Caen, 148, pp. 164–5. • **54**. Ibn al-Qalanisi, p. 61. • **55**. For Tancred taking possession of Edessa, Albert of Aachen, IX.42, p. 694; Fulcher of Chartres, II.27.5, p. 178; II.28, p. 180; Ralph of Caen, 151, p. 167; Matthew of Edessa, III.20, p. 194. For the Byzantine gains of 1104, Anna Komnene, XI.9–11, pp. 321–9. • **56**. Albert of Aachen, IX.46, p. 700–2. • **57**. Ralph of Caen, 152, pp. 168–9. • **58**. Anna Komnene, XI.12, pp. 329–31.

12 *The Consequences of the First Crusade*

1. For songs being sung in France, Orderic Vitalis, X.21, 5, p. 342. For the song cycles, see S. Edgington and C. Sweetenham (eds.), *The Chanson d'Antioche: An Old-French Account of the First Crusade* (Aldershot, 2011). • **2**. E. de Marneffe (ed.), *Cartulaire de l'abbaye d'Afflighem* (Louvain, 1894), pp. 19–21. • **3**. For many examples, see Riley-Smith, *The First Crusaders*, p. 150. • **4**. E.g. *De genere comitum Flandrensium notae Parisienses*, MGH, SS, 13, p. 259. • **5**. Suger of St Denis, p. 38; also see Riley-Smith, *First Crusade*, pp. 122–3. • **6**. Guy of Trousseau deserted at Antioch according to the *Gesta Francorum*, IX, pp. 55–6. His relationship through marriage with the king presumably explains sympathetic comments about him in a source close to the royal house of France. Suger of St Denis, p. 36. • **7**. Guibert of Nogent, VI.11, p. 243. • **8**. For Stephen's death, Albert of Aachen, IX.6, p. 644. For an example of his treatment in the song cycles, *Chanson d'Antioche*, pp. 285–6. • **9**. France, *Victory in the East*, pp. 141–2. • **10**. Gilbert of Mons, 27, p. 30. See William of Tyre, I, p. 298; Albert of Aachen, IX.52, p. 716. • **11**. Orderic Vitalis, X.24, 5, pp. 358–76. • **12**. Ibid., p. 354. • **13**. France, 'The Anonymous *Gesta Francorum*', pp. 39–69 and above all, Rubenstein, 'What is the *Gesta Francorum* and who was Peter Tudebode?', pp. 179–204. • **14**. Fulcher of Chartres, I.33. v–xxi, pp. 129–32; Albert of Aachen, VII.6, p. 494. • **15**. R. Hiestand (ed.), *Papsturkunden für Kirchen im Heiligen Lande* (Göttingen, 1985), p. 102; for several other examples, *Codice Diplomatico Barese*, 5, pp. 83–102. • **16**. Suger of St Denis, p. 44. • **17**. Romuald of Salerno, p. 203; Ekkehard of Aura, p. 293; William of Tyre,

XI.1, 1, p. 460. • **18.** Bartulf of Nangis, *Gesta Francorum expugnantium Iherusalem*, 65, p. 538; *Chronica Monasterii Casinensis*, IV, p. 493; Suger of St Denis, p. 48; Hiestand, *Papsturkunden für Kirchen*, p. 7, n. 2; *Codice Diplomatico Barese*, 5, pp. 79–80. • **19.** Albert of Aachen, VIII.48, p. 636. • **20.** See, for example, W. Whalen, 'God's Will or Not? Bohemond's campaign against the Byzantine Empire (1105–1108)', in T. Madden, J. Naus and V. Ryan (eds.) *Crusades – Worlds in conflict* (Farnham, 2010), pp. 115–23. • **21.** For Bohemond's itinerary, see L. Russo, 'Il viaggio di Boemundo d'Altavilla in Francia', *Archivio storico italiano* 603 (2005), pp. 3–42. • **22.** Orderic Vitalis, XI.12, 6, pp. 70–2. • **23.** Ibid., p. 70. • **24.** See for example W. Holtzmann, 'Zur Geschichte des Investiturstreites', *Neues Archiv der Gesellschaft für ältere deutsche Geschichtskunde* 50 (1935), pp. 280–2. • **25.** Orderic Vitalis, XI.12, 6, p. 68; William of Malmesbury, IV.407, p. 736. • **26.** J. Stevenson (ed.), *Chronicon Monasterii de Abingdon*, 2 vols. (London, 1858), 2, p. 46. There is no indication of date or the motivation of the embassy to England. • **27.** For example, Shepard, 'The "muddy road" of Odo Arpin', pp. 11–28. • **28.** Anna Komnene, XIII.12, p. 385. • **29.** Ibid., p. 386. • **30.** Ibid., pp. 392–4. • **31.** Ibid., p. 387; p. 389. • **32.** Ibid., p. 392. • **33.** Ibid. • **34.** Orderic Vitalis, X.24, 5, p. 356; William of Tyre, VI.23, 1, p. 340. • **35.** Anna Komnene, XIV.1, p. 397. • **36.** Anna Komnene, XIII.12, p. 395. • **37.** Ibid., p. 394. • **38.** Fulcher of Chartres, I.32, p. 128; Orderic Vitalis, X.12, 5, p. 276. • **39.** Anna Komnene, XI.7, p. 316; XII.1, pp. 332–3; Orderic Vitalis, X.23, 5, p. 350; X.24, p. 354. • **40.** *Gesta Francorum*, I, p. 5. • **41.** Ibid., p. 6; II, p. 10. • **42.** *Gesta Francorum*, II, p. 11. • **43.** Ibid., p. 17. • **44.** Raymond of Aguilers, I, pp. 18–19; II, p. 22. • **45.** Raymond of Aguilers, II, pp. 26–7. • **46.** Ibid., p. 23. • **47.** *Gesta Francorum*, II, p. 12. • **48.** Robert the Monk, VII.20, p. 176. • **49.** Barber and Bate, *Letters*, p. 20. • **50.** Ibid., pp. 22–5. • **51.** Matthew of Edessa, II.114, p. 167. For the Black Mountain, see *Regulations of Nikon of the Black Mountain*, in J. Thomas and A. Constantinides Hero (eds.), *Byzantine Monastic Foundation Documents*, 5 vols. (Washington, DC, 2000), pp. 377–424. Also see *Typikon of Nikon of the Black Mountain for the Monastery and Hospice of the Mother of God tou Roidiou* in ibid., pp. 425–39. • **52.** Ralph of Caen, 54, p. 80. • **53.** Raymond of Aguilers, XI, p. 88. • **54.** Hagenmeyer, *Epistulae*, p. 153. • **55.** Barber and Bate, *Letters*, p. 21. • **56.** *Gesta Francorum*, X, p. 72; Fulcher of Chartres, I.23.viii, p. 107; cf. Albert of Aachen, V.3, pp. 340–2. • **57.** Barber and Bate, *Letters*, pp. 30–3. • **58.** Ibid., p. 33. • **59.** Fulcher of Chartres, I.24.i–xiv, pp. 107–12. • **60.** Raymond of Aguilers, II, p. 23. • **61.** Ibid., pp. 22–3. • **62.** *Gesta Francorum*, X, p. 75. • **63.** Raymond of Aguilers, X, pp. 74–5. • **64.** Robert the Monk, VII.20, p. 176; William of Tyre, IX.13, 1, p. 437. • **65.** Robert the Monk, VI.16, p. 160. • **66.** Guibert of Nogent, I.5, p. 104. • **67.** William of Malmesbury, *History of the English Kings*, ed. R. Thomson, R. Mynors and M. Winterbottom (Oxford, 1999), III.262, pp. 482–4.

• **68**. Roger of Hoveden, *Rerum Anglicarum Scriptores post Bedam* (repr. Farnborough, 1970), p. 710. • **69**. William of Malmesbury, II.225, p. 412. • **70**. William of Tyre, X.12, 1, p. 467. • **71**. Edward Gibbon, *Decline and Fall of the Roman Empire*, ed. J. Bury, 7 vols. (London, 1909–14) 6, p. 335. • **72**. Anna Komnene, XIV.2, p. 401. • **73**. Albert of Aachen, IX.43, p. 696. • **74**. A. Wharton Epstein, 'The date and significance of the Cathedral of Canosa in Apulia, Southern Italy', *Dumbarton Oaks Papers* 37 (1983), pp. 85–6. • **75**. M. Ogle and D. Schullian (eds.) *Rodulfi Tortarii Carmina* (Rome, 1933), pp. 298–316. • **76**. See N. Paul, 'A warlord's wisdom: Literacy and propaganda at the time of the First Crusade', *Speculum* 85 (2010), pp. 534–66. Another source from this period also reports Bohemond as having got the better of the emperor, rather than the other way round. *Narratio Floriacensis*, pp. 356–62. • **77**. Barber and Bate, *Letters*, pp. 30–3. • **78**. *Gesta Francorum*, I, pp. 1–2. • **79**. Erdmann, *Die Briefe Heinrichs IV*, pp. 38–9. • **80**. Ekkehard of Aura, pp. 182–4; *Annales Hildesheimensis*, MGH, SS, 3, pp. 50–1. • **81**. Erdmann, *Die Briefe Heinrichs IV*, pp. 39–40. • **82**. *Patrologia Latina*, 163, cols. 108a–c. • **83**. Erdmann, *Die Briefe Heinrichs IV*, pp. 39–40. • **84**. For the treaty, Anna Komnene, IX.3, p. 244, and above, p. 146. For the stable and seemingly positive relations between Alexios and Kilidj Arslan, see, for example, Albert of Aachen, IX.34, pp. 680–2. • **85**. For Fulcher's emollient attitude to Byzantium, see L. Ní Chléirigh, 'The impact of the First Crusade on Western opinion towards the Byzantine Empire: The *Dei Gesta per Francos* of Guibert of Nogent and the *Historia Hierosolymitana* of Fulcher of Chartres', in C. Kostick (ed.), *The Crusades and the Near East: Cultural Histories* (Abingdon, 2011), pp. 161–88. • **86**. Albeit reaching rather different conclusions, note M. Carrier, 'L'image d'Alexis Ier Comnène selon le chroniqleur Albert d'Aix', *Byzantion* 78 (2008), pp. 34–65. • **87**. Anna Komnene, XI.8, p. 320. • **88**. Anna Komnene, XIV.2, pp. 402–3; Albert of Aachen, XI.4, p. 776. • **89**. P. Maas, 'Die Musen des Kaisers Alexios I', *Byzantinische Zeitschrift* 22 (1913), ll. 312–51. • **90**. H. Hoffmann (ed.), *Die Chronik von Montecassino* (Hanover, 1980), IV.46, p. 514. • **91**. Lilie, *Byzantium and the Crusader States*, p. 162. • **92**. Anna Komnene, XIV.4, p. 411. • **93**. Anna Komnene, X.2, p. 262.

Further Reading

Rather than include a comprehensive bibliography stretching to well over 2,000 books and articles, I thought it more useful to give some suggestions for starting points for the reader who would like to read more about the First Crusade in general, or about individual aspects of the expedition. Where possible, I have tried to list secondary works in English, though there are occasions when books and articles in other languages are unavoidable.

General

The Crusades have received a great deal of attention from historians, not least in recent years. Major volumes by Christopher Tyerman, *God's War: A New History of the Crusades* (London, 2006), Jonathan Phillips, *Holy Warriors: A Modern History of the Crusades* (London, 2009), and Thomas Asbridge, *The Crusades: The War for the Holy Land* (London, 2010) take different approaches to the Crusades. Each provides a compelling overview and demonstrates that scholarship about the subject is in robust health. The doyen of Crusade historians is Jonathan Riley-Smith, whose *The First Crusade and the Idea of Crusading* (London, 1986) is still indispensable. His many other works about the Crusades in general and about the first expedition to Jerusalem in particular are invaluable – not least *The First Crusaders 1095–1131* (Cambridge, 1997). John France's *Victory in the East* (Cambridge, 1994) provides a fine military history of the expedition to Jerusalem. Also see Thomas Asbridge's very readable *The First Crusade: A New History* (London, 2005).

There are a number of edited volumes based on conferences held to commemorate the nine hundredth anniversary of the Council of Clermont with collections of papers by leading scholars. The best are Jonathan Phillips' *The First Crusade: Origins and Impact* (Manchester, 1997), Michel Balard's *Autour de la Première Croisade* (Paris, 1996), and Alan Murray's *From Clermont to Jerusalem: The Crusades and Crusader Societies* (Turnhout, 1998). Other edited volumes to recommend include *Crusade and Settlement*, edited by Peter Edbury (Cardiff, 1985), and *The Experience of Crusading*, edited by Marcus Bull, Norman Housely and Jonathan Phillips, 2 vols. (Cambridge, 2003). Also see Thomas Madden's well-chosen collection of essays by leading scholars, *The Crusades* (Oxford, 2002). Alan Murray's bibliography for the First Crusade is also invaluable.

Modern Byzantine and Arab historians have written surprisingly little about this subject. One exception is Jonathan Harris' clear and useful *Byzantium and the Crusades* (London, 2003). Not to be missed is Paul Magdalino's 'The Byzantine background to the First Crusade', in *Canadian Institute of Balkan Studies* (Toronto, 1996), pp. 3–38. Likewise Ralph-Johannes Lilie's excellent study of Byzantine relations with the Crusaders, first published in German in 1981, available in a fine translation as *Byzantium and the Crusader States 1096–1204* (tr. Morris and Ridings, Oxford, 1993). Carole Hillenbrand's *The Crusades, Islamic Perspectives* (Edinburgh, 1999) is extremely helpful in looking at the west from the east.

Sources for the First Crusade

Anna Comnena by Georgina Buckler (Oxford, 1929) is still the only major monograph on the *Alexiad* and is excellent on the mechanics of the text, though less so on its interpretation. An important paper from the Belfast colloquium on Alexios I is essential, raising difficult questions about the composition of the text. The article by James Howard-Johnston in Margaret Mullett and Dion Smythe (eds.), *Alexios I Komnenos* (Belfast, 1996) is important and should be read alongside a slim but invaluable collection of essays edited by Thalia Gouma-Peterson, *Anna Komnene and Her Times* (New York, 2000). John France's 'Anna Comnena, the *Alexiad* and the First Crusade', *Reading Medieval Studies* 10 (1984), pp. 20–38 gives a western Crusade view of the text.

The best major deconstruction of the *Alexiad*'s chronology was done by Iakov Liubarskii 'Zamechaniya k khronologii XI Knigi "Aleksiada" Anny Komninoi', *Vizantiiskii Vremennik* 24 (1963), pp. 46–56, who examined the problems of Book XI of the *Alexiad*. This is reprised and advanced by Lilie in Appendix 1 of *Byzantium and the Crusader States*, pp. 259–76. The mistakes in the positioning of individual episodes elsewhere in the text have been noted by David Gress-Wright, 'Bogomilism in Constantinople', *Byzantion* 47 (1977), pp. 163–85; P. Gautier, 'Discours de Théophylacte de Bulgarie', *Revue des Etudes Byzantines* 20 (1962), esp. pp. 99–103; J. Gouillard, 'L'Abjuration du moine Nil le Calabrais', *Travaux et Mémoires* 2 (1968), pp. 290–303. Liubarskii's 'Ob istochnikakh "Aleksiady" Anny Komninoi', *Vizantiiskii Vremennik* 25 (1965), pp. 99–120 remains the best attempt to identify the range of sources available to Anna Komnene, as well as picking up on several other instances where the *Alexiad* is chronologically flawed. A major new study of Anna Komnene's work is needed to identify the full extent of the problems of the history's sequence of events.

For the western narrative sources for the Crusade, a good starting point is Colin Morris, 'The *Gesta Francorum* as Narrative History', *Reading Medieval Studies* 19 (1993), pp. 55–72. More recently, however, see John France's 'The anonymous *Gesta Francorum* and the *Historia Francorum qui ceperunt Iherusalem* of Raymond of Aguilers and the *Historia de Hierosolymitano itinere* of Peter Tudebode: An analysis of the textual relationship between primary sources for the First Crusade', in J. France and W. Zajac (eds.), *The Crusades and their Sources: Essays presented to Bernard Hamilton* (Aldershot, 1998), pp. 39–69. Also see France's 'The use of the anonymous *Gesta Francorum* in the early twelfth-century sources for the First Crusade', in Alan Murray, *From Clermont to Jerusalem: The Crusades and Crusader Societies* (Turnhout, 1998). pp. 29–42 and most recently, Jay Rubenstein, 'What is the *Gesta Francorum* and who was Peter Tudebode?', *Revue Mabillon* 16 (2005), pp. 179–204.

For Albert of Aachen, see Sue Edgington, 'Albert of Aachen reappraised', in Murray, *From Clermont to Jerusalem*, pp. 55–67. Also see Edgington's 'The First Crusade: Reviewing the evidence', in Phillips, *First Crusade*, pp. 57–77, and Marc Carrier's 'L'image d'Alexis Ier Comnène selon le chroniqueur Albert d'Aix', *Byzantion* 78 (2008), pp. 34–65. See R. Chazan, 'The Hebrew First Crusade Chronicles', *Revue des Etudes Juives* 133 (1974), pp. 235–54. Also Hillenbrand's 'The First Crusade: The Muslim perspective', in Phillips, *First Crusade*, pp. 130–41.

The letter from Alexios I to Robert of Flanders has been roundly dismissed, Peter Schreiner, 'Der Brief des Alexios I Komnenos an den Grafen Robert von Flandern und das Problem gefälschter byzantinischer Kaiserschreiben in den westlichen Quellen', and Christian Gastgeber, 'Das Schreiben Alexios I. Komnenos an Robert I. Flandern. Sprachliche Untersuchung', both in Giuseppe de Gregorio and Otto Kresten (eds.), *Documenti medievali Greci e Latini: Studi Comparativi* (Spoleto, 1998), pp. 111–40, 141–85, though also see Carole Sweetenham, 'Two letters calling Christians on Crusade', in *Robert the Monk's History of the First Crusade* (Aldershot, 2005), pp. 215–18. Both however consider the Byzantine position in Asia Minor to be positively healthy in the early 1090s. Note therefore Michel de Waha, 'La lettre d'Alexis Comnène à Robert Ier le Frison', *Byzantion* 47 (1977), pp. 113–25.

The papacy and western Europe at the time of the First Crusade

There are any number of outstanding studies about Europe on the eve of the Crusade. For the papacy, H. E. J. Cowdrey's *Pope Gregory VII, 1073–1085* (Oxford, 1998) and Alfons Becker's magisterial *Papst Urban II 1088–99*, 2 vols. (Stuttgart, 1964–88) are essential. Cowdrey's *The Age of Abbot Desiderius: Montecassino, the Papacy and the Normans in the Eleventh and Early Twelfth Centuries* (Oxford, 1983) is important, as is Josef Deér's *Papsttum und*

Normannen: Untersuchungen zu ihren lehnsrechtlichen und kirchenpolitischen Beziehungen (Cologne, 1972). Ian Robinson's *The Papacy 1073–1198* (Cambridge, 1990) provides a convincing commentary on Rome's struggles in this period. The same author's *Henry IV of Germany, 1056–1106* (Cambridge, 1999) is excellent on the crises in Europe in the late eleventh century. The collected works of Timothy Reuter, edited by Janet Nelson, *Medieval Polities and Modern Mentalities* (Cambridge, 2006), and Karl Leyser, edited by Reuter, in *Communications and Power in Medieval Europe: The Gregorian Revolution and Beyond* (London, 1994) offer much food for thought.

Steven Runciman's *Eastern Schism: A Study of the Papacy and the Eastern Churches During the Eleventh and Twelfth Centuries* (Oxford, 1955) still provides a clear narrative of the events of 1054, though Henry Chadwick's *East and West: The Making of a Rift in the Church: From Apostolic Times Until the Council of Florence* (Oxford, 2003) puts the schism in a wider context. Also worth seeing here is Aristeides Papadakis and John Meyendorff, *The Christian East and the Rise of the Papacy: The Church 1071–1453* (New York, 1994) and above all Axel Bayer's *Spaltung der Christenheit: Das sogenannte Morgenländische Schisma von 1054* (Cologne, 2002). Tia Kolbaba's *The Byzantine Lists: Errors of the Latins* (Urbana, 2000) is helpful on the rivalry between the Eastern and Western churches. For the investiture crisis, see Ute-Renata Blumenthal's *The Investiture Controversy: Church and Monarchy from the Ninth to the Twelfth Century* (Philadelphia, 1988) and Gerd Tellenbach, *The Western Church from the Tenth to the Early Twelfth Century* (Cambridge, 1993).

The Byzantine Empire in the late eleventh century

The Oxford History of Byzantium, edited by Cyril Mango (Oxford, 2002) and the *Cambridge History of Byzantine Empire, c.500–1492*, edited by Jonathan Shepard (Cambridge, 2008) provide introductions to the Byzantine Empire in general that are clear and often provocative. Angeliki Laiou's *The Economic History of Byzantium, From the Seventh Through the Fifteenth Century*, 3 vols. (Washington, DC, 2002) is also excellent, if monumental.

There are some outstanding collections of essays on Constantinople. See Cyril Mango's *Studies on Constantinople* (Aldershot 1993), and his *Constantinople and its Hinterland* (Aldershot, 1995) (with Gilbert Dagron). Paul Magdalino's *Studies on the History and Topography of Byzantine Constantinople* (Aldershot, 2007) offers much that is original and provocative. For a more general survey, see Jonathan Harris, *Constantinople: Capital of Byzantium* (London, 2007).

For the later eleventh century, the best secondary work is Jean-Claude Cheynet's *Pouvoir et contestations à Byzance 963–1210* (Paris, 1990). Alexander Kazhdan's seminal work on the Byzantine aristocracy is available in an

Italian translation, *L'aristocrazia bizantina: dal principio dell'XI alla fine del XII secolo* (tr. Silvia Ronchey, Palermo, 1997). Jonathan Shepard's brilliant 'Aspects of Byzantine attitudes and policy towards the West in the 10th and 11th Centuries', *Byzantinische Forschungen* 13 (1988), pp. 67–118 is a fine introduction to Byzantine attitudes to foreigners. Also see the same scholar's 'The uses of the Franks in 11th Century Byzantium', *Anglo-Norman Studies* 15 (1992), pp. 275–305, '"Father" or "Scorpion"? Style and substance in Alexios' diplomacy', in Mullett and Smythe, *Alexios*, pp. 68–132, and 'Cross-purposes: Alexius Comnenus and the First Crusade', in Phillips, *First Crusade*, pp. 107–29. Krinje Ciggaar's *Western Travellers to Constantinople: The West & Byzantium, 962–1204* (Leiden, 1996) shows just how cosmopolitan the city was in this period.

The reign of Alexios I Komnenos

Ferdinand Chalandon's *Essai sur le règne d'Alexis I Comnène* (Paris, 1900) is still the last major monograph on Alexios' rule. It remains lucid and very helpful. The proceedings of the 1989 Belfast symposium which appear in the Mullett and Smythe volume, *Alexios I Komnenos*, are excellent and contain a series of thought-provoking and important papers, above all those of Magdalino, Shepard, Macrides and Angold. I have written challenging the view of the emperor's family as the bedrock of Alexios' rule, highlighting the disgrace of members of his inner circle on the eve of the Crusade, P. Frankopan, 'Kinship and the distribution of power in Komnenian Byzantium', *English Historical Review* 495 (2007), pp. 1–34.

For the army under Alexios and his successors, John Birkenmeier, *The Development of the Komnenian Army: 1081–1180* (Leiden, 2002), though Armin Hohlweg, *Beiträge zur Verwaltungsgeschichte des oströmischen Reiches unter den Komnenen* (Munich, 1965) still has much to say. Paul Magdalino's *The Empire of Manuel I Komnenos 1143–1180* (Cambridge, 1993) is worth reading not only for Alexios' successors, but also as a backdrop to the composition of the *Alexiad*. For this, also see Paul Stephenson, 'The *Alexiad* as a source for the Second Crusade', *Journal of Medieval History* 45 (2003), pp. 41–54.

On the economy, see Alan Harvey, *Economic Expansion in the Byzantine Empire (900–1200)* (Cambridge, 1989) and his important piece on 'The land and taxation in the reign of Alexios I Komnenos: The evidence of Theophylakt of Ochrid', *Revue des Etudes Byzantines* 51 (1993), pp. 139–54. Michael Metcalf's *Coinage in South-Eastern Europe* (Oxford, 1979) is still essential, as is his article 'The reformed gold coinage of Alexius I Comnenus', in *Hamburger Beiträge zur Numismatik*, vol. 16 (1962), pp. 271–84. For the debasement of the currency in the eleventh century, see Cécile Morrisson, 'La Dévaluation de la monnaie byzantine au XIe siècle', *Travaux et Mémoires* 6 (1976), pp. 3–29.

Byzantium and its neighbours

Claude Cahen's seminal 'La première pénétration turque en Asie Mineure', *Byzantion* 18 (1948), pp. 5–67 dominated assessment of Asia Minor in the eleventh century, charting the rise of Turkish pressure before and after the battle of Manzikert. Jean-Claude Cheynet offered the first important corrective in 'Manzikert: un désastre militaire?', *Byzantion* 50 (1980), pp. 410–38. More recently, the same historian has gone further with 'La résistance aux Turcs en Asie Mineure entre Mantzikert et la Première Croisade', in *Eupsykhia: Mélanges offerts à Hélène Ahrweiler* 2 vols. (Paris, 1998), 1, pp. 131–47. Both provide crucial re-evaluations about the Turks and about Asia Minor. The importance of relying on archaeological evidence, as well as on the text, is clear from the work of Clive Foss, including 'The defences of Asia Minor against the Turks', *Greek Orthodox Theological Review* 27 (1982), pp. 145–205. New material from sites such as Strobilos, Sagalassos, Ephesus and elsewhere continue to challenge accepted views about the nature, extent and timing of Turkish settlement in Anatolia. For the rising pressure on Byzantium to the north of Constantinople, see Paul Stephenson, *Byzantium's Balkan Frontier* (Cambridge, 2000) which has supplanted previous works by scholars from this region.

The Norman conquest of southern Italy is brilliantly set out by Hartmut Hoffmann in 'Die Anfänge der Normannen in Süditalien', in *Quellen und Forschungen aus Italienischen Archiven und Bibiliotheken*, 47 (1967), pp. 95–144, though Graham Loud's pioneering work has moved this on in recent years, for example, *The Latin Church in Norman Italy* (Cambridge, 2007) and 'Coinage, wealth and plunder in the age of Robert Guiscard', *English Historical Review*, 114 (1999), pp. 815–43. Also see his *The Age of Robert Guiscard: Southern Italy and the Norman Conquest* (Singapore, 2000). Jean-Marie Martin's *La Pouille du VIe au XIIe siècles* (Rome, 1993) remains the benchmark for surveys of south-eastern Italy. The recent article by Paul Oldfield, 'Urban government in southern Italy, c.1085–c.1127', *English Historical Review* 122 (2007), pp. 579–608 also offers interesting insights into Norman control of southern Italy, as does his book *City and Community in Norman Italy* (Cambridge, 2009).

For Byzantine relations with the Normans, see Huguette Taviani-Carozzi, *La Terreur du monde – Robert Guiscard et la conquête normande en Italie* (Paris, 1997). Articles by William McQueen, 'Relations between the Normans and Byzantium 1071–1112', *Byzantion* 56 (1986), pp. 427–76, and Matthew Bennett, 'Norman naval activity in the Mediterranean c.1060–1108', *Anglo-Norman Studies* 15 (1992), pp. 41–58 offer helpful examinations of the attacks on Byzantium.

The trade treaty with Venice is of crucial importance, and has been looked at exhaustively. Thomas Madden's 'The chrysobull of Alexius I Comnenus to the Venetians: 'The date and the debate', *Journal of Medieval History* 28 (2002), pp. 23–41 is excellent; however, I have major doubts about the internal evidence in the text of the grant, not least about the date; see my article, 'Byzantine trade privileges to Venice in the eleventh century: The chrysobull of 1092', *Journal of Medieval History* 30 (2004), pp. 135–60. For concerns about other episodes in the 1090s, all stemming from problems with the chronology of the *Alexiad*, see pieces I have written on 'The Fall of Nicaea and the towns of western Asia Minor to the Turks in the later 11th Century: The curious case of Nikephoros Melissenos', *Byzantion* 76 (2006), pp. 153–84, and also 'Challenges to imperial authority in Byzantium: Revolts on Crete and Cyprus at the end of the 11th Century', *Byzantion* 74 (2004), pp. 382–402.

The First Crusade

In addition to the general works on the First Crusade noted above are added works that focus on specific aspects of the expedition. For the Council of Clermont and Pope Urban in France in 1095–6, see André Vauchez (ed.), *Le Concile de Clermont de 1095 et l'appel à la Croisade: Actes du Colloque Universitaire International de Clermont-Ferrand* (Rome, 1997). Many scholars cover the Crusade message very well, such as Penny Cole, *The Preaching of the Crusades to the Holy Land* (Cambridge, Mass., 1991), though also see H. E. J. Cowdrey, 'Pope Urban II's preaching of the First Crusade', *History* 55 (1970), pp. 177–88 and Robert Somerville, 'The Council of Clermont and the First Crusade', *Studia Gratiana* 20 (1976), pp. 323–7.

For the reactions and motivations of those who took part in the expedition, see Jonathan Riley-Smith, 'The motives of the earliest crusaders and the settlement of Latin Palestine, 1095–1100', *English Historical Review* 98 (1983), pp. 721–36; his 'The idea of Crusading in the Charters of Early Crusaders', in Vauchez, *Concile de Clermont*, pp. 155–66 is useful as well, as is Christopher Tyerman, 'Who went on crusades to the Holy Land?', in *Horns of Hattin*, pp. 13–26. Marcus Bull's *Knightly Piety and the Lay Response to the First Crusade: The Limousin and Gascony* (Oxford, 1993) provides a compelling and meticulous view of one region of France. Also note John France, 'Les origines de la Première Croisade: un nouvel examen', in Balard, *Autour de la Première Croisade*, pp. 43–56.

For millenarianism in the late eleventh century, see Hannes Möhring, *Der Weltkaiser der Endzeit: Entstehung Wandel und Wirkung einer tausendjährigen Weissagung* (Stuttgart, 2000), and Brett Whalen, *Dominion of God: Christendom and Apocalypse in the Early Middle Ages* (Cambridge, Mass., 2009). For more specialised studies on the impact and origins of the First Crusade, see Michele Gabriele, 'Against the enemies of Christ: The role of Count Emicho in the Anti-Jewish Violence of the First Crusade', in M. Frassetto (ed.), *Christian Attitudes towards the Jews in the Middle Ages: A Casebook* (Abingdon, 2007), pp. 61–82 and Robert Chazan, '"Let not a remnant or a residue escape": Millenarian enthusiasm in the First Crusade', *Speculum* 84 (2009), pp. 289–313.

Several recommendations can be made when it comes to practical issues to do with the expedition. *Logistics of Warfare in the Age of the Crusades*, edited by John Pryor (Aldershot, 2006) is a good start. Also see Alan Murray, 'The army of Godfrey of Bouillon 1096–9: Structure and dynamics of a contingent on the First Crusade', *Revue Belge de Philologie et d'histoire* 70 (1992), pp. 30–29; Jonathan Riley-Smith, 'First Crusaders and the costs of crusading', in Michael Goodrich, Sophia Menache and Syvlie Schein, *Cross Cultural Convergences in the Crusader Period* (New York, 1995), pp. 237–57; Matthew Bennett, 'Travel and transport of the Crusades', *Medieval History* 4 (1994), pp. 91–101; John Nesbitt, 'The rate of march of crusading armies in Europe: A study and computation', *Traditio* 19 (1963), pp. 167– 82 all raise sensible questions, as do Karl Leyser, 'Money and supplies on the First Crusade', in *Communications and Power*, pp. 83–94 and Sue Edgington, 'Medical knowledge in the crusading armies: The evidence of Albert of Aachen and others' in Malcolm Barber (ed.), *The Military Orders: Fighting for the Faith and Caring for the Sick* (Aldershot, 1994), pp. 320–6.

For Peter the Hermit, see M. D. Coupe, 'Peter the Hermit, a reassessment' *Nottingham Medieval Studies* 31 (1987), pp.37–45, Ernest Blake and Colin Morris, 'A hermit goes to war: Peter and the origins of the First Crusade', *Studies in Church History* 22 (1985), pp. 79–107, Jean Flori, *Pierre l'Eremite et la Première Croisade* (Paris, 1999), and Jay Rubenstein, 'How, or how much, to re-evaluate Peter the Hermit', in Susan Ridyard (ed.), *The Medieval Crusade* (Woodbridge, 2004) pp. 53–70. Biographical studies of the various Crusade leaders can be hit and miss and have been an unpopular genre in recent decades. Nevertheless, Ralph Yewdale's *Bohemond I: Prince of Antioch* (Princeton, 1924) is enduringly charming. Jean Flori's *Bohémond d'Antioche: Chevalier d'aventure* (Paris, 2007) is more up to date. For Raymond of Toulouse, John and Laurita Hill, *Raymond IV, Count of Toulouse* (Syracuse, 1962). For Robert of Normandy, William Aird's recent *Robert 'Curthose', Duke of Normandy (c.1050–1134)* (Woodbridge, 2008). For Godfrey of Bouillon, Pierre Aubé, *Godefroy de Bouillon* (Paris, 1985).

The massacres of the Jewish communities are covered by Robert Chazan, *European Jewry and the First Crusade* (Berkeley, 1987) and Gerd Mentgen, 'Die Juden des Mittelrhein-Mosel-Gebietes im Hochmittelalter unter besonder Berücksichtigung der Kreuzzugsverfolgungen', *Monatshefte für Evangelische Kirchengeschichte des Rheinlandes* 44 (1995), pp. 37–75. Eva Haverkamp's *Hebräische Berichte über die Judenverfolgungen während des Ersten Kreuzzugs* (Hanover, 2005) is now the seminal work on the pogroms of 1096.

For relations with Alexios in Constantinople, John Pryor, 'The oath of the leaders of the Crusade to the Emperor Alexius Comnenus: Fealty, homage', *Parergon* 2 (1984), pp. 111–41 is sensible, as is Ralph-Johannes Lilie, 'Noch einmal zu dem Thema "Byzanz und die Kreuzfahrerstaaten"', *Poikila Byzantina* 4 (1984), pp. 121–74. Absolutely crucial, however, is Jonathan Shepard's 'When Greek meets Greek: Alexius Comnenus and Bohemund in 1097–8', *Byzantine and Modern Greek Studies* 12 (1988), pp. 185–277.

On Antioch, see Bernard Bachrach, 'The siege of Antioch: A study in military demography', *War in History* 6 (1999), pp. 127–46; John France, 'The departure of Tatikios from the Crusader army', *Bulletin of the Institute of Historical Research* 44 (1971), pp. 137–47; Geoffrey Rice, 'A note on the battle of Antioch, 28 June 1098: Bohemund as tactical innovator', *Parergon* 25 (1979), pp. 3–8. Randall Rogers, *Latin Siege Warfare in the 12th Century* (Oxford, 1992), is an excellent guide to siege warfare of this period and the efforts against Nicaea and Antioch in particular.

For the kingdom established in the east in 1099 Jerusalem, Joshua Prawer, *The Latin Kingdom of Jerusalem: European Colonialism in the Middle Ages* (New York, 1972); Jean Richard, *The Latin Kingdom of Jerusalem* (London, 1979); Alan Murray, *The Crusader Kingdom of Jerusalem: A Dynastic History 1099–1125* (Oxford, 2000). For Antioch, see Thomas Asbridge's excellent *The Creation of the Principality of Antioch 1098–1130* (Woodbridge, 2000). Also see the important recent work by Christopher MacEvitt, *The Crusades and the Christian World of the East: Rough Tolerance* (Philadelphia, 2008). For the patriarch of Jerusalem, see Michael Matzke, *Daibert von Pisa: Zwischen Pisa, Papst und erstem Kreuzzug* (Sigmaringen, 1998).

For the Italian city-states, see Marie-Louise Favreau-Lilie, *Die Italiener im Heiligen Land vom ersten Kreuzzug bis zum Tode Heinrichs von Champagne (1098–1197)* (Amsterdam, 1988); for their relations with Byzantium, Ralph-Johannes Lilie's *Handel und Politik zwischen dem byzantinischen Reich und den italienischen Kommunen Venedig, Pisa und Genua in der Epoche der Komnenen und der Angeloi (1081–1204)* (Amsterdam, 1984) is still hard to beat.

For the Bohemond expedition against Byzantium, see John Rowe, 'Paschal II, Bohemund of Antioch and the Byzantine Empire', *Bulletin of the John Rylands Library* 49 (1966), pp. 165–202. Also see Luigi Russo, 'Il viaggio di Boemundo d'Altavilla in Francia', *Archivio storico italiano* 603 (2005), pp. 3–42.

For the creation of the history of the First Crusade, see James Powell, 'Myth, legend, propaganda, history: The First Crusade, 1140–c.1300', in *Autour de la Première Croisade*, pp. 127–41, and also two outstanding articles by Nicholas Paul, 'Crusade, memory and regional politics in twelfth-century Amboise', *Journal of Medieval History* 31 (2005), pp. 127–41, and also 'A warlord's wisdom: Literacy and propaganda at the time of the First Crusade', *Speculum* 85 (2010), pp. 534–66.

Index